Bioethics,
Health Care,
and the Law

A Dictionary

CONTEMPORARY LEGAL ⛪ ISSUES

Bioethics, Health Care, and the Law

A Dictionary

Richard Hedges

ABC-CLIO

Santa Barbara, California
Denver, Colorado
Oxford, England

Cataloging-in-Publication Data is available from the Library of Congress.

ISBN 0-87436-761-1

05 04 03 02 01 00 99 10 9 8 7 6 5 4 3 2 1

ABC-CLIO, Inc.
130 Cremona Drive, P.O. Box 1911
Santa Barbara, California 93116-1911

This book is printed on acid-free paper ∞.

Manufactured in the United States of America

Contents

Preface

Bioethics, health care, and the law—a fascinating web of society's values. Law is society's written definition of appropriate guidelines for human behavior. Health care is the behavior of caring for others. Bioethics are the moral and philosophical underpinnings of actions toward others in the health care context. These three areas of humanity are emotionally and intellectually challenging and ever developing. It is the goal of this book to provide the reader with more than an introduction to the key structures within each of the three areas, to expose the reader to the situations, the language, and the conditions that constitute questions that are not settled in society. Key medico-legal terms are used and, where appropriate, broken down into their prefixes and suffixes so that the reader can understand the technical language used and see how it is used in its technical context. These characterizations were written to be beneficial for readers at many educational levels, for health care providers, and for people outside health care.

In the United States, the legal system is fundamentally structured to follow English common law. Within this context, for centuries legal experts (judges) have been deciding the way that people are socially expected to treat one another. Curative health care and medicine is a relatively modern phenomenon. During the twentieth century, medical scientists have made wondrous advances in the treatment of human disease. There is no area of clinical work that has not experienced these advances, which include pharmaceuticals (drugs), surgical techniques, and biotechnology. These advances have the unchallenged support of the majority of society.

Determining whether a medical advance is truly therapeutic (clinically beneficial) or not requires scientific testing. Because the advances are intended to benefit humans, the final test must be carried out on humans—a human experiment. Many questions, notably bioethical questions, must be resolved before such experimentation occurs. These preparatory questions concern the likelihood of benefit, animal testing, and possible side effects of the intervention.

Health care in the United States is also influenced by the economics of the system. Most of the complex health care is paid for by someone other than the recipient of the service, usually an insurance company, the state, or the federal government. Because of this payment arrangement, most people do not have an idea of the true cost of health care procedures. Further, most don't care, because "their insurance covers it." This perspective results in the demand for greater health care regardless of cost. Where there is demand, supply will follow. Controlling the costs associated with this situation is both a social and a bioethical concern. It is social because people in the United States are spending trillions of dollars on health care. It is a bioethical question because technology should be developed to help people and, ideally, cost should not be an obstacle. But cost is an obstacle. Costs for health care are growing at an unprecedented rate. Where do we stop? How do we stop? To help the reader answer the question, payer arrangements are discussed.

Everyone is touched by these three areas. Often the issues are raised behind the scenes. At other times, the issue is brought to the forefront by media attention and subjected to public scrutiny. One thing we know for certain, all of us will be directly influenced by each of these areas by doing that which all humans do—by being born, by paying taxes, and by dying. Bioethics, health care, and the law are all interwoven into our existence.

To identify the many people who influenced this book is impossible. I am indebted to editor Alicia Merritt for her assistance and patience in the development of this effort. I am also indebted to Professor Martin Schwartz of Ohio University for his support and motivating commentaries. I would also like to express my thanks to the many students who have participated in my senior critical thinking class (Social Crises in Health Care), who helped me see many perspectives, and to the faculty in the School of Health Sciences at Ohio University, who have been supportive as I try to blend an academic career with that of a practicing attorney. Finally, I want to express my most sincere appreciation to my wife, Donna, and my parents, who encouraged me to pursue a never-ending intellectual challenge—the interface and integration of the art and science of bioethics, health care, and law.

Bioethics,
Health Care,
and the Law

A Dictionary

Bioethics, Health Care, and the Law

Welcome to one of the most challenging, diverse, and ever-changing areas of society. This area demands our special attention because it touches us in such an intensely personal way. Health care is an issue at the time of our conception, our birth, throughout our lives, and at the end of our lives. We all want our children born healthy; we want their mothers cared for; and we want to live with as little illness as possible. If we are sick, we want to be cured as rapidly as possible. And as to death, in our society we tend to want to put that off as long as possible.

The demand for perfect biological lives and a perfect quality of life raises other issues. What will we do to attain this level of perfection? What costs will be paid? What rights do people have to challenge these issues? What about death? Who decides about pain? These questions are all found in the delivery of health care. There are further implications for society. Who makes the decision in case of disagreement? Is there a right to personal choice? Is there a right to treatment? These are bioethical questions that confront people involved in health care.

Finally, there are some decisions that society believes are best "standardized" for all. These social decisions are placed into codes through the society's lawmakers. These decisions are applied to all of us and guide our decision-making options.

This introduction begins with an overview of the U.S. health care situation. Health clinicians will be characterized to show the variety of tasks that these occupations allow. A discussion on the types of health care organizations follows. Subsequent sections provide introductions to bioethics and to the American legal system. These issues are refined and focused in the terms defined and discussed in the body of this dictionary.

THE PROVISION OF HEALTH CARE

Health care is a complex micro-society within the greater society. This micro-society has its own unique social structure, language, hierarchy (or "pecking order"), and values. It includes the health providers (physicians, nurses, and other clinical health workers) who directly render services to patients. Providers work within the health care organizations (hospitals, nursing facilities, ambulatory clinics, etc.) that have the tools and support personnel to perform the highly technical tasks necessary to bring patients back to health. Because the provision of health care is a business in the U.S. system, there are a variety of ways to pay for the health care services.

The world of health care is an exciting, multifaceted microcosm of society. It has experienced (and the world has witnessed) extraordinary change in the past thirty years. To provide a sense of the magnitude of change, consider that antibiotics were introduced only sixty years ago. These antibacterial "golden bullets" were considered to be the answer to the world's ills! Problematically, we quickly found out antibiotics were no panacea. Chronic diseases rapidly replaced infectious diseases as the leading cause of death, and antibiotic-resistant strains of bacteria developed. So medical science continued to develop and progress. Today, we routniely practice what used to be science fiction. Cloning, i.e., the identical replication of existing cells, once a fantasy, is now a reality; identical animals can be reproduced through cloning, and these cloning techniques are now considered elementary science. As a tribute to technology, we have as an achievable goal the mapping all of the genes in the human body in the Humane Genome Project. From this map of the normal human genetic structure, scientists will be able to excise or remove abnormal genetic structures. Genetic diseases could become things of the past. Cryogenics (dealing with the effects of low, freezing temperatures) are used to freeze human embryos and sperm. They can be unfrozen later, joined in a laboratory, and implanted into the mother. Normal children have been the result.

The move from science fiction into reality is the result of an explosion of medical possibilities that has rapidly surpassed society's existing moral guidelines. New moral guidelines are needed, and as these are developed, the need for many more is confirmed. Our greatest challenges come from the need to deal with the wide variety of scientific changes encountered and the identification of their implications for human life and society. These realities cause society to consider the "what if's" from the health care system, bioethics, and the law.

THE HEALTH CARE SYSTEM

Health Care Providers
Health, illness, and the prevention of death are major interests in U.S. society. Trillions of dollars are spent annually on health and medical care. The value placed upon this social arena is reflected by its award of prestige. One of the most esteemed professions is that of the physician. A

"godlike" character has been attributed to many physicians because of their abilities to save lives. Only the brightest and most competent individuals are able to comprehend today's rapid, never-ending scientific and technological advances. Rigorous scientific preparation is required for admission to medical school and eventual admission to "physician" status. Most importantly, the graduation from medical school alone does not make one a good physician. A good physician is one who has also mastered the "art" of medicine, the intensely personal dynamic of the physician-patient relationship. Not every practicing doctor becomes a good physician. This country is blessed, however, with a wealth of good physicians.

The values of physicians (and other health care providers) are significantly influenced by the content of the professions. These people deal with human pain and suffering. Their goal is to eliminate pain by providing a cure for whatever causes it. Such cures may involve surgery, radiation treatment, or drugs. Each of these procedures or treatments may be fatal if the techniques are carried out incorrectly or negligently. Further, health care providers deal with the wonder of birth and the difficulty associated with death. These intensely personal and emotional working conditions shape the thoughts and beliefs of health care workers. For example, many people outside the health care professions believe that every possible medical intervention should be carried out to keep someone alive. Health care workers, on the other hand, may recognize that people cannot live without some minmum quality of life. Merely keeping someone alive may be more cruel than death could ever be. Health care workers cannot, however, dictate to the person's family what decision to make. Yet their recognition of the biological frailties (and strengths) of the human being create a unique perspective.

The art of medicine involves the recognition of the patient's individual rights and values. These individual attributes may conflict with the physician's own thoughts. Yet, as long as the patient remains competent, patients remain the ultimate decision makers over their treatment and future. Rather than place the burden of total decision making upon the physician (which may be requested by the patient), society has provided the physician with legal and philosophical assistance.

To further complicate the moral quandaries, health and medical care have their own unique structure and pecking order. The structure is an integration of business and science in which the physician is the principal player. The physician may practice general medicine or a specialty (e.g., pediatrics). The physician (usually) operates a private practice and has clinical privileges at one or more hospitals. This business side provides many of the tools and ancillary services for the physician's scientific endeavors, the diagnosis and treatment of disease.

Health Care Organizations

The variety of health care organizations is increasing with the growth and complexity of the health care industry. Specialty ambulatory (outpatient) practices such as one-day surgery centers and free-standing emergency rooms are increasing in number. These types of organizations, through their physicians, provide less complicated care and do not have the operational costs associated with the most complex procedures. Despite the variety in organizational forms, popular perceptions continue to recognize three major categories of services: ambulatory or outpatient care, hospitals or acute care, and nursing facilities or long-term care.

Ambulatory care is arguably the area of greatest growth among today's health care organizations. The growth in medical technology and therapy has resulted in increased needs for services that can be provided outside of the costly inpatient services. Through these organizations, patients can be treated and then return home to care for themselves alone or with visiting medical support. Ambulatory services involve physician offices, clinics, and other provider organizations. These services are increasing as patient treatments no longer require a hospital stay or call for a shorter length of inpatient treatment. For example, some laparoscopic surgeries require a minimal incision, thus allowing the person to go home within hours of the procedure. Before the development of these techniques, the surgery formerly required days in the hospital.

Ambulatory care is also less costly than other services. Cost has become an increasing issue, and where cost-lowering options are identified, they are usually pursued. The costs must be considered for their implications for society and for the health of the patient.

Hospitals remain the mainstay of the health organizations. Often physically large and intimidating, these organizations serve as the technological workshops of physicians and other clinicians. The hospital is a complex business organization, responsible for ensuring quality clinical care for both inpatients and outpatients.

Hospitals are, in many ways, still the physician's workshop. Early in the 1900s, medical technology was found to be prohibitively expensive for most physicians. The dramatic growth of medical technology furthered the need for some means to make the technologies available to physicians without requiring physicians to purchase them. Hospitals were that vehicle. Hospitals became the repository of medical technology. Most acute-care hospitals have laboratories, radiology, surgery suites, and other highly complex examination tools. These tools are used by the physicians to make their diagnoses.

The hospital hires nurses and other technologists to assist physicians in their efforts to return the patient to optimal health. Some physicians are hired or are on contract with the hospital, but most physicians are private businesspersons who have applied for and received "practice privileges" at hospitals. Each hospital's medical staff has a committee called the Credentialing Committee. Every physician who applies to practice at the hospital must go through this committee and have his or her medical license, medical education, and medical background investigated. If these credentials are acceptable, the physician is granted "privileges." These privileges may be general in scope or they may be restricted to medical practice in certain areas. In return for these practice privileges, the physicians serve on hospital committees and perform various hospital functions.

Behind the clinical activities are the hospital administrators and managers, whose job is to make the organization function effectively so that the clinical efforts are not interrupted. These people will manage personnel, billing and reimbursement, and the physical plant.

These highly complex organizations function as the premier showplaces of the U.S. medical system. There are about 6,500 hospitals in the United States. Their roles are changing. Hospital admissions are declining, yet the complexity of the medical problems of hospital patients is increasing. Futurists predict that hospitals may be getting smaller but the technology will continue to become more complex.

Long-term care is often erroneously considered to include only nursing facilities. Actually, long-term care involves any health organization that has an average length of stay beyond 30 days. Some specialty hospitals, such as psychiatric or rehabilitation hospitals, may fall into this category. Even the "nursing home" idea has changed. There are now continuing care retirement communities (CCRCs) that offer everything from apartments to skilled nursing areas. These multilevel organizations are attempting to meet the total needs of the elderly. The elderly person may enter the CCRC by purchasing an apartment, contracting with the CCRC for basic health care depending upon his or her needs. As the person ages and becomes more fragile, the person can move into assisted living. In this area, the person receives more support but remains primarily independent. Importantly, the security of remaining in the same place is to a large degree retained. Friends and acquaintances from the community remain available, which improves both physical and psychological well-being. As age complications increase, more traditional nursing facility may be needed. The facility is located on the same campus, again making contact available for friends and loved ones. These CCRC arrangements are increasingly available.

The three main organizational areas and their health providers are the major source of research and treatment in the U.S. health system. Like any group of people, they create their own perceptions and biases. The potential exists for these persons to project their ideas onto others. This projection cannot be accepted without review and scrutiny. Therefore another line of review exists, that of bioethics.

BIOETHICS

Bioethics arise from situations occurring in the provision of health care. An issue of the rights of a person, the limitations on the responsibility of the provider, and the limits of society's ability to direct health care onto a person are all fundamental questions of bioethicists. There are four principles that serve as guidelines to bioethicists.

The *principle of autonomy* holds that people have the right to make decisions themselves about what happens to them. The important concept of "informed consent" is derived from this principle. Informed consent requires that the health professional inform the patient what the procedure or treatment involves, what the risks are, and what the chances for success are. In other words, the patient receives complete, understandable information and then is permitted to make the decision about whether to accept or reject the treatment. The patient has the right to refuse treatment or to pursue a procedure with only limited chance of success. The important issue is that patients are able to make up their own minds.

The *principle of beneficence* is the principle of doing good. For bioethicists, the principle asserts an obligation to help others to further their goals and to actively prevent and remove harms that may stand in their way (Beauchamp and Childress, 1989). There are implications for beneficial actions. The benefits may cause risks to be incurred and the person may not wish to take the risk; the risk may be perceived as outweighing the benefit. Here the principle of autonomy must be considered and decisions reached by the integration of both these means of analysis.

The *principle of nonmaleficence* is another way of saying "do no harm." Upon receipt of a degree in medicine (whether allopathic or osteopathic medicine) the health provider traditionally takes an oath not to intentionally harm an individual (the patient). This specific principle is put to the test in health care. Physicians have to take the risk of invading human bodies to remove invaders (bullets, diseased organs, etc.). In some cases, the patient dies despite the best efforts of the physician. The physician's decision involves the balance between action and inaction. If there is an opportunity to help the person recover and the risk of major harm is smaller than the alternative, then the benefit can outweigh the harm done. The harm is not the sole consequence but a limited and controlled problem, part of the corrective process; but the options must be considered and explored with the patient.

Finally, there is the *principle of justice*. This principle states that equals should be treated equally. Only upon demonstration of relevant differences can people be treated differently (Beauchamp and Childress, 1989). In health care, a patient is a patient. The differences in treatment are directed by different diagnoses or different reactions to pharmaceuticals. The treatments are to be given to everyone; the poor person on Medicaid (i.e., a person on medical welfare) should be given the same treatment as the wealthy person when they enter the emergency room. The difference between the two people is not relevant to their treatment. It may be relevant to their ability to pay, but that is not the most important issue in this context. The person's life is most important.

All of these principles may come into play in any specific health development. The principles are thought-provoking and force bioethicists to consider the many alternatives possible. Further, they force bioethicists to consider what *may* be possible or may be a consequence. The issue then is to determine whether the negative consequence can be avoided or minimized and through what health care practices.

THE LAW

Society's structural character is written into codes called laws. These laws are intended to guide social behavior in a consistent and fair manner. Some behaviors are not controlled or guided because they have not been previously encountered. Equally, a new level of knowledge may have changed the behavior into something that requires guidance. Before a law is decided a trial is held. Before a statute is passed, extensive discussion occurs. When a new area requiring a decision is identified, much discussion and analysis of the issue must take place. In the arena of health care, bioethics is the initial forum for many of these debates and discussions. The parameters of the discussion and a focused issue must be identified. To be overly general in the identification of the situation makes further guidance too broad to be of societal use. When a bad outcome results, then very often the law and its structures are called upon to resolve the issue.

The law of the United States is based on English common law. This means that the law consists of both codes, written by the various levels of government, and judicial decisions, in which the codes are interpreted by judges as they are applied. Some issues are brought before the courts that are not clearly within the context of the written code. Therefore, the judge and jury will weigh the facts and apply the appropriate law, and a verdict will be reached. Once that happens, other courts under that court have to follow the same decision. This following of the decision is the legal principle of *stare decisis*, meaning that the decision is binding on the lower courts. A court that is not underneath the decision-making court does not have to follow the other court's reasoning, but it may be persuaded to follow the logic. This arrangement is called persuasive authority. The court may not want to follow the decision and may want to distinguish the new decision from the decision in the other court.

There are also two principal categories of law, criminal law and civil law. In criminal law, a person victimizes another. Society is affronted that the victim's rights are violated. The "state" becomes the complainant (plaintiff) and the accused becomes the defendant. The rights of the accused are to be considered innocent until proven guilty. In a criminal trial, the state must prove its case *beyond a reasonable doubt*. That level of proof means that the jury must be 98 or 99 percent certain that the defendant committed the offense against society. The reason for this significant level of proof is that a criminal offense may carry loss of individual freedom (jail) or loss of a typical citizen's privileges. There are personal rights taken away.

Civil law concerns the lawsuits of individuals against one another. The cases are not criminal and do not carry jail terms; the loser in a civil trial has to pay compensatory damages. The level of proof required by the plaintiff's attorney is *preponderance of the evidence*, meaning that the jury must be 51 percent sure that, for example, the contract was breached or someone was negligent when he didn't follow the rules and an accident occurred because of that lapse.

There are different rules for each type of law and different court procedures, each of which may be involved in health care issues.

The hierarchy of courts is an important element in the U.S. judicial system. All courts in the United States must follow the decisions of the U.S. Supreme Court on federal law. If the U.S. Supreme Court has not ruled on a matter of state law, then the highest court is the state's highest court, often called the state Supreme Court (called the Court of Appeals in New York). All state courts must follow decisions of the state's highest court. A court can deviate from the higher court's decision only if the lower court can distinguish the issue from one already ruled upon by the higher court. If the case is brought into federal court, the federal court applies state laws to guide its decisions. If federal law is the issue, then the federal or state court will apply the federal law.

In the case of bioethical situations, higher court rulings are not often found, especially in federal law. The judge will look for guidance to other decisions and to analogous cases, but there may not be another similar case, and the trial court judge may find him/herself involved the first step toward a landmark decision.

When the initial court (called the trial court) hears the case, often the holding (decision) is not the final hearing. If the case has many advocates and opponents, reasons to appeal the decision may be found. The case may leave the trial court and proceed to the Court of Appeals. From the

Court of Appeals, the issue may go the state Supreme Court and then to the federal Supreme Court. This process may take several years. Even if the case is appealed to the high courts, there is no guarantee that the highest courts will decide on the case. The highest courts will consider the issue and whether a ruling needs to be made. The justices may decide to send the case back to a lower court for a new hearing with some guidance on how a decision might be reached.

This legal process is arduous. Its goal is to ensure that equals are treated alike to the complete administration of the law, that is, to implement the principle of justice in society. The responsibility of the various courts is great.

CONCLUSION

The rapid growth of health care and the associated social interest has required the intertwining of bioethics, health care, and the law. Laws are introduced to protect the public and guide health practitioners in the performance of their responsibilities. The health care structure is intended to facilitate the provision of health care. Finally, as new areas are encountered, the forums presented by the bioethicists are available for discussion. Understanding the blend of these areas and their contributions is a fascimating challenge. The purpose behind this dictionary is to provide readers with a complete discussion of the key language and issues encountered in the intersection of these three areas. Equally, the author's goal is for the reader to have the tools to understand the key areas of undeveloped knowledge in health and medical care.

The encyclopedic dictionary is focused upon providing the student with the rudimentary language encountered in the various ethical and structural situations. Notably, the author has attempted to provide the student with medical language along with its common wording. For example, a heart attack to a health care provider is a *myocardial infarct* (myo—muscle; cardio—heart, indicating heart muscle; infarct—area of dead tissue caused by a blocked artery). The use of medical terminology is helpful for the student in relating to the health sciences and for understanding the specific nature of medical wording. Also introduced are legal terms, laws, and cases that will allow students to investigate the issues of interest more completely. Each entry is presented with as little bias as possible. The goal is for readers to review the information, investigate the issues further, and make up their own minds on these sensitive issues.

A

ABANDONMENT   Abandonment occurs when a person, usually in the position of a helper, enters into a helping-legal relationship with a victim, and the helper intentionally leaves the victim without fulfilling the relationship or turning the responsibility over to another. The relationship is one of dependence and reliance by the victim upon the helper. Abandonment may be identified by words from the helper (express abandonment) or by the helper's actions (implied abandonment). The provider abandoning the patient can be any health care provider, but the people most susceptible to the charges of abandonment are those providers licensed for independent or semi-independent practice such as physicians, dentists, podiatrists, physician's assistants, and nurse practitioners. If, however, a lay person agrees to help a victim and then intentionally decides to not complete the helping action, that person may be liable to a charge of abandonment.

This civil wrong or tort is often associated with breach of contract and negligence. As a breach of contract, abandonment may occur when the health care provider, usually a physician, has entered into a treatment relationship patient. (See **Physician-Patient Relationship**.) The courts have found this relationship to be one of contract because the physician and patient mutually consent to an exchange. The physician agrees to diagnose and treat the patient until the termination of the relationship. The patient agrees to pay the physician for services rendered. Either party may terminate the relationship. The physician usually terminates the relationship at the end of treatment, for example, after surgery and postoperative care has occurred. The contract covers the completion of the services to be rendered. When this treatment regimen or continuum of care is interrupted by the physician terminating the relationship, the issue of abandonment arises under breach of contract. The physician would not be complying with the agreement to provide complete treatment, as the physician-patient relationship would require.

Negligence occurs when the medical provider does not act as a reasonable provider would under the same or similar circumstances and the

11

victim is harmed by the act or failure to act by that provider. Abandonment with negligence would occur when the provider terminates the relationship with the patient in an unreasonable way according to the standard that other providers would follow under the same or similar circumstances. For example, if the physician were to end the treatments (interrupting the patient's treatment) because the patient was delinquent in paying the physician, the physician would be found liable for any patient damages due to negligence and abandonment by the majority of courts. The standard of medical treatment would clearly be violated, as a reasonable physician would not stop medical treatment on the basis of the patient's nonpayment of their bill.

Abandonment can occur in a variety of circumstances. It may arise in emergencies, during the normal health care relationship between the physician and patient, and during the relationship between the health organization and the patient.

In emergencies, the courts have held that an emergency medical technician (EMT) cannot stop rendering treatment until the patient has expired or until the responsibility for treatment has been turned over to another who is qualified to carry out the treatment. EMTs abandon the patient if they stop treatment and benefit to the patient is still possible. Once they reach the hospital emergency room, they may cease treatment and transfer responsibility to hospital emergency personnel. That transfer would be the defense against a charge of abandonment.

In nonemergency situations, physicians abandon patients if they terminate the treatment relationship and do not provide patients with alternative health care. The physician-patient relationship requires that the physician provide a list of alternative resources to the patient. The patient may investigate the resources to find a positive treatment provider; then the original relationship is terminated. Where there are many providers available, the physician need not provide a list of providers but must provide a reasonable time for the patient to find another provider. After a reasonable time, the relationship may be terminated. In both of these nonemergency situations, the requirement is for protection of potentially vulnerable patients, who are recognized by public policy as generally unable to treat themselves. Thus, if the physician unilaterally terminates the physician-patient relationship with an unprotected patient, abandonment may be considered to occur.

A classic example of this situation occurs when the physician becomes frustrated with the patient's lack of compliance with the medical regimen needed to achieve a cure. Further, the patient may blame the physician for not providing a cure. In exasperation, the physician may tell the patient that the relationship is terminated due to the lack of compliance, And the patient must find another provider. Based upon these facts alone, the courts would probably find the physician liable for abandonment because the physician did not take reasonable steps to protect the patient. If the physician provided a list of other physicians and gave a reasonable deadline to find another provider, then the physician would probably not be held liable for abandonment.

The hospital also may be judged to abandon the patient if through its policies and procedures, it interferes with the treatment of a patient, causing the treatment course not to be initiated or to be interrupted. The hospital is subject to potential liability in both emergency and nonemergency circumstances. Under emergency circumstances, hospital personnel assume responsibility for the patient upon receipt into the emergency department. These personnel are responsible for treating and stabilizing the patient before any other transfer or discharge is considered, presuming of course that the department has the technical capabilities to handle the problem confronted. If the emergency department transfers the patient and the patient's medical condition worsens, then the hospital would probably be liable for abandonment. (See **Emergency Medical Treatment and Active Labor Act**.)

Also in the nonemergency circumstance, hospitals, like physicians, have a legal standard of care to ensure that the patient's medical condition is not aggravated by discharge or transfer to another hospital. If the hospital discharges a patient and the patient is placed at a foreseeable unreasonable risk, the hospital is probably liable for abandonment. This action by the hospital is negligence. It is true that patients are not to be discharged without a physician's order under most hospital policies. However, in this time of pressure for cost containment, physicians are encouraged to discharge patients as quickly as medically realistic and professional judgment allows; thus the hospital is responsible to ensure that patients are not discharged prematurely.

ABORTIFACIENT   An agent, usually a drug, that causes an abortion (abortio—abortion; facere—to make or cause; also known as abortient or aborticide). In the United States, drugs are used to induce abortions during the second trimester of pregnancy. These drugs stimulate uterine contractions and labor begins, causing the fetus to be evacuated (aborted). A new abortifacient known as RU-486 halts the delivery of progesterone to the embryo, causing the body to reject the embryo. It is currently used in France and is reported to be 90 percent effective at evacuating the embryo in the first seven weeks of pregnancy. RU 486 involves an ethical issue because it has been perceived as a means of contraception rather than as an abortive technique. Traditional contraceptives prevent pregnancy by preventing ovulation. RU 486, on the other hand, causes the body to expel the embryo (a developed fertilized ovum, or eggs—which is abortion, not contraception. Opponents of abortion thus oppose RU 486 and have worked to block its approval for use in the United States, where it is not currently legal.

See also **Artificial Insemination.**

ABORTION   The term has both medical and legal definitions. Medically, an abortion may be defined as the premature expulsion of an embryo or nonviable fetus from the uterus (womb). An abortion may be accidental, spontaneous, or induced. Accidental abortions are caused by an accidental injury to the mother causing the body to abort the embryo or fetus. A spontaneous abortion is the body's natural response to an unviable embryo or fetus. An induced abortion, which often provokes legal disputes, is intentionally brought about by the mother and the physician. A subtype of induced abortion is a therapeutic abortion, which is performed when the mother's life or health is at stake or the pregnancy is the product of incest or rape. In general, legal disputes do not arise over accidental or spontaneous abortions. Though they may arise over the accidental cause, a cause of action is not available when the body decides to abort an embryo or fetus.

The legal definition of abortion incorporates the medical definition and adds stipulations concerning when abortions may be carried out. A legal abortion is defined by the U.S. Supreme Court decision in *Roe v. Wade*, 410 US 113 (1973). The cases that followed Roe have further clarified (some would argue "restricted") the right of a woman to purposely terminate her pregnancy. The principle underlying the *Roe v. Wade* decision was that a woman's right to choose what would happen to her physical being was a matter of individual privacy. Justice Blackmun has pointed out, however, that this right is not unqualified. Under *Roe v. Wade*, the woman was able to have a physician-induced abortion without state interference or regulation during the first trimester (first three months) of the pregnancy. During this period, the justices reasoned, maternal mortality from abortion was less than the mortality associated with giving birth, thus maternal rights to privacy held supremacy over state's interests.

A second-trimester abortion was also made available, but because the mother's mortality risk increased, the state was recognized to have greater responsibility to protect the health of the mother. As a result, the state was permitted to regulate abortions during the second trimester by requiring approved medical facilities, proper techniques, and licensed personnel.

The Court's finding on the issue of third-trimester abortion recognizes the state's interest in both the mother and the fetus. The fetus is now viable and has the potential to survive outside of the womb with artificial support. At the same time, maternal mortality associated with late-term abortion is significantly higher than at childbirth. Therefore, the Court reasoned, the state is required to provide much greater protection to both mother and fetus during this period. Thus the state has the right to regulate and restrict the woman's ability to have an induced abortion during the third trimester.

The Supreme Court decision in *Roe v. Wade* also recognized the right of privacy during the first trimester of the pregnancy. However, the state's interests increased as the fetus gained rights as a "potential life" through its potential for viability outside the uterus.

Some of the strongest critics of trimester timelines base their positions on the growth of biotechnology. They argue that biotechnology is increasing the "potential life" span of the fetus through the development of prenatal intensive care units and other modern life-sustaining equipment for neonates. However, other studies have indicated that the trimester approach recognizes the biological stages and that a fetus younger than 28 weeks simply does not have the organ development to survive. These arguments will continue, since improved timelines have not yet been identified.

In 1989 the U.S. Supreme Court allowed tightened Missouri state requirements in *Webster v. Reproductive Health Services, Inc.* According to the state statute at issue, public funds could not be used to pay for counseling for an abortion or for an abortion itself unless the mother's life was at risk. No public employee could perform an abortion, and no public facility could be used. The Court further permitted a requirement for extensive testing to ascertain fetal viability for abortions past 20 weeks where there was a reasonable medical basis to suspect viability.

In *Planned Parenthood of SE Pa. v. Casey* in 1992, the Court decided a case that challenged the principles of *Roe v. Wade*. At issue was whether to permit the implementation of the Pennsylvania Abortion Control Act of 1982 as amended in 1989. This act required that a woman seeking an abortion give informed consent and that she receive specific information 24 hours in advance. If the woman was a minor, then parental consent was required, although a judicial bypass was available. A married woman was required to sign a statement indicating that she had notified her husband of her intention to obtain an abortion.

The Court's complex opinion sustained the foundation of *Roe v. Wade*. The justices followed the precedent (the doctrine of stare decisis) and indicated that the basis for overruling precedent was when the prior case holding has proven itself unworkable. The Court held that the precedent of Roe was workable, and that it had not eroded any rights or principles. It had engendered disapproval but this disapproval was not enough to overrule the central holding of *Roe v. Wade.* However, those state rules that would not be overly burdensome on the right to abortion would be potentially permissible.

Fathers' challenges to abortions have never been successful. The father is recognized as contributing half of the genetic makeup of the fetus, but the woman carries the burden of the pregnancy. Therefore courts have consistently held that the father's objection to the woman having an abortion is to be denied.

Most states have favored guardian/parental consent as a prerequisite to an abortion for a minor. The state has a compelling interest in protecting minors from making hasty or short-sighted decisions and usually requires the consent of a parent or guardian. However, the approval of both parents is not usually required, and most states provide for exceptions to the rule of parental notification. In Ohio, for example, if the minor files an affidavit stating that she is in fear of emotional, physical, or sexual abuse from the parent to be informed and a sibling over 21 is available to be informed, then the parental notice is waived.

Most states also provide for a judicial bypass. In this case, the minor requests the court to recognize her own maturity and allow her to decide on her own to undergo the abortion procedure. She must state that she desires to have the abortion without any notifications and that she is mature enough to make the decision. The court must permit the abortion if the minor proves that she is mature enough or that the abortion is in her best interest. In Ohio, the court must respond within five days with its decision. (See the actual cases of *Roe v. Wade, Webster v. Reproductive Health Services, Inc.,* and *Planned Parenthood of SE Pa. v. Casey.*)

ABORTION AS CONTRACEPTION

The clinical difference between abortion and contraception is becoming increasingly difficult to identify with the development of drugs with different timing of "intervention." Part of the difficulty lies in varying definitions of the point at which pregnancy begins. That point could be defined as the joining of the sperm and egg (ovum), the ovum's attachment to the womb, or the development of a fetus with recognizable human features. There are other definitions. Contraceptives, as traditionally characterized, particularly barriers such as the cervical diaphragm and the sponge, are designed to prevent pregnancy from occurring. However, one can argue that intrauterine devices (IUDs) that prevent a fertilized egg from attaching to the womb are a form of abortion rather than contraception. With the drug RU 486 (mifepristone) the pregnancy intervention occurs within the seven weeks following conception. As RU 486 causes the body to expel the embryo, an abortion is technically the result. Because first-trimester abortions are legal, a clear legal distinction between abortion and contraception is not required at this time; but for many people the distinction involves the same ethical issues as abortion. This point is debated among both pro-choice and pro-life groups from a variety of legal and ethical standpoints. (See B. Furrow et al, *Bioethics: Health Care Law and Ethics* [1991].) It would appear, however, that if the Supreme Court decisions dealing with abortion are overruled, then these definitions would become subject to extensive legal scrutiny and the chemicals or devices placed into strict categories to determine legality or illegality.

ACQUIRED IMMUNODEFICIENCY SYNDROME (AIDS)   A fatal viral disease that attacks the immune (lymph) system. It follows infection with the human immunodeficiency virus (HIV), the identified cause of AIDS. Today the time period between infection with the HIV virus and the development of AIDS can be quite lengthy, ten years and more. The length of time is influenced by the physical condition of the infected person, how early the diagnosis occurred, and the combination of medications used. At this time, an "AIDS cocktail" is being used experimentally with some success to prevent or postpone the development of AIDS. (To take a famous case, Magic Johnson, formerly of the National Basketball Association's Los Angeles Lakers, was diagnosed as HIV-positive in the late 1980s. At the time of this writing, he is an active businessperson with the Lakers, and published reports indicate he is not suffering HIV consequences.) When AIDS does develop, the victim's immune system is progressively weakened and he becomes susceptible to a variety of diseases. Two diseases commonly diagnosed in association with AIDS are pneumocystis carinii pneumonia (PCP) and Kaposi's sarcoma (KS).

Since more than a decade may pass before a person who is HIV-positive contracts AIDS, people carrying these diagnoses have been placed into a legally protected class of disabled people. They are protected by the Americans with Disabilities Act of 1990, the Rehabilitation Act of 1973, and other civil rights legislation. (See **Americans with Disabilities Act of 1990; Rehabilitation Act of 1973.**) This protection was deemed necessary because of the negative social stigma attached to the disorder.

The stigma arose because the first social group recognized to have the HIV infection consisted of homosexual and bisexual males. The stigma was exacerbated by the scientific finding that intravenous drug users were also at high risk of HIV, especially those that used "dirty or pre-used" needles for their drug injections. The capstone for the stigma was the recognition that the diagnosis of HIV and AIDS was 100 percent fatal. Initially, therefore, the diagnosis of "HIV-positive" meant not only that the victim was under a death sentence, but that he was either a homosexual or a drug user, or both.

Initially, blood donations were not screened for the presence of HIV, and other groups using the untested blood supply became victims of AIDS. Thus hemophiliacs, who must receive blood transfusions so that they will not bleed to death from minor lacerations, were also among the initial groups at high risk for AIDS. Other victims included those who received HIV-positive blood donations while in surgery. Arthur Ashe, the great tennis player, and numerous others were unfortunately infected in this way.

Regardless of how they were infected, people with HIV and AIDS carried (and still carry) a social stigma. Suspicion about how they got the disease and "what kind of people they really are" still gives rise to discrimination, even though epidemiological studies indicate that the people at greatest risk today are white, middle-class females who do not practice "safe sex." Thus it is important to realize that AIDS is not a disease of a particular social group but a threat to all humans.

The technology is not currently available to "cure" AIDS. The intermediate goal is for people to be able to live with AIDS as diabetics live with their disease. We don't have a cure for diabetes, but we do have the ability to help diabetics cope with the problems of the disease and reduce the side effects. AIDS researchers want to be able to do the same for people with AIDS.

CONFIDENTIALITY

Because of the social stigma associated with AIDS and people's fear of being infected, all health care workers have been mandated to practice *universal precautions*. Universal precautions, now called Standard Precautions, require that all health workers protect themselves by taking precautions with all patients. The HIV, as well as other diseases, is spread by interpersonal contact with an infected individual's bodily fluids. Standard precautions include hand washing with antimicrobial soap, wearing gloves and eye protection, and wearing fluid-resistant gowns. The goal of these precautions is to prevent contact with potentially infectious fluids while maintaining the ability to use the touch required for diagnosis and treatment. (See **Standard Precautions.**) If standard precautions are taken with everyone entering the health care system, one patient cannot be differentiated from another by the precautions taken and the confidentiality of HIV-positive patients can be preserved.

Because of the discrimination that often results from the fear of being infected, the confidentiality of an HIV or AIDS patient is a strong ethical obligation for health care providers. If the confidence is broken, an HIV or AIDS victim has several causes of legal action stemming from invasion of privacy to breach of contract to statutes that require patient confidentiality by health workers. Victims can recover damages for any harm done economically and to their reputation from the loss of confidentiality.

In health care, patient confidence is a big part of the health provider–patient relationship. To breach this confidence is grounds for a review of the provider's conduct and possibly the loss or suspension of license and practice privileges. In some states, this breach of confidentiality has become a recognized cause of action by the victim. Many states have statutes indicating that health care workers who learn that someone has AIDS while rendering health care many not confirm or disclose that the patient has HIV in any way. They may share the information that a patient has HIV/AIDS on a need-to-know basis only. (See, for example, Ohio Revised Code 3701.243(A)(1) et seq.)

However, the diagnosis of HIV and AIDS may not be completely confidential. Some states have passed legislation to identify who outside of the health care setting may be informed of a person's HIV-positive status. Most often, physicians may inform the spouse, the parent or guardian of a minor, and the person's private physician. In circumstances where criminality is involved, law enforcement officials and the district attorney may be informed, if necessary. But only those persons with a legitimate interest may be informed.

The physician also has ethical and legal responsibilities to report the HIV/AIDS diagnosis under certain conditions. For many contagious diseases, notably sexually transmitted diseases, the Centers for Disease Control and Prevention (CDC) mandates the reporting of the diagnosis. HIV/AIDS falls in that mandated category. The patient's name is not identified, but the record of the diagnosis and general patient characteristics are submitted to the Centers for Disease Control and Prevention (CDC). This federal agency has the responsibility for compiling and analyzing health and medical statistics that can be used to prevent the spread of disease or stop its progression. Because it is extremely important for epidemiologists to have accurate information on the spread of a dangerous disease, the requirement that physicians report the diagnosis is legally mandated. The diagnostic information helps them and other biomedical scientists and physicians identify who is at risk and where they are at risk. It also helps them identify risk factors that the general public can be encouraged to avoid.

Confidentiality can also be broken when the infected person is uncooperative and refuses to tell sexual partners of the diagnosis. Health workers have a duty to inform people at serious risk of harm and prevent the harm from occurring, especially when significant harm is foreseeable. In *Tarasoff v. Regents of the University of California* (551 P.2d 334 (Cal.1976]), a psychotherapist failed to inform an individual (a former girlfriend) that threats of imminent harm had been made against her by the therapist's client, and the client finally did kill the woman. The California Supreme Court held that the therapist did have a duty to warn *when the harm is foreseeable.* The states are not consistent on this duty to break confidentiality and warn others of a potentially dangerous situation. Confidentiality has also been held to be appropriately broken if imminent harm exists from contagious diseases. The people eligible to receive the information include anyone who might suffer imminent harm. However, the physician needs to be cautious in relaying this information. Physicians regarded as "spreading gossip" may be ordered by the court to pay damages. To avoid this consequence, the physician needs to make sure the sex partner or partners are at serious risk of exposure.

The specific issue of confidentiality currently receiving the most extensive ethical analysis arises when an employee receives a health physical that is paid for by the employer. If the employee tests positive for HIV, should the employer be notified? A minority of cases suggest that the employer should be notified. In that case, what can the employer do with that information and how confidential must the employer keep the diagnosis? If the employee has signed a consent form to release medical records, the problem does not arise. But if consent is unclear, employer confidentiality may become suspect. The employer does not gain the right to spread gossip or to read a person's private records to discuss the information in public. The tort of invasion of privacy is a clear cause of action to provide a remedy for that employer act. Equally, medical records are not freely accessible to all areas of management. Only a select few would have access to such information. But in today's world, where information technology can pose threats to privacy and confidentiality and employers have a stake in keeping health care costs, and thus employer-paid insurance premiums, as low as possible, employees need to make sure their medical records are kept as confidential as possible.

LIABILITY FOR INFECTING OTHERS

People entering into a sexual relationship should be equal partners, but they cannot be equal if knowledge is held by one and not the other. This is especially true when a person is aware that he is HIV-positive and fails to inform his or her partner. People who are infected, not only with HIV/AIDS but with any contagious disease, have a moral and ethical duty to inform their partners that they are being placed at risk. (Many sexually transmitted diseases are permanent once transmitted, e.g., genital warts and herpes. Others can be treated but if left untreated can cause many health problems for the recipient and their future children, e.g., syphilis, gonorrhea, chlamydia).

A negligence cause of action is also applicable if one knowingly exposes another to a contagious disease. Fundamentally, negligence may be defined as occurring when one has a legally identifiable duty to another and fails to carry out that duty, resulting in damages or injury. Such breach of duty would appear to occur if one partner fails to inform the other of his or her HIV status. This duty would appear to be even more socially binding in the case of HIV/AIDS, since the disorder is always fatal.

MANDATORY HIV TESTING FOR HEALTH WORKERS

Should health care workers be required to be tested for HIV? A test is required for all blood and tissue donors to protect potential hemophiliac and surgery patients from transmission of HIV. Some argue that a logical extension of this protection would require that health workers who practice any type of invasive techniques, such as surgery and injections, should be mandated to take an HIV test. An alternative argument is that health workers should be tested only after an accidental needle stick or laceration.

DISCLOSURE OF HIV STATUS TO PATIENTS

Because of the stigma attached to the disease, many HIV-infected health care providers believe that informing patients of their status would cause economic disaster and invade their privacy, as confidentiality rules do not apply to the lay public. Further, existing epidemiological evidence on the transmission of HIV from HIV-positive health providers to patients has shown that it virtually never occurs. The most notorious case involved a Florida dentist, who later died from complications of AIDS, whose practices allegedly infected at least one patient. The dentist was practicing invasive techniques such as tooth extraction, fillings, and other general dental procedures without, allegedly, practicing universal precautions of wearing gloves and a mask. Through these inappropriate acts, he transmitted HIV to one or more patients. However, the actual transmission has not been proven, and many allegations and counterallegations have surfaced.

There have not been any other reported infections given to patients by their health workers. To ensure prevention, testing of all donated blood and standard precautions were implemented in 1985. (See **Standard Precautions**.) Therefore, the health care providers argue, it is unnecessary to advise patients of their HIV-positive status. Patients, on the other hand, argue that they have the right to know whether their health care provider is placing them at risk, no matter how small the risk may be. Because the disease is always fatal, many contend that patients do have a right to know the status of their physician. There is little current consensus, however, on this hotly debated question.

ADOPTION AND BIOLOGICAL PARENTS' RIGHTS

Adoption is a state-guided legal process that terminates the parental rights of the biological parents and transfers parental rights to adoptive parents. Parental rights include the right to make decisions in the care, development, education, and punishment of the child. This parental right includes assuming economic support for the child, which typically includes providing clothing, food, housing, and health care.

Rights of an adopted individual include the right to inherit from adoptive parents. They are subject to the control and responsibilities of their adoptive parents in the same way as biological children. Many, if not most, psychologists advocate that these children have the right to know that they are adopted.

Adoptions may be accomplished through a state agency or by a licensed private adoption agency. These agencies are often guided by an attorney, because court approval is required to complete an adoption. The biological parents' consent to the adoption is required in most states. In instances where the biological father is unknown, however, only the mother's consent is required.

Can the biological parents offer their consent and then revoke it? The answer depends on the situation. In most states, if parental consent is given before the child is born, the mother is allowed a period after delivery to reconsider; if consent is given after delivery, the period for reconsideration is just a few days. The time periods and conditions for revocation are set by the respective states.

An ethical issue that often arises among adoptive families is the debate about identifying unknown biological parents. Some biological parents request privacy and sealed records in order to terminate the relationship. Others choose to allow personal information to be divulged. The debate surrounds whether or not the biological parents should be contacted by the biological child even though they have requested anonymity. Those individuals who help adoptive children locate their biological parents report wonderful as well as disastrous meetings. It is precisely that lack of consistency, coupled with an undesired invasion of personal privacy, that causes strong, ongoing debate.

ADVANCE DIRECTIVES

Guidelines in which an individual indicates actions to be taken on her behalf if she should become incapacitated or incompetent to make the decisions herself. Advance directives can take several forms; the two most common are the living will and the durable power of attorney for health care.

A living will is a document that identifies what a person wants done in case she is incapacitated or becomes incapable of giving the decision to others. In many states, statutes require that a patient write a living will upon admission to the hospital. This document is signed by witnesses and advises the medical provider what the patient's wishes are, should a medical crisis arise. It becomes effective only when she is incapacitated and cannot make her own health care decisions.

The content of living wills is statutorily constrained in many states. In general, most of the living will forms deal with the artificial prolonging of death. Do you want to be maintained on a respirator where death is imminent? The problem with a living will is that death is not always imminent when you need to give someone directions—for example, if you are in a persistent vegetative state or coma or other unconscious condition that may last for years. These conditions are often not covered by living wills. Therefore, many provisions that a person might write to deal with these circumstances are not legally binding. One way to avoid this situation is to have an attorney draw up a document creating a durable power of attorney.

A durable power of attorney for health care authorizes another to make decisions for you after you have become incompetent or incapacitated. It is an extension of the power of attorney (POA) concept, which allows you to appoint another to make decisions for you under identified conditions. The power of attorney may be general or specific. The general POA allows the person to make a wide array of decisions, and the specific POA restricts the person to one or two decision areas.

The concept of durability was added to allow the person holding the power of attorney to make decisions after the principal had become unable to make such a decision, such as after a medical incident or an incapacitating accident. In most states, a statute indicates the form and structure of the document. A person writing a durable power of attorney must remember that she can only authorize decisions that she herself could make under other circumstances. For example, if a patient enters into brain death, in most states she could authorize, through durable power of attorney, the decision for placing her on life support or denying her life support machinery. Alternatively, if she authorized physician-assisted suicide after she became incompetent from Alzheimer's disease, her wish would not be allowed because it is illegal in all states.

AMERICAN BAR ASSOCIATION (ABA) HEALTH LAW SECTION   The principal national association of attorneys and jurists, initiated in 1878. Membership is open to attorneys in good standing in any state. Its original purpose was to help make regulations uniform and improve civil and criminal court procedures. This purpose has evolved into a broader role focusing upon improving the services provided by attorneys and the related administration of justice.

Its subsection, the Health Law Section, identifies legal concerns and implications in bioethical issues that arise in medical practice. It also clarifies new regulations and laws to health law section members.

Each state has its own bar association (not affiliated with the American Bar Association) for attorneys and jurists practicing in that state. These state associations provide significant assistance to state attorneys, because they tailor their activities around the key activities of the local attorney membership. These state associations may or may not have sections dealing with bioethical issues.

AMERICAN CIVIL LIBERTIES UNION (ACLU)
Founded in 1920 by Roger Nash Baldwin, this nonprofit legal organization attempts to use the law and the legal system to protect civil and constitutional freedoms of United States Citizens. Today, the ACLU is dedicated to the enforcement and preservation of rights and civil liberties guaranteed by the federal and state constitutions. According to Norman Dorsen, president of the ACLU, the organization is a limited-purpose organization focusing upon protecting the rights of freedom of inquiry and expression, due process of law, equal protection of the laws, and privacy. Its membership is unrestricted, and it is supported by annual dues and contributions. There are state chapters in most states.

The ACLU characterizes itself as nonpolitical. It encourages and protects diverse ideas, as guaranteed by the federal and state constitutions. Its actions include challenging governmental activities and legislation that violate citizen rights. In many cases, the ACLU acts as amicus curiae, or "a friend of the court." In this role, the ACLU is not a formal party in the trial or appellate hearing. Rather, the ACLU attorneys file a legal brief (called an amicus brief) that encourages the court to attend to a point or points that might be otherwise overlooked or minimized.

The ACLU has been involved in several cases dealing with bioethical issues, including housing for people with mental health problems and mental disabilities, abortion rights, and cases involving privacy issues as well. The ACLU has also published a broad array of handbooks that inform people of their rights, including G. J. Annas's *The Rights of Patients: The Basic ACLU Guide to Patient Rights,* 2d edition (1989).

AMERICAN HOSPITAL ASSOCIATION (AHA)
The AHA, founded in 1898, is a voluntary hospital association with over 42,000 individual and organizational members. It has been and continues to be very influential in developing and promoting hospital com-

pliance with established standards of quality care and was instrumental in developing programs emphasizing quality. It was also a major contributor to the introduction of the Joint Commission on Accreditation of Hospitals (JCAH), which places a heavy emphasis on quality of care. The JCAH, now the Joint Commission on Accreditation of Health Care Organizations, is known as the Joint Commission. (See **Joint Commission on Accreditation of Healthcare Organizations**.)

The AHA developed a Patient's Bill of Rights in 1973 to serve as a guide to physicians and members in achieving greater patient satisfaction as part of the healing process. It recognized that health care is an intimate and personal interaction, and that it is incumbent upon health care organizations and providers to understand the unique trust patients place in them.

A Patient's Bill of Rights

The patient has the right to considerate and respectful care.

The patient has the right to obtain from his physician complete current information concerning his diagnosis, treatment, and prognosis in terms the patient can be reasonably expected to understand. When it is not medically advisable to give such information to the patient, the information should be made available to an appropriate person in his behalf. He has the right to know, by name, the physician responsible for coordinating his care.

The patient has the right to receive from his physician information necessary to give informed consent prior to the start of any procedure and/or treatment. Except in emergencies, such information for informed consent should include but not necessarily be limited to the specific procedure and/or treatment, the medically significant risks involved, and the probable duration of incapacitation. Where medically significant alternatives for care or treatment exist, or when the patient requests information concerning medical alternatives, the patient has the right to such information. The patient also has the right to know the name of the person responsible for the procedures and/or treatment.

The patient has the right to refuse treatment to the extent permitted by law and to be informed of the medical consequences of his action.

The patient has the right to every consideration of his privacy concerning his own medical care program. Case discussion, consultation, examination, and treatment are confidential and should be conducted discreetly. Those not directly involved in his care must have the permission of the patient to be present.

The patient has the right to expect that all communications and records pertaining to his care should be treated as confidential.

The patient has the right to expect that within its capacity a hospital must make reasonable response to the request of a patient for services. The hospital must provide evaluation, service, and/or referral as indicated by the urgency of the case. When medically permissible, the patient may be transferred to another facility only after he has received complete information and explanation concerning the needs for and alternatives for such a transfer. The institution to which the patient is to be transferred must first have accepted the patient for transfer.

The patient has the right to obtain information as to any relationship of his hospital to other health care and educational institutions insofar as his care is concerned. The patient has the right to obtain information as to the existence of any professional relationships among individuals, by name, who are treating him.

The patient has the right to be advised if the hospital proposes to engage in or perform human experimentation affecting his care or treatment. The patient has the right to refuse to participate in such research projects.

The patient has the right to expect reasonable continuity of care. He has the right to know in advance what appointment times and physicians are available and where. The patient has the right to expect that the hospital will provide a mechanism whereby he is informed by his physician or a delegate of the physician of the patient's continuing health care requirements following discharge.

The patient has the right to examine and receive an explanation of his bill regardless of source of payment.

The patient has the right to know what hospital rules and regulation apply to his conduct as a patient. No catalogue of rights can guarantee for the patient the kind of treatment he has a right to expect. A hospital has many functions to perform, including the prevention and treatment of disease, the education of both health professionals and patient, and the conduct of clinical research. All of these activities must be conducted with an overriding concern for the patient, and, above all, the recognition of his dignity as a human being. Success in achieving this recognition ensures success in the defense of the rights of the patient.

This bill of rights recognizes the multifaceted nature of health care. As currently provided, health care is fragmented. Physicians, for the most part, are private business people, and the hospital, through its board of directors, grants them practice privileges, which define the extent of their use of hospital facilities. Physicians are not usually hospital employees. Because the hospital and physician are separate, their business goals and objectives may conflict, leading to strained relations. Recognizing this possibility, the AHA is attempting, through this document, to ensure that the patients know who is responsible for their care.

AMERICAN MEDICAL ASSOCIATION (AMA)

Founded in 1847, the AMA is a national society of 287,000 physicians and surgeons with headquarters in Chicago. Its mission is promoting the science and art of medicine, and safeguarding the interests and upholding the standards of the profession.

Predominately, this organization represents people holding M.D. degrees—that is, those physicians trained from the allopathic perspective of medical treatment and therapeutics. (See, for comparison, the **American Osteopathic Association**, which represents people holding the D.O. degree.) The allopathic physician practices a system of medical therapeutics (drugs, surgery, other medical interventions) in which diseases, syndromes, and other clinical health conditions are treated by producing a physical condition incompatible with or antagonistic to the condition to be cured or alleviated. For example, an allopathic physician may treat a bacterial infection with an antibiotic because antibiotics create a physical condition that can inhibit or destroy the infection. The AMA promotes this viewpoint politically, and its legal arm writes amicus curiae (friend-of-the-court) briefs on major cases in an attempt to influence the outcome.

The AMA demands of its members compliance with the Code of Ethics, thus guiding the art and science of medical practice. However, not all allopathic physicians are members of the association, and there is no legal requirement to join.

Code of Ethics (1980)

Preamble:

The medical profession has long subscribed to a body of ethical statements developed primarily for the benefit of the patient. As a member of this profession, a physician must recognize responsibility not only to patients, but also to society, to other health professionals, and to self. The following Principles adopted by the American Medical Association are not laws, but standards of conduct which define the essentials of honorable behavior for the physician.

Principles:

I. A physician shall be dedicated to providing competent medical service with compassion and respect for human dignity.

II. A physician shall deal honestly with patients and colleagues, and strive to expose those physicians deficient in character or competence, or who engage in fraud or deception.

III. A physician shall respect the law and also recognize a responsibility to seek changes in those requirements which are contrary to the best interests of the patient.

IV. A physician shall respect the rights of patients, of colleagues, and of other health professionals, and shall safeguard patient confidences within the constraints of law.

V. A physician shall continue to study, apply, and advance scientific knowledge, make relevant information available to patients, colleagues, and the public, obtain consultation, and use the talents of other health professionals when indicated.

VI. A physician shall, in the provision of appropriate patient care, except in emergencies, be free to choose whom to serve, with whom to associate, and the environment in which to provide medical services.

VII. A physician shall recognize a responsibility to participate in activities contributing to an improved community.

Like most other codes, this code does not attempt to deal explicitly with every specific bioethical situation a physician might confront. Instead, the code is written as a guide for the practitioner. From the key values it expresses, the practitioner can extrapolate the ideals that should guide decisions on bioethical situations. Consider, for example, this issue: The physician strongly advocates a particular medical procedure because of its effectiveness, but the patient, for personal reasons, does not want that procedure under any circumstances. Should the physician ignore the patient's wishes? Principle IV states that the physician shall respect the rights of the patient. Doesn't the patient have the right to ultimately decide what and how something is done to his or her body? The individual patient's rights in this situation supersede the physician's right. These guides do not operate in a vacuum. They are intertwined with many other concepts, which make them valuable to the practitioner. Informed consent requires the physician to advise the patient and make sure the patient understands the procedure(s). If, after informed consent, the patient continues to refuse that treatment, the physician is obligated to follow the patient's directives. There have been patient directives that resulted in the patient's death. If the patient is mentally competent to make such a decision, that decision must be respected.

▆ AMERICAN NURSES ASSOCIATION (ANA)   This

association, founded in 1896, is the principal professional organization for registered and licensed nurses, serving over 200,000 members.

At the most general level, a nurse can be defined as an individual who is professionally trained to care for the sick person. Nursing goes far beyond simply caring for the sick, however, to include promoting and restoring health, preventing illness, and alleviating suffering. Nurses are skilled at assessing and treating the sick, making nursing diagnoses, providing medication and treatment at the orders of the physician, and teaching the patient how to deal with an illness and prevent further problems.

There are two major levels of nursing certification determined by the amount and type of training received: registered nurses (RNs) and licensed practical nurses (LPNs), also known as licensed vocational nurses (LVNs) in some states. The LPN is a graduate of a nursing program, typically lasting about 13 months, that involves basic classroom and clinical training. Upon completion of their course work, LPN candidates take a licensing examination. If they pass, they are allowed to practice nursing within the boundaries of their state license. In the clinical hierarchy, these nurses are supervised by the RN.

A registered nurse has successfully completed the requisite classroom and clinical experience and passed the national nursing registration examination. Currently, the minimum education necessary to take the registration examination is completion of the 24-month associate degree in nursing (ADN). Before the expansion of associate degree nursing programs, the preparation for nursing was a diploma in nursing program. Hospitals created schools of nursing (which had to be accredited like college training programs) that generally offered a three-year program with a heavy clinical emphasis. Certain diploma programs can still be recognized by the shape of the graduates' caps. Graduates of these two programs may pursue the bachelor of science degree (BSN) in nursing. The BSN is increasingly demanded by health organizations for positions as director of nursing or vice president of nursing service. There are also graduate degrees in nursing, such as the master of science in nursing (MSN), the doctor of nursing science (Dr.N.Sci.), or a Ph.D. in nursing.

Nurses may also pursue certification in a clinical area, such as intensive care, emergency nursing, or surgery by passing an exam. Certification is voluntary but is valuable in helping take advantage of career opportunities. One can also specialize via education to become a nurse practitioner or nurse anesthetist.

The ANA recognizes a fundamental belief in the nature of individual needs and rights, the roles of nurses, and the relations between nurses, health, and society. Like many other health care organizations, the ANA developed a code for nurses' direction and guidance.

Preamble

The Code for Nurses is based on belief about the nature of individuals nursing, health, and society. Recipients and providers of nursing services are viewed as individuals and groups who possess basic rights and responsibilities, and whose values and circumstances command respect at all times. Nursing encompasses the promotion and restoration of health, the prevention of illness, and the alleviation of suffering. The statements of the Code and their interpretation provide guidance for conduct and relationships in carrying out nursing responsibilities consistent with the ethical obligations of the profession and quality in nursing care.

Code for Nurses

The nurse provides services with respect for human dignity and the uniqueness of the client unrestricted by considerations of social and economic status, personal attributes, or the nature of health problems.

The nurse safeguards the client's right to privacy by judiciously protecting information of a confidential nature.

The nurse acts to safeguard the client and the public when health care and safety are affected by the incompetent, unethical, or illegal practice of any person.

The nurse assumes responsibility and accountability for individual nursing judgments and actions.

The nurse maintains competence in nursing.

The nurse exercises informed judgment and uses individual competence and qualifications as criteria in seeking consultation, accepting responsibilities, and delegating nursing activities to others.

The nurse participates in activities that contribute to the ongoing development of the profession's body of knowledge.

The nurse participates in the profession's efforts to implement and improve standards of nursing.

The nurse participates in the profession's efforts to establish and maintain conditions of employment conducive to high quality nursing care.

The nurse participates in the profession's effort to protect the public from misinformation and misrepresentation and to maintain the integrity of nursing.

The nurse collaborates with members of the health professions and other citizens in promoting community and national efforts to meet the health needs of the public.

AMERICAN OSTEOPATHIC ASSOCIATION (AOA)

The national association of osteopathic physicians and surgeons. People trained in osteopathy use similar diagnostics, therapeutics, and other interventions to allopathic physicians in addition to osteopathic manipulative procedures. Graduates of osteopathic medical schools hold the D.O. degree, which leads to eligibility for a license for medical practice of therapeutics and surgery in all 50 states.

Like most if not all professional societies, the AOA also demands adherence to a Code of Ethics of its members.

AOA Code of Ethics (1985)

The American Osteopathic Association has formulated this Code to guide its member physicians in their professional lives. The standards presented are designed to address the osteopathic physician's responsibilities to others involved in health care, to patients, and to society.

Section 1. The physician shall keep in confidence whatever he may learn about a patient in the discharge of professional duties. Information shall be divulged by the physician when required by law or when authorized by the patient.

Section 2. The physician shall give a candid account of the patient's condition to the patient or to those responsible for the patient's care.

Section 3. A physician-patient relationship must be founded on mutual trust, cooperation, and respect. The patient, therefore, must have complete freedom to choose his physician. The physician must have complete freedom to choose the patients he will serve. However, the physician should not refuse to accept patients because of the patient's race, creed, color, sex, national origin, or handicap. In emergencies, a physician should make his services available.

Section 4. A physician is never justified in abandoning a patient. The physician shall give due notice to a patient or to those responsible for the patient's care when he withdraws from the case so that another physician may be engaged.

Section 5. A physician shall practice in accordance with the body of systematized and scientific knowledge related to the healing arts.

A physician shall maintain competence in such systematized and scientific knowledge through study and clinical applications.

Section 6. The osteopathic profession has an obligation to society to maintain its high standards and, therefore, to continuously regulate itself. A substantial part of such regulation is due to the efforts and influence of the recognized local, state, and national associations representing the osteopathic profession. A physician should maintain membership in and actively support such associations and abide by their rules and regulations.

Section 7. Under the law a physician may advertise, but no physician shall advertise or solicit patients directly or indirectly through the use of matters or activities which are false or misleading.

Section 8. A physician shall not hold forth or indicate possession of any degree recognized as the basis for licensure to practice the healing arts unless he is actually licensed on the basis of that degree in the state in which he practices. A physician shall designate his osteopathic school of practice in all professional uses of his name. Indications of specialty practice membership in professional societies, and related matters shall be governed by rules promulgated by the American Osteopathic Association.

Section 9. A physician shall obtain consultation whenever requested to do so by the patient. A physician should not hesitate to seek consultation whenever he/she believes it advisable.

Section 10. In any dispute between or among physicians involving ethical or organizational matters, the matter in controversy should first be referred to the appropriate arbitrating bodies of the profession.

Section 11. In any dispute between or among physicians regarding the diagnosis and treatment of a patient, the attending physician has the responsibility for final decisions, consistent with any applicable osteopathic hospital rules or regulations.

Section 12. Any fee charged by a physician shall compensate the physician for services actually rendered. There shall be no division of professional fees for referrals of patients.

Section 13. A physician shall respect the law. When necessary a physician shall attempt to help to formulate the law by all proper means in order to improve patient care and public health.

Section 14. In addition to adhering to the foregoing ethical standards, a physician should whenever possible participate in community activities and services.

The AOA's code of ethics reflects its concerns with bioethical issues. The code's authors assume that the osteopathic physician will be aware of unsettled issues surrounding the care and treatment of patients. They intend for the code, which is relatively short and general, to provide guidance to practitioners as they encounter a wide range of specific circumstances. The practitioner is expected to apply the generalized precepts to the specialized circumstance.

AMERICAN SOCIETY OF LAW, MEDICINE, AND ETHICS (ASLME)   Formerly the American Society of

Law & Medicine, ASLME differs from other professional organizations like the AMA because it is a multidisciplinary association of people with interests in law, medicine, and ethical philosophy. According to its 1988 bylaws, the association provides a professional, nonpartisan forum for the discussion of issues that touch law, medicine, and ethics through its publications and annual meetings. This forum offers the opportunity for intellectual discourse, interchange, criticism, and contribution from multiple perspectives. Its primary activity is to sponsor continuing education conferences and printed materials.

AMERICANS WITH DISABILITIES ACT OF 1990 (ADA)   The ADA (42 U.S.C. § 12111) is a federal law passed

in 1990 that extends protection against employment discrimination based on disability to private and public employees. Specifically, the ADA prohibits discrimination "against a qualified individual with a disability because of the disability of such individual in regard to job application procedures, hiring, advancement, or discharge of the employee, employee compensation, job training and others terms, conditions, and privileges of employment." A "qualified individual with a disability" is one who "with or without reasonable accommodation, can perform the essential functions of the employment position that such individual holds or desires." If the applicant is able to perform the essential functions of the position, the employer is required to offer the applicant reasonable accommodation, unless implementing such accommodation would impose an "undue hardship" on the employer.

The statutory definition of disability follows the definition found in earlier legislation (see Section 504 of the Rehabilitation Act of 1973, 29 U.S.C. §§ 701–796). Disability is defined as (1) a physical or mental impairment that substantially limits one or more of the major life activities of such individual; (2) a record of such an impairment; or (3) being regarded as having such an impairment. An employer who is faced with a disabled but otherwise qualified individual is obligated to make reasonable accommodation for the disability. These definitions raise several issues that are still being clarified by regulatory agencies and the courts, including the meaning of "essential functions of the position" and "reasonable accommodation by the employer."

It has been argued that the phrase "essential functions of the position" implies that a handicapped person need not be able to perform all of the position requirements, only those that are essential. Therefore it is argued that a form of discrimination against nonhandicapped people exists, since they would be required to perform all of the position requirements.

The ADA notes that reasonable accommodation requires two modifications: (1) making facilities readily accessible and usable, and (2) job restructuring; part-time or modified work schedules; reassignment to vacant positions; acquisition or modification of equipment or devices; appropriate adjustment or modification of examinations, training materials or policies; the provision of qualified readers or interpreters; and other similar accommodations for individuals with disabilities (42 U.S.C. § 12112). This definition of reasonable accommodation has been criticized as unclear and overly broad. The courts have been asked to clarify this requirement, but a succinct, broadly applicable statement has not yet been rendered.

The courts have recognized the employer's claim of undue hardship as a defense against a request for reasonable accommodation. To qualify as an undue hardship, the accommodation must present a significant challenge and/or be extremely costly. The authors of the legislation recognized that the type of company, its location, and the structure of the work force are factors in determining undue hardship, along with the size of the organization. The cost of accommodation may appear high if only one person is involved and the organization is small. In large organizations, however, the cost decreases as it is dispersed across a large area where many could benefit. Although larger corporations will incur greater expenses, they are also more capable financially of making reasonable accommodation. The essential consideration is whether the person's job can be modified without seriously penalizing the employer; if so, then the accommodation must occur. If the employer can prove that an undue hardship would be created, then the courts will not require that the employer comply with the requested accommodation.

The ADA has also raised several bioethical issues, because its definition of disability includes conditions that are both communicable and fatal, such as AIDS. The ADA recognizes an HIV-positive person as one with a handicapping condition. The employer is required to hire the qualified person with a disability, which gives rise to the question of risk to co-workers. AIDS is transmitted by the exchange of bodily fluids, and the potential for such exchanges on the job are debated issues. Many jobs do not provide the opportunity for physical contact, but even so, accidents such as a bloody nose or a machine laceration could bring about the exchange of fluids. Other occupations are more hazardous, including that of health care workers. It is remotely possible that an HIV-positive health care worker could pass fluids from herself to others. At risk here are not only the worker's colleagues but also the patients. However, statistics indicate that patients are at exceptionally low risk of receiving HIV from health care workers—only one such case has been reported. Ironically, health care workers face a much higher risk of contracting AIDS from their patients, since many do not advise the health care worker of their HIV-positive status.

Should these HIV-positive people be permitted to work and thereby place other workers at risk? According to the ADA, the answer is yes. To do otherwise is to illegally discriminate against a disabled person. This AIDS issue and others like it are debated by bioethicists. At issue is the balance between the consequence of discrimination versus the risk of contracting the disease.

AMNIOCENTESIS   The removal of fluid from the amniotic sac through the abdomen (amnio—membrane around the fetus; centesis—perforation). The amniotic fluid is entirely fetal in origin. It contains characteristics from both parents and allows identification of recessive chromosomes passed from the father that would be unrecognized in maternal fluid testing. Amniocentesis is typically used to evaluate the fetus for sex determination, chromosomal analysis, and enzyme studies. Many abnormalities such as anencephaly (a congenital disorder in which the baby is born without brain development) can be determined by this test.

Two major ethical issues arise with amniocentesis. First, in this test, the fetus is placed at risk. The risk is small and fetal risk is decreasing as the test becomes more common. Nevertheless, many critics believe that the womb should not be invaded for nonessential information. They argue that the test should be performed only if questions of serious disease or malformation are potentially present.

The second bioethical issue is related to the first. Often these tests are performed when a fetal medical problem is believed to exist. If a problem is discovered, the issue becomes whether or not to terminate the pregnancy (have an elective abortion). The debate on whether or not an abortion is appropriate when parents learn that their child is not completely healthy is extensive and emotional. Many parents of children with handicapping conditions shudder at the thought of possibly having had the opportunity to abort their child. They adamantly maintain that helping such a child grow is exceptionally rewarding. Many people who support the abortion option argue that the decision of whether or not to bring a seriously handicapped child into the world should be left to the parents who will be responsible for the child.

ANATOMICAL GIFTS   The gift of all or part of a body, to take effect upon or after the death of the donor (See **Organ and Tissue Donation, Uniform Anatomical Gift Act of 1987**). The federal government has recognized the right of people over 18 to indicate on their driver's license their intentions to donate their organs. Their decision is usually indicated by a tag on their license or an accompanying card, though states vary in their means of identifying of donors. Other donors indicate their willingness to make an anatomical gift through their living will, which allows a more complete statement of donor intentions. (See **Living Will.**)

Anatomical gifts do not always occur at death, however. In the case of kidney transplantation, for example, a living donor can provide one of his or her kidneys to a recipient and still live a fully normal life. Many siblings, once determined eligible, have donated a kidney to a brother or sister with end-stage renal (kidney) disease. These familial transplants are among the most successful due to the biological similarities between donor and recipient.

Can a person become a donor without indicating the intention to donate? Yes. The surviving family members have the right to make an anatomical gift of all or part of the decedent's body for an authorized purpose. However, if the decedent has indicated an unwillingness to be a donor, those wishes are honored. Regardless of the decision, if intentions regarding anatomical gifts have been communicated, the pressure of making such a decision is removed from the family members and they can comply with the decedent's wishes.

An important consideration for donors is whether or not they can revoke their decision, should they change their minds. The donor may revoke the donation by signing a revocation statement, orally communicating that intention to two people, advising a physician, or informing the recipient in writing.

ANENCEPHALY   A congenital neurological disorder in which the newborn has an essentially normally formed torso but an incompletely developed head. Notably there is an absence of the cerebral hemispheres. The top of the head may be covered with skin or it may be exposed. This condition is the most common severe birth defect in the United States and is always fatal. There are no therapeutic interventions for the fetus or for the infant after birth. In these cases, the infant is usually stillborn or expires within a few days after birth. Often the fetal condition is identified during the pregnancy and the mother will elect to have the pregnancy terminated.

TRANSPLANTATION ISSUES
Because the torso of the infant is apparently fully formed, questions of giving birth to the child and using its body for purposes of transplantation have arisen. The attractiveness of infant transplantation is derived from three factors: the ability of infant tissue to adapt to its new host, the favorable size of the organs for transplantation to other children, and the rarity of available infant organ donors. The principal concern with anencephalic transplantation is that a child with several congenital malformations often has other organ abnormalities that make them inappropriate for transplantation, including inadequate formation and mutated growth. Nevertheless, many parents wish to have their children considered for potential donation so that the child's short life will have had a meaning.

This exact situation arose in 1992 (*In re T.A.C.P.* 609 So.2d.588 [Fla.1992]). When a Florida mother gave birth to an anencephalic child, both parents agreed to donate the child's organs. The parents made immediate arrangements for donation, knowing that organs sustained by life support deteriorate quickly. The problem was that the child had not died. The partially functioning brain stem was maintaining a heart rhythm and physiologic activity, meaning that the child was not brain dead. In fact, the child was not dead under any organ donor guidelines (See **Death, Uniform Determination of Death Act**.) The family petitioned the Florida court to allow the transplantation to go forward, but the court denied it. After only a few days, the case reached the U.S. Supreme Court. The Court sustained the Florida courts and the infant died shortly thereafter. There were no reports of any organ transplantation.

The ethical debate surrounding these infants raises questions of life and death. The anencephalic infant does react to tactile stimulation and pain. However, the infant does not have a formed cerebral hemisphere, which guarantees death. Whether the infant is an appropriate donor or not begs the question: Should an infant with a known extremely short life span have its life taken on behalf of others needing transplants? Many people fear the slippery slope consequence that the question could be applied to others. In other words, other patients at different ages who have known extremely short life spans could also be justifiably used for transplantation. An example of syllogistic slippery slope logic suggests: (I) organ harvesting should occur as rapidly as possible in order to avoid organ deterioration. (2) The process of dying causes organs to deteriorate rapidly, making time a critical factor in organ transplantation. Therefore, if anencephalic infants are recognized as dying, then the organs are deteriorating rapidly and require rapid organ harvesting.

Complicating this logic, however, is the fact that these infants are not dead but dying. This issue is, therefore, if death is absolute certainty, can organs be harvested? Clearly, this is a bioethical issue with implications for many other medical situations, e.g., car accident victims and other trauma victims.

ANIMAL EXPERIMENTATION

The use of animals in biomedical and pharmaceutical experiments prior to using the drugs, procedures, and techniques on humans. A variety of animals are used to test the effectiveness of clinical interventions and to ascertain what dangers may exist to the recipient. Under common clinical standards, animal testing is virtually required prior to sending evaluation results of an activity to the federal Food and Drug Administration (FDA). Vivisection is the term used when surgical procedures are tested on animals.

Harvard University's New England Regional Primate Center uses monkeys to test a vaccine designed to protect people from human immunodeficiency virus (HIV). In 1991, two macaque monkeys were inoculated with simian immunodeficiency virus (SIV). Normally, the SIV is virulent and the monkeys would be dead within two years. However, these monkeys had been vaccinated in 1989 with an experimental vaccine containing an attenuated (weakened) form of SIV. The monkeys did become ill but not significantly. The immune system reaction was exceptional, however. Tests carried out in 1997 indicated that despite the 1991 inoculation of the SIV, the animals were not hurt because the vaccination somehow enabled their immune system to fight off the real SIV. These findings give rise to research that might help humans protect themselves from infection by HIV.

ANIMAL RIGHTS

Society has essentially recognized the need to use animals in clinical education and experimentation. Animals are used in laboratories in medicine, veterinary medicine, psychology, and other scientific disciplines to assist in the progression of knowledge. In the training of physicians, for example, animals are used to teach medical students how to treat diseases. In clinical experimentation, animals are test subjects used to ascertain the presence or absence of adverse consequences.

The prevailing rationale for using animals in this is that by exposing animals to the drugs or procedures, problems are identified and minimized or eliminated. In this way, humans are protected from harm. To not expose animals would place humans in danger. As humans are higher on the evolutionary scale (having the ability to think and act independently without instinct), humans should be protected.

Although protecting humans is important, animals too are recognized as having rights. For example, they have the right not to be subjected to cruel and inhumane treatment, not to be used in experimentation that lacks scientific justification, and to be protected from unnecessary painful treatment. Therefore, anesthesia is used whenever possible (unless the experiment requires its absence), and the animal is euthanized upon conclusion of the experiment to avoid any prolonged difficulty. The adherence to these rights by the researcher is voluntary, although there are also laws against animal abuse.

Most scientists and many animal rights advocates strongly believe in and promote adherence to these guidelines. A variety of companies place "No Animal Testing" on their ingredient labels because they do not believe in subjecting animals to the social whims of human beings. In other words, if humans are not directly threatened with significant or substantial harm by the product, then animals should not be subjected to pain or death in order to manufacture the product. For example, hair shampoo has been tested on rabbits to ascertain the discomfort associated with getting shampoo in the eyes. Animal rights advocates oppose testing animals for these purposes. A growing number of more radical animal rights groups espouse total avoidance of animal use in experimentation or scientific practice.

XENOGRAFTS

Also called heterografts, these are tissue exchanges (including blood and organs) between different species of animals. Many scientists are experimenting with the possibility that interspecies transplants can be successful. Current experiments involve growing organs within animals, and organs or tissue taken from animals and transplanted into humans. These grafts range from whole organs to bone marrow. Not all xenografts are experimental. The most common xenograft used today is implantation of porcine (derived from pigs) heart valves into humans. Proponents of these procedures point out the lack of available human donors and that animals are an appropriate alternative under the proper conditions. (See **Xenotransplantation.**)

ARTIFICIAL INSEMINATION   Any procedure placing the sperm into the woman's cervical canal accomplished by artificial techniques rather than natural means. For example, semen placed into a syringe and injected into the cervical canal is a very basic form of artificial insemination. Presuming a normal female anatomy and ovulation, a successful pregnancy can result.

If couples encounter problems when attempting to achieve pregnancy, many turn to their physicians to find out what is wrong. The physicians conduct studies to determine the presence or absence of anatomical or physiological problems such as a low sperm count or an inability to ovulate. Either the man or the woman could be sterile. The woman could be affected by her methods of contraception, the medication remaining in her system. Once these obvious problems have been eliminated, many patients are simply encouraged to "keep on trying." They are often encouraged to have sexual intercourse every third or fourth day to allow the male's sperm count to be at its maximum. They are also encouraged to determine the woman's ovulation cycle and tie their reproductive behavior to those times.

In some cases, one of the many artificial insemination techniques can result in a pregnancy.

ARTIFICIAL INSEMINATION–HOMOLOGOUS (AIH)

This medical procedure involves the use of the husband's sperm to inseminate the wife. There have been few challenges to this procedure outside of some religious objections to the necessity of masturbation to obtain semen.

ARTIFICIAL INSEMINATION–DONOR (AID)

In this procedure, sperm from a donor other than the husband is used to inseminate the wife. The sperm may have been taken from a known donor, a physician's office set of donors, or anonymously from a sperm bank. (For information on sperm bank donor quality standards, contact the American Fertility Society or the American Association of Tissue Banks for guidance in selecting the right resource.)

Under modern law and case decisions, the donor is not considered the father. Historically, the parent-child relationship has been an issue for child support and parenting obligations. The Uniform Parentage Act (UPA) of 1974 guides the resolution of these issues and provides guidance for courts in jurisdictions that have not adopted the UPA. The husband is recognized as the adoptive parent and incurs all of the associated responsibilities. Legal challenges can still occur because the UPA applies only (1) if the woman who is inseminated is a wife; (2) if she proceeds with the consent of her husband; and (3) the procedure is carried out under the supervision of a licensed physician. If any of these conditions are not met, the UPA is inapplicable.

In those situations where the UPA is inapplicable, the courts look to contract law. For example, cases have arisen when the husband did not provide a written affidavit accepting the donor insemination. Modern court decisions have recognized a presumption of consent to donor insemination where the husband holds the child out as his son/daughter. This decision is also consistent with the Uniform Status of Children of Assisted Conception Act, which has not been adopted in all jurisdictions.

One of the major questions that arises with any form of fluid donation involves the transmission of HIV or other serious disease. Screening of candidates and screening of fluids have become serious issues, although semen can be evaluated for HIV and several other diseases. Candidate histories and assurances of their accuracy have been demanded, but at this time no state guidelines or medical requirements exist. Other considerations include the requests for the opportunity to select donor eligibility more fully. The recipient and husband may wish to exclude some potential donors from the list of possible donors.

IN VITRO FERTILIZATION (IVF)

This term is used to indicate fertilization outside of the body and in the medical laboratory. The process begins when several ova (eggs) are surgically removed from the woman and placed into a glass containing appropriate amounts of semen. Once they are fertilized, they are placed into the uterus for natural growth and development. Usually this procedure is preceded by administration of fertility drugs to the woman so that more eggs are produced. The multiple eggs increase the chances of successful fertilization but also create potential problems. When multiple eggs are fertilized, the possibility of multiple births is greater. There is also a greater spontaneous abortion rate—some studies report twice the rate of normal pregnancies.

GAMETE INTRA-FALLOPIAN TUBE TRANSFER (GIFT)

This form of fertilization uses partial in vitro fertilization techniques. The ova and semen are combined and then injected into the fallopian tubes, where fertilization takes place.

CRYOPRESERVATION OF OVA

Cryopreservation is one of the modern techniques used to evaluate the genetic structure of the ova or pre-embryo. Ova are removed from the woman and frozen. Research has ascertained that about half of the frozen embryos are viable for implantation, although length of appropriate containment and adverse effects from the freezing are unknown.

Tennessee courts have been the legal hotbed for the status of frozen pre-embryos. In the divorce case of *Davis v. Davis* (842 S.W.2d 588 [Tenn.1992]), Mary Sue Davis wanted to use the pre-embryos for conception, but her husband did not want children. The trial court held that she should have possession of the pre-embryos because it was in the pre-embryo's best interest. Appellate court Justice Franks noted that "the sole issue on appeal is essentially who is entitled to control seven of Mary Sue's (cryopreserved) ova fertilized by Junior's sperm through the in vitro fertilization process." The appellate court reversed the trial court, giving the parties "joint custody" over the pre-embryos, which would require permission from both before the pre-embryos could be implanted. The Tennessee Supreme Court affirmed the appellate court decision but indicated that pre-embryos were not children or property and pre-embryos had no legal rights. The court recognized an ownership interest by both Davises that could be used as a guide in balancing the interests involved.

This area is ripe for bioethical and legal controversy because conception and children are involved. Malpractice charges and damages in obstetrics are noteworthy because of the sensitivity to any form of damages to a newborn.

Bioethically, an issue already exists in the status of pre-embryos. One state, Louisiana, gives them the status of children (La. Stat. Ann. Rev. St. 14:87.2). However, *Roe v. Wade* would seem to suggest that pre-implanted fertilized eggs have no such status. As biotechnological innovations increase, further challenges will arise.

ARTIFICIAL NUTRITION

The administration of nutrition to a person, usually by latex tubes inserted into the body. Artificial nutrition is used when a person is unable to feed herself. The most frequently used procedure is to entubate the person by placing the tube into the nose, then down the throat into the stomach. This type of tube placement is known clinically as a naso-gastric (or NG) tube (naso—nose; gastric—stomach). Another tubal method is the surgical implantation of a gastrostomy (ostomy—surgery creating artificial opening) tube. An incision is made in the patient's abdomen and the tube is placed into the stomach. Both techniques use commercial complete food formulas, often supplemented with chemically defined essential nutrient diets requiring little or no active digestion. Intravenous fluids may be added to ensure proper fluid intake and output.

Complications to these forms of feedings, such as diarrhea and gastrointestinal upset, are normally controllable. The NG tube follows normal anatomical channels, minimizing most complications—as long as the patient is carefully monitored. The gastrostomy potentially creates more side effects because of the necessity of surgery and the placement of the tube near multiple major organs.

The most difficult problems arising form artificial nutrition concern its termination. A competent adult has the right to accept or reject nutrition (and other life-sustaining interventions) and to specify the conditions under which termination of nutrition is to be considered. A living will may include instructions (advance directives) for care, should circumstances arise warranting their use. (See **Living Will.**)

When artificial nutrition is administered to incompetent people or people in a persistent vegetative state, it allows their bodies to continue functioning indefinitely after their minds have ceased normal functioning. (See **Nonmaleficence, Principle of.**) Two bioethical issues arise with respect to cessation of artificial nutrition. The most commonly followed issue concerns whether or not the person's can actually be improved. To resolve the issue, both the courts and physicians recognize guidelines focused upon therapeutic intervention. The guidelines have come from cases where people have lived for long periods of time in persistent vegetative states, such as *Matter of Quinlan* in 1976. Since then, there have been over 170 cases that give guidance in the decision to continue life-extending care. The various national medical associations have also developed guidelines. The guidelines suggest that the decision maker consider whether there is a chance of therapeutic intervention and recovery for the patient. If there is a chance, even a small chance, then withdrawal of nutrition and hydration should not be considered. Alternatively, if there is no chance for a return to "life," then nutrition and hydration can be withdrawn.

The second issue concerns the perception of the discomfort of dying from lack of nutrition and hydration. People assume that hunger pangs of terminally ill people resemble the hunger pangs of a fully competent, healthy person. This is an incorrect presumption. Medical research indicates that people experiencing the throes of an incurable and irreversible condition do not experience these same feelings of discomfort.

An incompetent person presents the most difficult ethical problem to those who must decide whether to withdraw nutrition and hydration. Many bioethicists argue that there is no single definition of an incompetence, and thus incompetence must be defined situationally. To pronounce a patient incompetent, the physician must recognize a lack of mental capacity in the patient and the inability to make decisions regarding her own care. However, mental incompetence alone is not enough. Physicians must make their determinations based upon the summary of mental and physical circumstances and consider the patient's possible recovery. The courts have made clear that if the patient's mental capabilities fluctuate between lucidity and incompetence, decisions made during lucidity must be recognized and followed. Where there is no chance for recovery, decisions for withdrawal of nutrition will consider the totality of circumstances. The family or significant other people will be consulted where possible.

A person in a persistent vegetative state exists in a condition where motor reflexes are exhibited but lacks cognitive function. (See **Persistent Vegetative State**.) The body will respond in terms of reflex. None of the person's actions or reactions are derived from thought. In this condition, "life" can be sustained by providing a complete diet. But is this treatment beneficial to the patient or greatly burdensome? (See *Cruzan v. Director, Missouri Department of Health.*) If the treatment is more burdensome than beneficial, then the courts will allow the withdrawal of nutrition.

AUTONOMY, PRINCIPLE OF   This principle, also called the right of self-determination or self-rule, requires recognition of the individual's right to determine his or her own future without interference from others. This principle is fundamental to U.S. legal and political convictions that the autonomous person has the right to act according to his or her own self-determined plan. The term *autonomy* is derived from the Greek *autos* (self) and *nomos* (rule or law).

According to T. L. Beauchamp and J. F. Childress in *Principles of Biomedical Ethics,* the extent to which human behavior is autonomous may be analyzed in terms of those people who act intentionally, with understanding, and without controlling influences that determine their action. These people act purposefully and knowledgeably without external controls on their selection of decision or behavior. The individual accepts the consequences of his or her decisions. Social protections established in order to prevent harm to others do not reduce the value of this principle of autonomy because it is based upon other equally powerful principles, such as the principles of justice or nonmaleficence.

The principle of autonomy is a basic guide for health care providers. Adherence to this principle requires respect for the person and the decisions he made, whether or not the care giver agrees with the decision. One of the main applications of the principle of autonomy involves informed consent. (See **Informed Consent**.) To make a decision, one needs complete and understandable information about the situation, the alternatives, and the possible consequences. For example, an attorney was diagnosed with a serious, rapidly developing cancer. After researching the disease and the treatment alternatives, he elected to not participate in any curative procedures because of the personal burden that would be involved. Instead, he chose pain medication and used his remaining time to tie up his personal and professional life. Was there the possibility of a cure? There was a small chance. Should he have pursued that chance? He investigated his options and intentionally decided not to participate in medical interventions other than palliative care. Whether the care givers agreed with his decision or not is not the issue. According to the principle of autonomy, he has the right to autonomous self-determination and to end his life on his own terms.

The principle of autonomy is one of the underlying themes guiding many legal and medical decisions and actions, such as the physician-patient relationship and the various codes of patients' rights. Though it may be unstated, its presence is easily recognized. Rarely does this principle occur in isolation, however. Competing principles may also be recognized, and the circumstances of the situation will require analysis to determine which principle is most determinative.

AUTOPSY   Also known as post mortem examination or necropsy, an autopsy is the examination of a dead body to determine cause of death. This examination is usually required by statute if the death is unexpected or associated with crime—that is, if the death was violent, a suicide, or occurred in a suspicious or unusual manner. Guidelines for conducting autopsies are often found in state statutes, usually associated with directions to the coroner.

Because of the unusual nature of the death, an autopsy may interfere with the decedent's intention to donate organs. The priority of accurately determining the cause of death under suspicious circumstances will void organ donation. The time and conditions required for an adequate autopsy would negate any possible organ viability for transplantation. If consent is required for the autopsy, the order of people legally acceptable to provide consent is indicated by statute.

B

BENEFICENCE, PRINCIPLE OF   This principle requires that the medical practitioner act in the best interests of the patient. It is an obligation assumed by practitioners to help patients gain benefits and interests in reaching their best outcomes. This rule, according to many bioethicists, follows the principle of autonomy in priority and becomes dominant when patients are unable or incompetent to communicate their personal choices. The rule complements the principle of nonmaleficence by prioritizing the patient's right to services in his or her best interest.

When the patient makes a decision that most believe is not in his or her best interest, the principles of autonomy and beneficence conflict. Unless there are statutes or common law precedents guiding the decision, the principle of autonomy is considered dominant when the individual is competent to make her own decisions. Where the individual is incompetent, then autonomy cannot be communicated and beneficence is the guide.

An example of the application of these principles occurs when a patient loses the ability to indicate his or her decisions and has not communicated them at an earlier time. The priority of recognizing a person's autonomy is considered first. Once it is determined that the patient is incapable of exercising autonomy, clinical science is obligated to determine how it may contribute to the patient's welfare, with guidance from a surrogate if one exists. Justice Sandra Day O'Connor, in her concurrence in *Cruzan v. Director, Missouri Department of Health* (492 US 261 [1990]), indicated that "the Constitution permits a State to require and convincing evidence of Nancy Cruzan's desire to have artificial hydration and nutrition withdrawn [Principle of Autonomy] . . . does not preclude a future determination that the Constitution requires the States to implement the decisions of a patient's duly appointed surrogate. Nor does it prevent States from developing other approaches for protecting an incompetent individual's liberty interest in refusing medical treatment. . . . the more challenging task of crafting appropriate procedures for safeguarding incompetent's liberty interests is entrusted to the 'laboratory' of the States [Principle of Beneficence.]" In short, the state can require clear evidence of the person's requests before accepting the word of a surrogate decision maker. The person's individual rights are foremost.

These principles are incorporated into modern medical decision making even when not consciously recognized. They also allow a justiciable balance for modern court decision making, offering guidelines for balancing benefits and harms.

BEST INTERESTS OF CHILD STANDARD   The policy guideline used by the court that requires evaluation of the activities done on behalf of a child to be in the "best interests" of that child. Children, infants, and especially young children are considered unable to make a competent decision when that decision requires knowledge and exposure the child would not have or would be unable to comprehend. Under federal and state constitutions, parents or guardians have the responsibility to make those important decisions. The fundamental belief is that the parents will reach a conclusion for the child that would yield the best results. Circumstances warranting the use of this standard arise when a parent or guardian is responsible for making decisions for the child(ren), yet the decision appears to contradict societal notions of correctness or public policy.

Making decisions for the provision of health care exemplifies the application of the best interests of the child. A person under the age of 18 is considered a minor and thus requires guardian or parental consent in health care decisions. Competence is a legal prerequisite to receiving health care. Where a person is incompetent, the parent or guardian are responsible for providing the necessary consent. Several exceptions exist because competence can be gained, and because society accepts certain conditions as indicative of competence. For example, a 17-year-old may be married, a mother, a member of the armed forces, or living independently. Under these circumstances, it is clearly necessary for the child to be capable of consenting to or refusing a medical procedure. Also, "mature minor" rules allow an unusually capable "child" to give or refuse treatment consent without parental approval.

For the majority of children, however, parental consent to a health care procedure is required, and in the vast majority of decisions, parental consent is not challenged. Certain circumstances have, however, call into question a parental decision. *Bowen v. American Hospital Association* (476 US 610 [1986[), which is actually a set of three cases, provides guidance for parental decisions. The case began in 1982 when Baby Doe was born in Bloomington, Indiana, with Down's syndrome (technically known as trisomy 21), a condition in which an extra chromosome of a particular type is present in an otherwise balanced cell. The baby was also born with an abnormal passageway in his throat (tracheoesophageal fistula) requiring surgery to allow him to eat and drink orally. After being informed of the complete condition of the child, the parents denied the surgery. They permitted only the administration of morphine and Phenobarbital to negate discomfort for the six days prior to the baby's death, and the physicians followed the parents' wishes. However, legal interventions were attempted by interested third parties through the Indiana courts, and the case did reach the U.S. Supreme Court. There it was declared moot, because Baby Doe had died.

These parents refused to consent to surgery specifically because of their child's Down's syndrome. Advocacy groups, state and federal human service agencies, and politicians, including President Ronald Reagan, all questioned the parents' right to make such a decision based upon a handicapping condition. President Reagan directed the federal Department of Health and Human Services (DHHS) to determine a means of preventing this consequence should a similar situation occur. The DHHS determined that Section 504 of the Rehabilitation Act of 1974 (29 U.S.C.A. § 794) would allow funds to be withheld from health care organizations participating in federally funded activities if they were found to discriminate against infants on the basis of handicap. Signs announcing nondiscriminatory policies towards handicapped infants were ordered posted in pediatric units and infant/pediatric intensive care units, and a toll-free telephone number was created to encourage reporting of instances of discrimination. However, these activities were later rescinded because appropriate implementation procedures were not followed.

New child protective laws were then created in the early 1980s that clearly specified federal and state governmental agency involvement. These actions resulted in the third step of the case sequence, a 5–3 decision by the U.S. Supreme Court. Unfortunately, there is no written majority opinion. Thus the result was a policy compromise that gave the major responsibility for intervention to state human service agencies. Since that time, the courts have intervened and denied parental wishes in similar cases where the child was likely to survive.

Perhaps in response to the nature of the Court's decision, Congress created the Child Abuse Prevention and Treatment Act in 1987 (45 C.F.R. Part 1340). In this act the concept of medical neglect was introduced, making it possible to prosecute physicians who withheld treatment from a disabled infant with a life-threatening condition. Physicians were forbidden to withhold medical interventions that could correct the problems. Only if the infant is incurably comatose or the treatment would simply prolong futility, could medical treatment be legally withheld.

Two other examples of applications of the best interests of child standard involve religious beliefs and surrogate parenting. The exercise of religious beliefs is protected by the First Amendment of the U.S. Constitution and applied to the states by the Fourteenth Amendment. Competent adults can decide, on the basis of their religious beliefs, to allow their lives to end. But is it in the best interests of the child to follow the parents' religious precepts? This question has been analyzed in a variety of situations. Arguably, *The Application of the President and Directors of Georgetown College, Inc.* (331 F.2d 1000 [D.C. Cir.1964]) provides the modern decision. The mother in this case was a Jehovah's Witness, a denomination that does not allow medical intervention. Following this religious belief, the mother denied a blood transfusion for her child. The judge weighed the issue of whether the state or the mother had the greater right to make a decision. Constitutional issues are often decided on this rational basis test, in which the court asks, Does the state have the greater obligation (called a compelling state interest) to protect the victim of the decision or does the religious belief take priority? The judge indicated that the state as parens patriae (that is, the state is allowed to act as legal guardian) will not permit a parent to allow a child to die, and that the state has a compelling state interest in the life of the child. The circuit court held that a religious belief can be overcome, even though freedom of religion is a constitutionally guaranteed right.

This same religious question has been raised regarding religious healers. The Church of Christian Science has accredited practitioners who perform spiritual healing. Almost all states recognize these healers, because the states have no compelling reason to forbid this form of exercise of religion. In 1996, the Christian Science Church was called into court for these practices. As a result, the church's healers were more strictly confined in their practices, and medical procedures were determined to be mandated in more situations than the church desired. However, this decision was not considered a violation of constitutional religious protections.

Surrogate parenting typically takes place when a couple is incapable of having a child. To remedy that condition, and in order to make the child as biologically close as possible, a legal contract is written between the husband and another woman, who is artificially inseminated with the man's sperm. The contract stipulates that she carry the baby and at birth, give the child to the couple for adoption. However, there have been instances where the birth mother has had second thoughts about giving up the baby. One argument for repudiating the contract has been the "best interests of the child" standard. The argument is that the biological mother is best suited for raising the child because of the natural chemical ties that arise with the infant during gestation and the birthing process. This argument has carried weight with bioethicist George Annas, who characterizes surrogate mothering as harming real children by making them into commercial products and legally separating them from their natural mothers. (See **Surrogate Mothering**.)

BIOETHICS Bioethics, also known as biomedical ethics, is the empirical and intellectual examination of moral issues in health and medical life. This bioethical analysis includes the roles of people uniquely trained in therapeutic and palliative care and their decisional rights toward the right to life and the right to die, and considers the extent to which these people influence human behavior. Proponents of this field of inquiry argue that there are responsibilities, obligations, and situations unique to this arena. The kinds of issues that arise almost daily in the medical field make this form of moral analysis more application-oriented than other ethical categories. These unique issues require analyzing facts, identifying inherent moral challenges, and analyzing alternatives according to broader moral principles and concepts. (See pp. 6–7 for extensive discussion.)

BIOMEDICINE The application and use of the natural biological sciences in clinical medicine. Clinical medicine takes its fundamental tools from the basic biological sciences such as biology, biochemistry, and zoology. Biomedicine and related subjects provide the basic knowledge required for students studying to become medical practitioners and other clinical professionals. These subjects are introduced in secondary education science programs, then further developed in college and university programs. Specialized application of biomedicine to different careers occurs in select program curricula, with many of these careers requiring university related graduate education and postgraduate training in hospitals and research settings.

BIOTECHNOLOGY An association between technology and human life and its application within the health, medical, and pharmaceutical sciences. Biotechnology involves a wide range of investigations. For example, the pharmaceutical company Genentech has identified therapeutic interventions naturally achieved by a healthy body. They have taken the natural substance and used it for the same purposes as nature intended, but in greater dosages. Specifically, Genentech sells a natural substance entitled TPA™, which stands for recombinant tissue plasminogen activator. This drug is a natural substance recognized for its clot-dissolving (thrombolytic) properties and is useful in ameliorating heart attack (myocardial infarct) and stroke (cerebrovascular accident). Genentech carries a U.S. patent on its development, a normal protection for an organization that has developed a significant product. This protection is under fire, however, because TPA™ is a product of biotechnology. Since TPA™ is a natural substance that all humans produce, some public policy proponents advocate that companies should not have the right to patent the procedure developing it.

Another example of biotechnology's potential is the artificial heart. Perhaps the best-known of the mechanical heart transplants was the December 2, 1982, implantation of the Jarvik–7™ mechanical heart into the body of a 62-year-old Indiana dentist by surgeon William DeVries. Dr. Barney Clark agreed to be the subject of a heart experiment that involved the removal of his biological heart and its replacement with a permanent mechanical heart. Was the surgery successful? The answer depends upon the evaluator. Dr. Clark lived for only a short time—112 days— after the implant. He was able to go out of the hospital only in a medical van because he had to remain attached to his external power source. He was never discharged from the hospital and died from a pulmonary embolus. One of the ironies of this biotechnological experiment was that at the moment of Dr. Clark's death, the clicking of his mechanical heart valves could still be heard. The experiment was considered a success in the sense that a person did live with an artificial heart. It also showed that there is still a long way to go before this practice becomes entirely acceptable.

BIRTH   Birth is the complete separation of the fetus from its mother after it has proceeded through a gestation period. A fetus may be stillborn (born dead) or may be born via cesarean section, a medical procedure in which the obstetric surgeon delivers the baby through an incision in the abdominal and uterine walls.

From a bioethical-legal standpoint, the definition of birth is not as clear. The written decision of the U.S. Supreme Court in *Roe v. Wade* (410 US 113 [1973]) considered the gestation period prior to birth to consist of three trimesters. (See **Abortion** for discussion of *Roe v. Wade*.) The third trimester is characterized by fetal movement (quickening) and the ability of the fetus to survive outside of the womb with medical assistance. This ability gives the state a compelling interest in what happens to the fetus. Thus the definition of birth here appears to be whether the fetus could survive if the birth were to happen at each period.

PREMATURE BIRTH

Occurs when the mother initiates delivery of the fetus despite the fact that the gestation period (and fetal development) is incomplete. Medical science has the ability to recreate a mother's womb (artificial womb) in a neonatal intensive care unit (NICU), and the youngest fetus to survive premature birth was at approximately the fifth month of pregnancy. However, the medical sophistication required is at the apex of biotechnology, and the cost of survival is extraordinary. These children are potentially confronted with a myriad of developmental problems, and their prognosis for survival is often not positive. The state is often forced into the position to support such costly endeavors. The principle of beneficence recognizes that medical science should do what is best for each person. (See **Beneficence, Principle of**.) Within beneficence falls the converse, principle of nonmaleficence, which recognizes that the physician has an affirmative obligation to do no harm. (See **Nonmaleficence, Principle of.**) According to scholars, for example, B. R. Furrow et al. in *Bioethics: Health Care Law and Ethics*, these principles are priority guidelines for the physician when the patient cannot articulate his or her personal intentions. The courts also apply these principles in evaluating the physician's decisions affecting that patient.

The bioethical principles guiding medical science and advancing biotechnology have caused a debate over policies concerning the application of science and technology to the situation of extreme premature birth. The decisions that have been reached on sustaining life for these infants are inconsistent and unclear. There appears to be an opportunity for "wrongful life" causes of action when death might be the preferred option in the face of inadequate fetal development. There are also opportunities for discrimination claims against the state when these sophisticated technologies are not applied uniformly. Finally, in today's cost-conscious society, policy analysts are cognizant that the costs of sustaining life may be extreme and the benefits are probably not commensurate with the high costs.

BIRTH CONTROL   *See* CONTRACEPTION

BLOOD TRANSFUSION   A blood transfusion is blood administered to a patient during a medical procedure or surgery. Blood for transfusions is derived by two primary means: autologous transfusions and person-to-person donation. In autologous transfusions, people donate blood for their own use in an upcoming surgery. This

method insures that compatibility is not an issue and that the patient will not be exposed to any diseases from other donors.

Blood is also donated by volunteers through organizations such as the American Red Cross, which operate blood banks. The blood donation is extensively tested to prevent any possible disease from being passed from the donor to the recipient. Throughout this process, blood banks are extremely cautious. They take every possible step to protect the donor and the recipient. New, sterile needles are used and then destroyed. Tests of blood samples are conducted upon the donated blood before the blood is considered for transfusion to make sure it is not the vector of transmission of a serious disease.

Blood transfusions are lifesavers to hemophiliacs, who must receive blood transfusions because their own blood lacks clotting factors. Without these transfusions, a small scratch could potentially cause a victim of this disorder to die from blood loss. The bleeding simply would not stop. Blood containing the clotting factors is administered and many lives are made much longer and happier.

There are also potential problems involving transfusions. In the early 1980s, before the new, more stringent tests were introduced, the human immunodeficiency virus (HIV) was passed by blood transfusions. Many people are familiar with the cases of Arthur Ashe and Ryan White. Ashe, one of the world's greatest tennis players, and White, a happy young boy with hemophilia, were infected with HIV from blood transfusions. Their widely publicized experiences exposed the dangers of transferring body fluids, but it also gave rise to the erroneous notion that one can get HIV from donating blood. Not true. When the blood bank is following standard procedures, new needles are used and used ones are immediately destroyed, there is no chance for transferal of blood between people.

Because of the publicity these two cases received, autologous blood donation remains a popular option. However, blood testing today is extensive, these situations rarely if ever occur. The motivation to further improve the sensitivity and specificity of blood testing for other diseases potentially transmissible via transfusion continues to increase.

BOUVIA, ELIZABETH   The case of Elizabeth Bouvia was one of the most compelling examples of the controversy surrounding the right to die. Bouvia, at age 28, had suffered with cerebral palsy and was a quadriplegic. She was incapable of self-mobility or caring for her most intimate needs, and was a patient in a public hospital. Despite her physical challenges, she was mentally very alert and had completed her college degree. However, as a result of these living conditions, she expressed her request to die by voluntary starvation. The clinical staff had entubated her with a nasogastric tube (see **Artificial Nutrition**) contrary to her express instructions. When the hospital staff would not permit her to carry out her fully informed decision, she initiated legal action.

In *Bouvia v. Superior Court (Glenshur)* (225 Cal. Rptr. 297 [Cal. App. 2 Dist.1986]) the trial court upheld the clinical staff's interventions. Appealing the decision, Bouvia argued that a patient has the right to refuse medical treatment even if the removal creates a life-threatening result. The appellate court overturned the trial court decision and held that an adult person who is in sound mind has the right to control what happens to his or her body, even if death is the consequence. The justice writing the majority opinion recognized that decision making was a right as fundamental as the right of privacy. As such, it is constitutionally guaranteed. Simply put, a competent person has the right to decide her future. Bouvia could spend 15–20 years in this condition, being further subject to the deteriorating complications of arthritis and cerebral palsy. In view of these realities, Bouvia, as a competent and knowledgeable person, has the right to make her own moral and philosophical decision. It is not the role of her physicians or the courts to make such a decision on her behalf. The hospital should not practice medicine against her stated desires but should, as a matter of practice, alleviate her pain and suffering. Bouvia died peacefully shortly thereafter.

Bouvia reflects the application of the principle of autonomy. The patient has the right to choose a consequence that others may not select. Nevertheless, the patient is making the decision for herself and herself only. This right to this result must be respected. However, the principle of beneficence was also considered, since the physicians are obligated to help her avoid unnecessary pain and suffering. The benefit is furthered by the court's instructions that she should be allowed to die with ease and dignity. This decision has received widespread support from the bioethical, legal, and medical communities.

 BOWEN V. AMERICAN HOSPITAL ASSOCIATION (1986) *See* BEST INTERESTS OF CHILD STANDARD

 BRAIN DEATH See DEATH, UNIFORM DEFINITION OF DEATH ACT; PERSISTENT VEGETATIVE STATE

BREAST IMPLANTS   Surgically inserted, soft and malleable plastic pouches designed to enhance the female breast. Most often implants are used after a woman has had a partial or radical mastectomy (partial or full breast surgical removal) to recreate the breast. This surgery can have positive psychological benefits for a victim of breast disease by returning her perception of her femininity. Implants have also been used for cosmetic breast augmentation purposes.

Today, implants often contain saline solution, a solution of sodium chloride in purified water. In the past, the implants contained silicone. Initially, the silicone implants created few if any problems. But as they aged, some problems arose when the silicone leaked into the breast tissue. In several cases, breast cancer resulted from the leak. The victims sued the manufacturers, primarily Dow Corning, under a products liability cause of action. As a result, the company was forced into Chapter 11 bankruptcy reorganization and continued to settle claims.

C

CARDIOPULMONARY RESUSCITATION (CPR)

Cardiopulmonary resuscitation ("cardio" refers to the heart, "pulmonary" to the lungs) essentially means to bring back or to restart the heart and lungs by some action. CPR is an emergency rescue technique used to restore heartbeat and respiration to a victim whose heart and breathing have stopped. The rescuer breathes into the lungs and compresses the chest to act as a pumping heart.

Many people believe that everyone should be educated and certified in the use of CPR, which has helped many victims who have suffered a heart attack (myocardial infarction) or nearly drowned. Although CPR is not always successful, it is a very substantial tool in our repertoire of lifesaving techniques, especially for the first people on the scene.

There are times, however, when CPR should not be used. CPR should not be attempted on a person who has a pulse, even a very weak pulse. In this case, the chest compressions by the rescuer would not assist the heart in its action, but would interfere with the normal sequence of the heartbeat, causing the heart to beat irregularly. These cardiac arrhythmias (also called dysrhythmias) are potentially fatal, notably the form of arrhythmia called cardiac fibrillation. In this form of arrhythmia, each of the four chambers of the heart beat of their own accord and in their own rhythm. Though the heart in this condition seems to quiver, resembling a shaking bowl of gelatin, the quivering is really an irregular, nonsequential beat that eliminates the pumping capability of the heart. If the heart is not returned to a sequential, pumping rhythm (called sinus rhythm), the victim will die. Cardioversion (electric shock to the heart) is frequently used when a victim's heart is fibrillating to return the heart to sinus rhythm.

CPR also presents an ethical challenge under certain circumstances. First, consider the physical realities associated with CPR. CPR is not a light massage. To make the heart beat, the provider must compress the chest with some degree of force. The rescuer is substituting the compression for the heart muscle moving the blood throughout the body. Considering the physical force required, should CPR be attempted on a fragile person? Brittle ribs could break with the force of chest compressions. Under the principle of beneficence, the damage done to the chest of the person may be more painful than death, and the broken bones may puncture a lung or cause the person's death in another way. On the other hand, aren't rescuers obligated to prevent death? Again, the ethical considerations are raised without clear answers. An analysis of circumstance at the point of intervention will be required. Ideally, the victim's advance directives will have notified the health provider of his or her wishes in advance.

Ironically, several cases of "wrongful life" have resulted from CPR. In one notable case in Cincinnati, Ohio, the patient had authorized his physician to write Do Not Resuscitate (DNR) orders onto his medical chart. The orders were clearly written, yet when the individual's heart stopped, CPR and other life-sustaining interventions were used. The patient was resuscitated and lived for approximately two more years, dying of a stroke (cerebrovascular accident). Before the patient died, he sued the hospital and won. The hospital staff were held by the court to be liable for wrongful life because their staff did not follow the patient's and his attending physician's orders not to resuscitate him.

These wrongful life cases are rare, however. When they do occur, the problem most frequently arises from a violation of a living will or DNR order. In other words, they occur in health care settings where health care providers attempt to postpone death for victims in violation of their known directives. In few instances outside of the health care organization or with in-home health care situations would one be at risk of being sued for wrongful life.

CHILD PROTECTIVE LAWS   Federal and state laws written to deal with issues involving whether or not the child has been denied the essentials of life, that is, clothing, education, food, housing, and medical care. In health care, legal issues arise concerning the protection of children with regard to medical treatment.

All states have developed guidelines for child abuse and neglect. They are used to determine whether a child has been denied the essentials for life and the state should assume custody. The people susceptible to questions of neglect are most commonly the child's caretaker—a parent, grandparent, relative, or teacher. To initiate the question of neglect, the state must have probable cause (the legal term for a reasonable belief that something improper has occurred) to believe that neglect occurred. If the state demonstrates this reasonable belief, then it may obtain temporary protective custody. The more severe the neglect and degree of proof met, the longer the state may retain custody of the child.

Health care workers have become central players in those protective laws dealing with child abuse, especially emergency department personnel. Many states require the health care worker (physicians, nurses, social workers, etc.) who suspects a case of abuse or neglect to report it to the child protective services agency. Some states penalize these workers for failing to report cases of suspected abuse. However, the requirement that health workers turn in suspected cases of child abuse may discourage parents from bringing children into the health care setting for fear of these reports. This chilling effect has not been clearly researched, and the issue is remains a concern.

MEDICAL NEGLECT

If a health care provider has failed to provide medical treatment, neglect has probably occurred. The concept of medical neglect gained recognition in *Bowen v. American Hospital Assn.* (1986), a case in which the medical staff followed the parent's directives and did not treat the child. The child had Down's syndrome and an intestinal blockage. Even though the blockage could be corrected surgically, the parents did not wish the medical intervention. A political firestorm followed as the parental decision and medical adherence to it was soundly criticized. The result was the amended Child Abuse Prevention and Treatment Act (42 U.S.C. § 5101). Medical neglect was defined as the withholding of medically indicated treatment from disabled infants with life-threatening conditions. Medically indicated treatment is treatment that, in the physician's reasonable medical judgment, will most likely be effective in ameliorating or correcting the infant's medical conditions and result in reasonable survival. The legislators recognized that some infants' problems may not be medically correctable (if the child is comatose and irreversibly deteriorating, for example). If the child's condition is not correctable or the intervention would simply prolong the process of dying, then intervention is probably not warranted, and withholding treatment in this instance would not constitute neglect.

PARENTAL NEGLECT

The issue of parental neglect arises primarily in cases where parents adhere to a religious belief that does not permit health care or types of medical treatment for their children. Because parents are the natural decision makers for minor children and the state traditionally defers to parental judgments, the removal of parental authority is a complicated action. When the state believes it is necessary to intercede in the parental authority, it is recognizing a form of intentional child neglect. This intentional neglect occurs when the course of parental action results in the child not receiving appropriate health care interventions and may result in significantly impaired health or death. Under these circumstances and upon proving probable cause, the state will be able to gain custody of the child for the short term. To remove the parental decision making authority more permanently, a full court hearing is usually required. Custody often involves the appointment of a guardian for the child who has the authority to approve the health care procedure or treatment. The state must prove by clear and convincing evidence that it has complied with statutory requirements and should assume responsibility for decision making on behalf of the child on a more permanent basis. (See **Standards of Proof**.) Unless this intermediate standard of proof is met, the state is unable to maintain custody and parental rights are primary.

Parents who knowingly refuse (which is considered implied intention) to allow their children to have medical interventions have been criminally prosecuted. Charges of murder, negligent homicide, manslaughter, and others have been filed when the child died of apparent parental neglect.

See also **Best Interests of Child Standard.**

CHOICE IN DYING　Few experiences in life are more personal than the process of dying. People want to control their circumstances and means of dying as much as possible. They especially want to avoid the situation where they are incompetent to make their own decisions and the family is left with the burden of deciding what to do. In California during the 1980s, a group of people wanted to create the means to stipulate how death would occur even though they were unable to decide for themselves. For example, if a person is near death when she is admitted to the hospital, should all modern technology be used to help extend her life at great expense? This group's final product was a model document that became the forerunner of today's Living Will. Since that time, many states have passed legislation on Living Wills, which allow individuals to indicate their desires for technology and treatment should a deadly situation arise. (See **Living Will**.)

CHOICE OF EVILS DEFENSE　This defense is also called the "damned if you do and damned if you don't" defense. It is used in response to a situation where a person had to take the life of one person to save the life of another. The choice of evils is the recognition that to save a life, sometimes you must take a life. It is clearly a defense to be used as a protection to a person confronted with a last resort type of action.

A hypothetical example of this dilemma: A parent and two children are thrown overboard from a boat. The children are thrashing about in fear.

Because of these conditions, the parent can save only one of the two children. Which is saved? A horrible decision to be made, yet one that must be made.

A situation exemplifying the choice of evils decision occurred in the 1995 Lakeberg conjoined twin surgery, although the case did not go to trial. Amy and Angela were conjoined twins (also called Siamese twins). A large portion of their bodies was joined, and they shared single organs. The infants were believed incapable of survival in their conjoined state. If one was to survive, the shared organs had to be taken from the other, and without vital organs, the second infant would die. The question for the doctors to answer was which one? Death was inevitable for one of the children.

The choice of evils defense can be found in civil and criminal trials. The analysis, according to Professor George Annas, involves justification of the allocation of best interests. He asks, Is it ever in society's best interests for someone to die? Leaving this question unanswered, he notes that the weight of the decision is based on how well society recognizes the fairness of the decision about who lives and who dies.

CHRISTIAN SCIENCE, CHURCH OF   This religious denomination advocates spiritual healing and natural healing. It is recognized among bioethicists and health care practitioners for a unique aspect, that of the Christian Scientist healer. The healer is a religious person rather than a physician, nurse, or other therapist. This individual attends to the sick through ministrations of prayer. Reports have indicated a higher disease and death rate among Christian Scientists than nonpractitioners. The influence of Christian Scientist healers was severely curtailed in 1997 with new court decisions on children's treatment.

CIVIL RIGHTS ACT OF 1964   As amended by the Equal Employment Opportunity Act of 1972, a very influential act for health care organizations in issues concerning employment. It was passed initially in 1964 and has been amended several times to include newly identified groups under its protective umbrella. The act is now intended to prevent discrimination on the basis of age, color, national origin, pregnancy, race, or religion. Individuals who fall within each of these categories are considered members of "protected classes." Membership in one of these protected classes is fundamental to claiming discrimination. Discrimination may occur in terms of disparate treatment of an individual on the basis of his or her protected class. Or, the individual may be a representative of a protected class that the policies of the employer discriminate against, called disparate impact.

Title VII is a particularly important section of the Civil Rights Act (42 U.S.C.A. §§ 2000e et seq.), which is administered by the Equal Opportunity Employment Commission (EEOC). People who consider that they have been discriminated against on any one of the bases noted in the act should contact an employment attorney about filing a Title VII discrimination claim with the EEOC. Time requirements are strict; a complaint must be filed within 180 days (six months) of the incident. Most states have an equivalent to Title VII and the EEOC, which enables a person to potentially pursue both a federal and state legal option.

Title VII influences the relationship between physicians and the health organization. Under the current organizational framework, physicians are not employees of the hospital where they practice but private business people whom the hospital has granted practice privileges. Practice privileges are applied for by the physician and indicate the extent of practice the physician is allowed. For example, an attending physician has admitting and complete practice privileges at the hospital. A physician given courtesy privileges is granted the opportunity to indicate an affiliation with the hospital but does not have true practice privileges. A new physician, new either to the hospital or to the practice of medicine, has provisional credentials because she is still learning the practice of medicine at this specific location. As she demonstrates competency, her privileges are increased.

These practice privileges can be construed as an employment relationship if the hospital has control over the physician's access to patients, that is, control over the economic relationship. Under some forms of health care organization, such as a health maintenance organization, physicians are hired as employees with complete Title VII protections.

COMA   A state of unconsciousness resembling very deep sleep from which the patient cannot be awakened; consciousness, or a responsive brain, is suspended during a comatose state. A coma may or may not be reversible. In a light coma, the body may move in response to discomfort, and for these, the prognosis is usually good. The more commonly held perception of a coma is the deep coma, in which motor and psychological responses to stimulation are lost. The deep coma is severe and the patient is considered in a critical medical condition. Clinicians and researchers hold differing opinions on the extent of the victim's loss of sensation in a deep coma. There have been claims that the comatose person may be able to hear or understand some external activities even though they are unresponsive. Comas occur under a variety of circumstances: within the natural process of dying, as a result of accident or disease, or as induced by physicians to assist the patient to survive.

Different chemical and physiologic changes are associated with the different causes of a coma. In comas induced by alcoholism, one of the leading causes of hospital admission for coma, the chemical and physiologic changes include slowed brain rhythms, odor of alcohol on breath, reddened skin, and possibly convulsions and heart conduction problems.

Comas may also be caused by certain diseases, such as Type I or Juvenile Onset diabetes. This type of coma results from uncontrolled diabetes mellitus, that is, from a person not taking insulin properly, thereby causing the body to react in a way that may result in death. A diabetic coma is not a sudden occurrence. Its onset may be extended over a few hours or even a few days. In fact, the onset may be so gradual that the person is not aware of the problem until the coma causes severe consequences.

Physicians have also induced comas in serious cases where the patient needs to heal. Drowning is a classic example. In severe cases, physicians may induce a coma to take the physical strain off of the body during healing. The induced coma, under these circumstances, allows the victim the opportunity to slowly recover and heal while avoiding normal stressors.

COMMERCIAL SURROGACY   A form of surrogate mothering in which the substitute mother is hired to become pregnant on behalf of an infertile woman. Where possible, the sperm and egg are taken from the biological parents and implanted artificially into the surrogate's womb, which is, in effect, rented. (See **Surrogate Mothering**.)

Typically, the arrangement is contractual. The people desiring the child agree to pay an amount as a down payment, some funds per month, and funds at the end. All health care costs of implantation and monitoring of fetal development are paid for by the parties contracting for the surrogate. The contract may be with a company who hires surrogates or directly with the surrogate.

The question of renting or using a part of a woman's body has been controversial. Some critics have argued that this form of surrogacy is baby selling and must be prohibited. Proponents believe that paying the person for carrying the child offers women who are infertile the opportunity to have a child. State laws are varied but several issues can arise, such as the ability to contract for this service and questions surrounding the licensing of contracting agencies. This issue is not as controversial as it once was because of the development of new fertility treatments and other interventions.

COMPETENCY   The capability of individuals to rationally make decisions for themselves. Under the law, competency is presumed for a person who achieves legal age—18 in most states. The decision maker is presumed capable of considering options thoughtfully and deciding upon an appropriate course of action. The decision reached does not have to be the same as the decision most people would make in those circumstances. It must simply reflect an understanding of the situation.

This concept is made more complex by health care circumstances. Some people (those in comas, for example) are obviously incompetent to make decisions, others float in and out of competency, and still others only incompetent to make decisions at the moment. On the most basic level, infants and children are not considered competent to make critical decisions. They are not considered to have the mental development or experience to understand the complexities and implications of their decisions. Some people with physical illnesses and mental disorders may also be deemed incompetent.

When a person's competence is questioned, legal hearings may be held to determine whether a person has the mental capacity to make competent decisions. These hearings occur in both the civil and criminal context. For example, in the criminal trial of the notorious Jeffrey Dahmer, a man accused of serial murder and cannibalism, the defense lawyers attempted an insanity defense to explain the defendant's actions. Such a defense must prove that he was incapable of understanding the difference between right and wrong and is thus not competent to stand trial for his acts. In the civil context, an illness may require the appointment of a guardian if an individual has become incompetent to care for his or her own affairs.

Competency, like virtually all legal terms, can be controversial. An person can be temporarily incompetent from stress or personal disaster. A person who is a legal infant (under legal adult age) may be competent to decide which parent they want to live with. The circumstances considered in determining competency are frequently situational, requiring consideration of the totality of the circumstances.

An example of a decision that challenges competency occurs when an adult is brought into the emergency department of the hospital. She is seriously injured and needs a blood transfusion to save her life. The transfusion is normal medical procedure. However, upon consultation, she declines the blood transfusion knowing that she will certainly die. The average person may not make this decision, but if this individual is competent to understand the nature of the situation and the implications of her actions, the decision will stand. The clinical providers will experience a sense of extreme futility, though, and will probably try to challenge the person's beliefs. However, the result is clear. The person is competent and the decision will stand, even though the person dies.

CONFIDENTIALITY   In the health and legal context, this term refers to privileged communication between the attorney and client or doctor and patient. The information communicated is private and may not be shared with the public. The privilege extends to legal and clinical personnel who may be also be working with the individual. Violation of this privilege is a very serious breach of professional ethics and is sanctionable.

Though the idea of confidentiality is conceptually simple, it is very complex in its applications. In certain exceptional situations, for example, privileged communication should be violated. In the case of *Tarasoff v. Regents of Univ. of Cal.*, 551 P.2d 334 (1976), a patient told his psychotherapist that he was going to kill another person. The patient was clear in his intention and the therapist believed the patient would carry out the crime. However, the therapist did not warn the potential victim, who was indeed killed by the patient. The California court decided that the therapist should have breached confidentiality and taken reasonable steps to protect the intended victim. Similar cases have provided guidelines on violating the privilege. If there is clear probability that they will be seriously harmed or killed, the therapist or lawyer must warn the potential victims of the danger.

AIDS

Confidentiality is a major concern for people with this disease. The issue stems from the fact that as of this writing, AIDS is always fatal. (See **Physician-Patient Relationship.**) The possibility of discrimination against a patient who is HIV-positive can occur should there be a breach of confidentiality. People with access to the patient's records may identify this person in such a way that the patient is set apart or humiliated, and clinical people may not want to associate with the patient. In one instance, a patient described his initial hospitalization as the loneliest, most distasteful experience of his life. The doctors, nurses, and other providers visited only when required. Volunteers with magazines did not visit, although they did visit other patients down the hallway. Social interaction was nonexistent because the patient was HIV-positive and because others in the hospital knew of his condition. If the above description was an accurate portrayal of an HIV-positive person's experience in a health care setting, imagine the reaction by the general public to such a person. His isolation stemmed directly from his loss of confidentiality. Notice that this example does not indicate a breach of confidentiality, since health care providers were entitled to know of his condition.

🏛 **CONJOINED TWINS**   Twin children born sharing body extremities or organ systems are known as conjoined twins or Siamese twins. These twins are the product of a single ovum. The fetal cells do not separate into two distinct children, however, so the two always have the same chromosomal composition and sex. Seventy-five percent of the these twins are attached at the chest, sharing a single heart. Because the heart is not strong enough to support two people, their life expectancy is usually less than one year.

Conjoined twins may share organs other than the heart. Depending on the circumstances, these children potentially could be surgically separated and have a chance at a relatively normal life. Since there are two kidneys, one could go with each child. In the case of single organs, an artificial substitute could conceivably be introduced in one of the children to make survival a possibility.

The bioethical issue that arises with conjoined twins concerns both the quality of life of the children and the question of choice. The quality of life question arose when the parents of one set of twins elected not to have them separated. They shared minor internal organs and their arms and legs. To separate the two children would be to seriously physically handicap both children. The parents elected not to put that burden on the children. They left them together. Here is the quality of life issue: Most people have difficulty relating to seriously handicapped people, even though this situation is not particularly unusual. One person with two heads, however, is definitely unusual. Can such a person have an enjoyable life? Both alternatives are hard, but which would provide the children with a better quality of life?

When the children are joined on key organs, often the difficult choice confronting the parents is the survival of one child. Both children cannot survive because there will be a loss of important organs for one child. That one child will die. Which one will it be? (See **Choice of Evils Defense**.)

These choices are very difficult for all involved. Under today's laws, there is also the early recognition of the conjoined twin status so that abortion becomes another option. If the parents let the children live, will they be introducing children to a world where they would be outcasts? Or, is there terrible guilt for the surviving child, knowing that his twin brother died so that he could live?

The decision criteria used are often the objective medical indications. Emotion is usually kept out of the decision, to the extent possible, and pure medical objectivity allowed to determine the best decision. This decision method does not provide a satisfactory solution, but it does provide an acceptable one when the options are all exceptionally difficult.

CONSENT (INFORMED)   A right derived from the basic rights of liberty and privacy under the United States Constitution. Consent may be characterized as the recognition that a competent adult patient has an absolute right to consent to or to refuse any suggested medical treatment. Providing medical treatment over the objection of a competent adult patient may expose the physician or other provider to liability. Liability may also be imposed if the treatment or procedure goes beyond what was consented to (*Pugsley v. Privette*, 263 S.E.2d 69 [Va.,1980]).

To inform the patient, the physician must provide her with complete information about the proposed treatment and the alternatives in a method understandable to her. The patient can then make a knowledgeable decision about whether to proceed. The underlying premise is the belief in the individual's ability to make the correct decision when provided with clear, complete, and understandable information. Informed consent is an extension of the principle of autonomy and is required by international decree (Nuremberg Code), in many state statutes, and in administrative guidelines (for example, the Joint Commission on Accreditation of Healthcare Organizations, or JCAHO).

When is the patient adequately informed? There are two standards, one based upon the actions of the health provider and the other based upon the understanding of the patient. Many courts follow the reasonable physician standard (also called the professional practice standard). This standard requires the clinician to tell the patient what a "reasonable physician in the same specialty" would tell under the same circumstances. The patient must be informed of the procedures, the risks involved, and the alternatives. This standard has permitted the production of mass-produced informed-consent information for many frequently performed procedures. However, criticism of this mass-produced information is justified. The personal explanation needed by the patient may not be provided adequately. The physician may assume that the patient understands the procedure when, in fact, she does not. Also, patient fear may not be effectively addressed with by this technique.

The reasonable patient standard evaluates the informed consent by assessing whether the patient is told the key information she would need to evaluate the procedure, its risks, and its alternatives. This standard requires that the same information be provided but suggests a more extensive question and answer communication between the patient and physician to ensure understanding. It evaluates whether the patient received the information that is material to her. Currently a minority viewpoint, this perspective can be expected to become adopted in more jurisdictions as a result of the changing health care delivery system.

Who may consent is a question of competency. An adult is presumed competent until proven otherwise. If the patient is a child, the parents or guardians are considered the appropriate decision makers for the procedure. (See **Competency**.)

EXPRESS CONSENT

Verbal or written consent clearly and directly given on the subject such that interpretation is not required. This form of consent is the best and provides the best evidence indicating the provider or organization complied with the law on informed consent. Upon admission to a hospital, the patient (or family member or guardian) signs a consent form indicating his or her willingness to be treated in the hospital. This document does not excuse the hospital from negligence or malpractice, because a patient cannot consent to these actions.

IMPLIED CONSENT

Anything implied is more difficult to interpret that something directly expressed, because it requires the interpretation of one person's actions by another. To determine whether implied consent has occurred, the question asked is whether the person's signs, actions, or inaction indicated consent to the treatment or procedure. If, for example, during a surgical procedure that has been consented to, additional techniques are required to complete the procedure, the surgeon will document the reasons for the extra procedures and presume consent. The objective of the surgery remained the same but the procedure was necessarily changed.

Implied consent does not allow the physician to complete one procedure and begin another simply because the patient is already within the surgical suite. For example, if the surgeon is removing the patient's spleen and notices an area on the patient's lung that looks suspicious, the surgeon may document the suspicious area but is not allowed to remove the spot since it is outside of the scope of the consent. The removal would be considered an illegal battery (unconsented touching). Alternatively, if during the removal of the spleen, the patient has a heart attack (myocardial infarct), the surgeons have implied consent to attempt to interrupt the heart attack and minimize the damage to the heart, even though the actions exceed the scope of the original consent.

Consent implied in law is found in most if not all state statutes for treatment in the case of medical emergencies when the person is unconscious or incapable of giving express consent. This form of consent is necessary to protect people from dying unnecessarily. For example, a driver is involved in an automobile accident. He is unconscious due to bleeding inside the skull after hitting his head on the windshield. In order to save his life, the surgeons must relieve pressure on his brain. However, he is from another state and attempts to contact the family have been unsuccessful. If express consent were required, the driver might die or might suffer extensive brain damage. Consent implied in law requires only that the clinical providers document that the patient was incapable of responding and that the situation was an emergency.

CONSOLIDATED OMNIBUS BUDGET RECONCILIATION ACT (COBRA) This act is the compilation of legislative actions that concern federal governmental financing. The actions contained vary with the year of submission and passage. A portion of the 1985 COBRA, dealt with patient dumping (see **Patient Dumping**) and passed the Emergency Medical Treatment and Active Labor Act (EMTALA). One piece of legislation in COBRA 1994 covered managed care. Another COBRA dealt with health insurance for divorced people with health conditions that made insurance difficult to obtain, whose ex-spouses carried the health insurance. COBRA laws cover a wide range of activities. They also have the power to enforce their requirements because if these legislative efforts are not complied with, the offending organization may lose all its federal funding. For hospitals, federal reimbursement could be jeopardized. These acts are important for health organizations and providers to be aware of because COBRA directly affects how health care is delivered and practiced.

CONTRACEPTION The temporary prevention of pregnancy. A variety of methods are available; none, other than abstinence, is infallible. But some, such as the rhythm method, are significantly less effective than others. Most methods of contraception are used by women. For people electing to participate in sexual activities, using safe sexual practices to prevent the spread of sexually transmitted diseases is strongly recommended. These practices involve both parties protecting themselves. The male should wear a latex condom and the woman should wear one of the recently introduced female condoms. Both forms of condoms should include spermicidal cream.

Nonprescription methods of contraception are the rhythm method, the condom, spermicidal foams and creams, the sponge, and the diaphragm.

RHYTHM METHOD

Involves abstaining from intercourse on the days when one is most likely to get pregnant. This method requires considerable personal responsibility. To practice this method effectively, the woman must monitor her biological "rhythms" by maintaining a record of her basal body temperature and the dates of her menses. She should also check herself for vaginal secretions. These data should be collected for several months to make sure that the time of ovulation is identified. Two more factors must be considered. The woman must remember that the life span of the sperm and unfertilized egg is several days. To avoid pregnancy, therefore, intercourse cannot occur in the days prior to ovulation and during the life cycle of the egg after ovulation.

The rhythm method, even when practiced carefully, is at best unreliable. Many women have irregular periods, making it difficult to predict the periods of high potential for pregnancy, and the method also requires extended periods of sexual abstinence.

CONDOM

A sheath made of plastic or other material placed over the penis and designed to capture the male ejaculate. The recommended condom design incorporates a small pouch at the end of the condom that serves as a semen receptacle and contains a spermicide solution. The condom must remain in place until completion of the semen exchange.

The condom is strongly advocated because of the physical barrier it provides. A barrier method of contraception protects the participants from direct genital contact. Consequently, the condom barrier provides added (but not complete) protection against sexually transmitted diseases as well as pregnancy. Condoms made of latex are preferred because of their ability to contain the HIV. Condoms made of natural materials do not contain the virus. They may prevent pregnancy but may not prevent the transmission of sexually transmitted diseases (STDs).

Even if their partners are using condoms, women need to employ their own contraceptive measures. Condoms may rupture or some spillage may occur, and unless the woman uses additional protection, the sperm could survive and fertilize the egg, leading to pregnancy. A new form of condom has been designed for women. Made of latex, the condom is much larger than the male condom and is intended to protect the entire vaginal surface from exposure to sperm.

The male condom is approximately 85 percent effective. The greatest risk of pregnancy occurs because of spillage of semen into the vagina during withdrawal, if the end of the condom is not held. The complaint of many users, however, is that pleasure and sensation are lost when condoms are used. The barrier interrupts the natural sensations associated with sexual interaction and, as a result, people may avoid their use.

SPERMICIDE

Usually in the form of a cream, foam, or jelly, spermicides are applied into the vagina and are intended to kill the sperm in the semen on contact. Available without a prescription, spermicides should be applied within 30 minutes of intercourse and must be reapplied prior to each subsequent act of intercourse.

Used as a stand-alone contraceptive, a spermicide is about 85 percent effective when used consistently. Multiple applications are required to make it most effective, however, because of the natural change from cream, foam, or jelly to a liquid in a warm location. This characteristic reduces the spermicide's ability to serve as a chemical barrier, thereby increasing the potential for pregnancy. To compensate for this chemical change, spermicides are best used in conjunction with other forms of contraception such as the condom, diaphragm, or sponge. The spermicide can be applied into the condom, into the cap of the diaphragm, or into the sponge.

Used alone, spermicides provide a chemical barrier but are not a physical barrier. They will not serve as prevention for sexually transmitted diseases, and other STD preventive measures should be taken.

SPONGE

A small, soft, disposable sponge containing spermicide. It is inserted into the vagina and must remain in the vagina for several hours after intercourse. The sponge is designed to provide both a chemical and physical barrier to semen. Removing the sponge too early can lead to a higher chance of undesired pregnancy. The sponge must not be left in place longer than 24 hours, however. After this length of time, the possibility of toxic shock syndrome (TSS) increases. Toxic shock syndrome is associated with a material's absorbency. The sponge may act as a breeding ground in which toxins are produced.

The effectiveness of the sponge is approximately 75 percent, although some of the newer sponges have claimed to prevent pregnancy more effectively. The sponge is not intended to prevent sexually transmitted diseases nor act as a physical barrier for the HIV.

DIAPHRAGM

A soft, pliable, dome-shaped rubber insert with a supportive wire around the edges intended to seal the cervix from fluids in the vaginal area. The fit of the diaphragm around the cervix is best measured by a physician, since a good seal is critical to the diaphragm's effectiveness.

By itself, a diaphragm is inadequate for contraception. To be effective, a diaphragm must be used with spermicides. The diaphragm barrier is intended to catch and contain the semen, and the spermicide then eliminates the chance of pregnancy. The diaphragm and spermicide are inserted approximately two hours before intercourse and are not to be removed for approximately eight hours afterwards. With an appropriately fitted diaphragm and strict adherence to insertion procedures, this method of contraception is reported to be about 95 percent effective.

The difficulties associated with the diaphragm are getting the appropriate fit and putting it into place and keeping it there. It can be moved out of place during sexual activities, which can go unnoticed, substantially increasing the risk of pregnancy.

The diaphragm is intended as a physical barrier to prevent semen from reaching the cervix. It does not cover the area necessary to prevent STDs.

The second group of contraceptives must be prescribed by a physician. These contraceptives include injectables, intrauterine devices (IUDs), implants, and oral contraceptives (the Pill).

INJECTABLES

Contraceptives injected intramuscularly that last for several months. Depo-Provera® is the principal example. Injected once every three months, it contains a chemical similar to the hormone progesterone, which inhibits the ovaries from releasing an egg. A prescription is required as is the service of a nurse or physician for the injection. Depo-Provera is reportedly 99 percent effective, and under these circumstances, very convenient and simple. The side effects are minimal for most people, primarily weight gain and menstrual irregularities. However, this method does not provide a physical barrier and thus should be used in combination with a barrier method to prevent the spread of STDs.

INTRAUTERINE DEVICES (IUDs)

One of the older contraceptive techniques, an IUD is a small device with attached nylon threads or copper wire that is placed into the uterus by a physician. The reason this device inhibits pregnancy is unknown, but it is believed that that the presence of a foreign body prevents the egg from attaching itself to the uterus. The woman must check the placement of the IUD regularly and must have it replaced at regular intervals by a physician (the plastic type is replaced annually and the copper is replaced every six years).

Though the IUD is considered 95 percent effective, it is not appropriate for many women. There are risks to the uterine wall during insertion, and immediately following insertion there is a risk for bacterial infection. Bleeding and pain occur in about 15 percent of patients during the first year and about half of that during the second year. Because of these problems, a substantial proportion of women have IUDs removed. The IUD may also be expelled by the bearer and the woman may not be aware of the expulsion. The woman needs to check the IUD prior to any type of sexual intercourse.

Like the injectable, an IUD gives its user considerable freedom. However, women under 25 with multiple sexual partners should not use IUDs, nor should those at risk for pelvic inflammatory disease and diseases of the fallopian tubes (salpingitis). Users of IUDs must also remember that it is not a physical barrier method and does not provide any protection against sexually transmitted disease.

IMPLANTABLE CONTRACEPTIVES

Long capsules containing the hormone progestin, which are surgically implanted by a physician under the skin (subcutaneously) in the upper arm. These capsules stop ovulation and 99 percent effective for five years. The capsules are not biodegradable, however, and must be removed and, if desired, replaced. The best-known example of implantable contraceptives is Norplant®. Many patients appreciate the freedom these capsules provide for an extended period of time with a minimum of discomfort.

The problem that has arisen with the implants is difficulty in removal. After five years, the capsules become well situated within the arm. Thus the tissue that has surrounded the capsules must be moved, a process sometimes associated with discomfort. Another difficulty has been the rare instance when the capsules have moved down the arm, requiring premature removal. Finally, the implantable contraceptives must be used with a physical barrier to prevent STDs.

ORAL CONTRACEPTIVES (OCs)

These pills consist of hormones taken daily for three weeks and then inert pills for one week. They are provided in varying dosages depending upon the characteristics of the woman. The OC contains either a combination of progestogen and estrogen or progestogen only. Both approaches are 98–99 percent effective at stopping the ovaries from releasing an egg. The pills are provided to the woman in a packet indicating the day the pill is to be taken, the first hormone-containing pill to be used the first day after the end of the menstrual period. Since the responsibility for taking the pill rests with the user, one of the chief complaints is the fear associated with forgetting to take the pill. The OC does have the positive consequence of regulating irregular periods, an alternative use for OCs.

Before beginning OCs, a complete physical examination is recommended along with a substantial clinical history. There are risks with OCs, notably among smokers. Young women smokers taking OCs are at substantially greater risk of stroke (cerebrovascular accident, CVA) than their nonsmoking peers. Blood clots in the lungs and legs are also more common in these women.

▥ COST CONTAINMENT   The attempt by nonmarket forces to influence the costs involved in providing goods and services. Cost containment measures are characteristic of governmentally regulated enterprises, but health care as an industry is not considered regulated, and directly it is not. However, due to political and social pressures, both governmental and private forces have taken steps to indirectly control the costs of providing health care. Why? Because we believe that health care should be affordable. However, for most people health care is not affordable without health insurance. The costs of health care are also increasing faster than those of virtually all other industries. Therefore, many approaches are being considered to slow down the increasing health care costs. These measures have generally focused upon controlling the costs associated with health care organizations and providers.

CERTIFICATE OF NEED (CON)
The certificate of need (CON) concept began in the mid-1970s and was the primary federal and state regulatory strategy for controlling health care costs. This planning approach required hospitals to obtain government approval for capital investments, which meant that the purchase of virtually all biotechnological innovations needed government preapproval. The approval or rejection of the CON would be determined by a state committee, typically appointed by the governor. The committee would evaluate whether or not the proposal duplicated existing services in the region, and if the service was needed, the CON was approved. If duplication or need was not found, the CON was rejected. Although the federal government has now moved to other approaches, CON programs still exist in many states.

CON criteria vary from state to state. Some federal mandates required that the people submitting the CON proposal consider the state health plan, the long-range plans of the entity seeking the CON, the needs of the population served by the entity (including the special populations served), the medically underserved populations, availability of resources for the project, the quality of care provided, and the effect of the project on competition. States have the option to add further criteria. This approach was really a form of rationing health resources, that is, restricting services according to certain financial limits.

The basic premise of the CON was that demand for medical treatment increases as supply increases. Underlying this premise is the argument that patients neither understand the causes of, nor the solutions to, their medical problems and therefore must trust physicians to decide what medical care to purchase. Realizing this, hospitals compete to attract physicians rather than patients and attempt to make any capital expenditures that increase their attractiveness to physicians. Physicians, believing that there is a beneficial treatment available, make arrangements for the patient to receive it. Therefore, they will admit the patient to the hospital with the best biotechnology.

The process of determining whether or not to write a CON proposal begins with identifying the community's need—that is, what do the physicians' want? The need is identified by discerning the level of demand for health services and then determining the amount of health resources needed to meet this demand. If the available resources of the region do not meet this demand, the CON is submitted for approval. If the committee finds that the resources are already available, the CON is denied. The result is an authorized, planned health resources supply that has been allocated among institutional health providers through the CON program.

Studies have shown that a CON can have a positive effect on cost, but the CON politicized decision making processes, which sometimes resulted in erroneous decisions and thus an oversupply of technology. The majority of states have dropped this process.

PRO-COMPETITION COST CONTAINMENT

Many health economists argue for pro-competition, which means restraining health costs by creating competitive marketing conditions via incentives for both consumers and employers who purchase group health insurance policies. This concept, introduced in the early 1980s, includes income tax deductions for corporations, encouragement for raising the threshold for expenses, and multiple choice health insurance programs (cafeteria options). Unfortunately, these options had little effect on costs overall. Today cafeteria-type programs are still available, and some of the tax breaks remain. However, for the little company, many of the benefits never truly existed.

PROSPECTIVE PAYMENT SYSTEM OF COST CONTAINMENT

Concurrently with the pro-competition program was the implementation of the federal Prospective Payment System (PPS) (1982). Under the PPS, hospitals are reimbursed by Medicare for inpatient services through a payment system based on predetermined rates per discharge for diagnosis-related groups (DRGs). Payment bears no direct relationship to length of stay, services rendered, or costs of care. For a given discharge, a hospital with actual costs below the designated PPS rate for a particular DRG is permitted to keep the difference in payment. If discharge costs exceed the payment level, the hospital is required to absorb the loss.

DRG reimbursement has both influenced and been used as a format for many states' Medicaid programs as well as plans offered by many private insurance companies. DRGs were applied to acute care hospital inpatients because they could be averaged and were to a large extent predictable. Other types of patient characteristics could be averaged too. We now have prospective payment for outpatient activities in physicians offices under Medicare Part B, Ambulatory Patient Groups (APGs), and payments based upon resources used by the patient rather than diagnosis. The PPS is, arguably, the form of reimbursement that the government is actively focusing upon to ensure cost containment. (See **Managed Care; Medicaid/Title XIX; Medicare.**)

Cost containment policy analysts have now begun to evaluate its economic position. Earlier forms of cost containment focused upon controlling the supply of health care resources. Capitation-based cost containment focuses upon controlling the demand for health resources. (See under **Managed Care.**) This is the approach taken by managed care companies. In managed care, employees are usually required to select a primary care physician from a list of approved physicians who will coordinate the entire medical experience for the person. The key to capitation cost containment rests with these physicians, who are paid a lump sum in advance (usually monthly) to treat all of the employees who come to them. The physicians receive a set amount of money per employee for all services contracted, and thus they are financially encouraged to avoid unnecessary tests and procedures. In other words, the physician is recognized as the key to controlling demand for health resources. Physicians are given money up front to spend as they desire, though they must provide a complete package of services. If they spend more on the patient than allowed, the physicians lose money. If the physician diagnoses the problem at the earliest stages, then the cost of cure is relatively inexpensive and the physician can make more money. So it is argued that cost containment is achieved by controlling physician behavior (demand) and encouraging early diagnosis and treatment (changing patient demand). This idea is catching on throughout the country.

CRUZAN V. DIRECTOR, MISSOURI DEPARTMENT OF HEALTH (497 U.S. 261 [1990])   This case is one of the most influential Supreme Court decisions concerning a person's right to die under unexpected circumstances. The exceptional circumstances involved an automobile accident victim in her twenties who had not left any written directions of her wishes should an unexpected catastrophe occur. The victim's family and friends wanted to speak on her behalf. The problem was, despite admirable intentions, Cruzan's family and friends had only limited evidence to prove the victim's wishes. They had to proceed all the way to the U.S. Supreme Court before they were able to obtain permission to allow Cruzan to die, and Cruzan had to endure seven years of "life" in a persistent vegetative state. These facts demonstrate the need for all adults to discuss their wishes with their physicians and to execute a durable power of attorney and a living will.

On January 11, 1983, Missourian Nancy Cruzan was involved in an automobile accident. When discovered, she was not breathing and her heart was not beating. Emergency personnel restored her respiration and heart activity. After she reached the hospital, doctors determined that she had been without oxygen for 12–14 minutes, permanently damaging her brain. Cruzan never awakened. She deteriorated into a persistent vegetative state in which her body continued to function as long as she was artificially fed and given water (hydration), though there was no chance of her recovering. The family requested the removal of the life support. The hospital staff would not do so without a court order. Cruzan had become a ward of the state so that the state could bear the costs of her care, which was custodial and without a cure. The case was taken to court.

The trial court decided that a person in this condition has a fundamental right under the Constitution to accept or reject the artificial support. This court also determined that Cruzan had made comments to a housemate indicating she would not wish her life continued in this abnormal manner. The withdrawal could proceed.

The Missouri Supreme Court reversed the trial court.

The U.S. Supreme Court held that a person has the right to decide whether or not she wishes to be maintained in such a condition. To prove that such a decision has been reached by one who is now in deteriorated state, the petitioners must prove by clear and convincing evidence that the victim would have wanted the life-sustaining equipment withdrawn. "Substituted judgment" by close family members and friends is not enough by itself. But coupled with indicators of the patient's desires, their judgment can be used to conclude that the support may be withdrawn. According to Justice O'Connor, the decision is a protected liberty interest. A person has the right to refuse medical treatment, and this refusal may be inferred by a person's prior acts and decisions.

The decision was welcomed by the family and friends of Nancy Cruzan. The artificial support was withdrawn and she died a quiet death.

The difficulty with the Cruzan decision is that the degree of proof required places a great legal-procedural burden on the petitioners (on behalf of the victim). It may keep people alive inappropriately and contrary to their unknown wishes. The strength of the decision is the emphasis upon the right to make such a decision for oneself. A further strength, many argue, is that it allows the states to create their own right-to-die laws.

D

DEATH The end of life. Traditionally, death has been characterized and identified by the stopping of one's heart and breath. For people dying of natural causes, such as old age, this definition remains in use. For people dying from accidents, however, the definition has become more complicated. Our technology has allowed medical practitioners to continue a person's biological functioning with mechanical support (life support). The desired result of this life support is to allow the individual every opportunity to be healed. The problem arises when the person's brain is damaged and he can no longer function. In these situations, the ability to think has become the key characteristic differentiating between life and death. Terms like *brain dead* or *brain death* are now used to identify a condition of death where the body's functioning may be sustained but the person is legally dead.

This alternative characterization of death is important for organ transplantation. Medical science is now capable of taking the body organs from one person (called organ harvesting) and placing them into the body of another. We harvest hearts, lungs, kidneys, eyes, and other organs for transplantation. People who are brain dead may be candidates for organ donation. (Many states allow people to indicate whether they wish to donate their organs on their driver's licenses.) Should an accident resulting in brain death occur, then life support is initiated and the person is evaluated for harvesting. (**See Anatomical Gifts; Organ and Tissue Donation.**)

The desired donor is young, and the desired organs are damaged as little as possible. Harvesting should occur as quickly as possible, because the loss of the brain's functioning negatively affects other body organs. Because the need for organs is much greater than the supply of available organs, protections for the potential donor must be identified. Because we must make absolutely sure that the donor is actually brain dead so that we don't take a viable life, we have developed definitions and procedures to ensure that this doesn't occur. The majority of states have adopted the Uniform Determination of Death Act or a variant of it.

UNIFORM DETERMINATION OF DEATH ACT (1980)

This statute was written by the National Conference of Commissioners on Uniform State Laws as a model for states to follow in writing their own legislation. In Section 1 the authors defined brain dead: "An individual who has sustained either (1) irreversible cessation of circulatory and respiratory functions, or (2) irreversible cessation of all functions of the entire brain, including the brain stem, is dead. A determination of death must be made in accordance with accepted medical standards."

To declare a person brain dead, according to the authors of the Merck Manual (a standard physician reference manual), the following must be missing for at least 12 hours: behavioral or reflex activity above the neck, including eye responses, reflex actions and any respiratory movement. Spinal reflexes can remain. If organ harvesting time is short, the physician can indicate the absence of clinical indicators for only six hours. To use the six-hour observation, the physician should support the determination of death by an electroencephalogram (a test that shows brain activity) indicating no mental activity for 30 minutes or an angiogram (a medical tool that allows evaluation of circulation).

The definition promoted by the Uniform Act has been criticized, because it requires that the entire brain be dead. Any part of the brain that reflects activity would remove the person from the category of brain dead. Critics have promoted the alternative of higher brain death. This proposed modification to the definition would allow a person to be declared brain dead even though activity in the brainstem and high spinal cord is present. The rationale is that the brain functions that control the ability to communicate and think are found in the higher brain. The brain stem controls the most basic or reflex activities. The distinction that is being identified is the philosophical, not scientific, concept of humanness.

Responses to the higher brain death modification typically ask for specification of anatomical parts of the brain that must be nonfunctioning in order to declare the person brain dead. Many point out that the understanding of the brain is not adequate to make such absolute distinctions. Therefore, the definition requiring whole brain death is preferable because is protects the victim most effectively. Another response from a more emotional perspective: if the higher brain death is all that is required, one consequence could be that a person who is breathing could be buried. Many people would have great difficulty if confronted with that situation.

DEONTOLOGICAL THEORY   An ethical perspective that maintains that some human actions are right or wrong no matter what the consequences. (See **Utilitarianism, Theory of**.)

Often the consequences of an action are the reason it is prohibited. For example, recklessness, negligence, and wantonness are wrong because their consequences could be dire and harmful. Driving recklessly through a subdivision with children is wrong under the law, even though the person driving the car may be very skilled and may enter and leave the subdivision without doing harm. It is wrong because a child may run out in front of the car and the reckless driver would be unable to stop. The potential for harmful consequences makes the behavior wrong.

Deontologists believe that there are more fundamental issues by which we can evaluate human actions. They promote the idea that moral values such as truthfulness and justice are correct without regard to consequences. These moral values are pure and ideal. For example, people have a moral imperative to tell the truth. Maintaining truthfulness makes society a better place, where people are able to relate to one another with trust. Such pure values, when followed, will result in a quality human existence. Consequences are not an issue.

Bioethicists, the health care establishment, and the legal system all use deontologically recognized ideals. The foundation of these social groups' credibility, for example, is based upon society's belief in their adherence to the "right" principles, that is, those that are acknowledged by the majority as what's best. People place great trust in the recognized professions such as clergymen, lawyers, and physicians. Their trust is encouraged because of the codes of ethics that these groups follow; for physicians that code is the Hippocratic Oath, promising to "Do no harm. . . ." The trust that people place in their attorneys and physicians is an obligation that receives the greatest of professional recognition. These principles are stated in the professions' codes of ethics, and sanctions are in place to correct professionals should they breach these principles.

One of the problems that deontological theories encounter is in the ranking of the concepts. Which concept should be considered first? Second? There are health care situations where these esteemed concepts conflict. Another difficult question is, can consequences ever be truly avoided? For example, truthfulness between physician and patient is considered inviolate. Yet circumstances commonly arise where the complete truth may hinder or harm the healing process. For example, a physician may learn that her patient is dying, though there is a possibility that he could survive. She knows that a major influence on his survival is his mental attitude. Knowing that many people become seriously depressed when they learn they have a terminal illness, and knowing that a positive mental attitude is critically important to therapy, should the physician tell the patient? The concept of complete truthfulness would indicate an answer of yes. The belief in nonmaleficence (do no harm) would say no. Which principle should be followed? Deontologists encounter difficulty with this situation.

The reason for using such a theory is to provide an analytical perspective to the study of situations. Choices between actions or policies can be evaluated in terms of their commitment to rightness or closeness to moral values.

 **DO NOT RESUSCITATE ORDERS**   Commonly known as DNR orders, these instructions, included by the physician on the patient's medical chart, express the patient's wish not to be resuscitated if her heart or breath stops. The DNR order indicates that the patient has indicated that she wishes to be allowed to die without any heroic interventions by the staff. Unless these orders are indicated on the medical chart or in a Living Will, emergency implied consent will be applied—that is, it will be assumed that the patient has given consent to CPR and other interventions, should a cardiac or respiratory arrest occur.

DNR orders are becoming more common as patients seek to avoid being hooked up to modern technology where their bodies are maintained indefinitely. Not only are these devices uncomfortable, but they are also extraordinarily expensive. Because of these extras, the last six months of a person's life has been documented as the most expensive for most people. Furthermore, the patient's quality of life is poor.

Many people indicate their wishes via their Living Will or through their Durable Health Care Power of Attorney. From these documents or by direct communication with the physician, DNR orders may be added to the medical chart.

When patients indicates their wishes and refuse interventions but are resuscitated anyway, they can sue for wrongful life. One such instance arose when the DNR orders were not followed. Heroic interventions were used and the patient survived his heart attack. However, the patient's orders were clearly indicated on the medical chart. He sued and won damages. The life remaining to him was not one of quality, and he had to undergo two more years of hospitalization before he died. The costs and other expenses were unnecessary. The court held the hospital liable for wrongful life and ordered it to pay damages.

DNR orders are indicators of patients' rights to control the final stages of their own lives. Most people in the health care and legal systems believe that to ignore these last requests is to intrude upon the individual's right to choose.

DOCTOR-PATIENT RELATIONSHIP   *See* PHYSICIAN-PATIENT RELATIONSHIP

DUE PROCESS (CONSTITUTIONAL)   A concept of American law, found in the Fifth Amendment of the Constitution, which states that no person shall be deprived of life, liberty, or property without due process of law. This amendment, coupled with the Fourteenth Amendment, explicitly restricts all government bodies from taking life, liberty, or property from a person without a formal process.

The form of due process that most people encounter is procedural due process, which requires government to provide a fair process through which a person can protect life, liberty, or property. It requires notice of the hearing and fairness within the hearing. In other words, the government cannot conduct the hearing in secret, and both sides must be given a chance to explain their actions. It is also implied that a fair arbitrator or judge will make the final decision. The federal right government's Administrative Procedures Act (APA) specifies the procedures to be followed.

Due process is a protection guaranteed to many health care workers in terms of their state certification, license, or registration to practice. The license to practice is one's property. To remove such a license is to remove a person's livelihood, so the removal is not something to be taken lightly. If allegations are made claiming a medical technologist committed malpractice, due process rights must be protected. Notice of the charges to the technologist is required. An investigation of the allegations is then conducted according to the procedures outlined in the administrative procedures act. If enough evidence is found, an adjudicatory hearing is held. If the allegations are proven, the license may be removed, suspended, or the technologist may simply be reprimanded. If the allegations are proven false, the individual will not be penalized.

The due process requirements can extend to the local community hospital. Because it is a governmental entity, its physicians and employees are entitled to due process protections. For example, a physician was accused by peer heart surgeons of having a high patient death rate when conducting open heart surgery. In view of the seriousness of the surgery, it is known that some patients will not survive. Even so, the death rate is low for surgeons who actively practice the procedure, and this surgeon conducted these procedures frequently. The surgeon was notified of a due process hearing. At the hearing, an evidentiary review of the documents and statements by peer heart surgeons resulted in a loss of practice privileges for the physician at that hospital.

DURABLE POWER OF ATTORNEY FOR HEALTH CARE   This document is the means by which advance directives are made, guiding what will happen if health care decisions need to be made, and ensuring that the patient's autonomy will be respected, even when she is unable to communicate her decisions. Essentially, this document specifies who (the agent) will be making decisions for the patient (principal) and under what conditions. Advance directives indicate the patient's wishes regarding who will make decisions for her if she is unable to make them.

The requirements for an effective power of attorney may be reflected in state statutes. In Ohio, for example, the Ohio State Bar Association and the Ohio State Medical Association developed a state form for use by attorneys, physicians, hospitals, and the public. The law requires that the principal's signature to be witnessed or notarized. The document can be written at any time, however, and several states indicate the presence of such documents on the driver's license or other form of state identification. Copies should be brought with the patient to the hospital and given to the attending physician and the agent given the power of attorney, at minimum.

These powers of attorney are usually specific to a time period of health incompetency and specify the conditions under which the durable power will be effective. The document also specifies or limits the scope of decisions the agent may make and sometimes the methods of making decisions. If, for example, the circumstance arises where a principal might be taken off artificial respiration, the principal might want the decision to rest with certain members of the family. Or, in the case of a less life-threatening situation, the principal may wish the agent to have control over the principal's finances. This situation is commonly encountered when a person enters a nursing facility for an extended recovery and needs someone to handle the daily expenses.

The durable power of attorney for health care should be consistent with a person's living will. The agent may confront issues not addressed by a living will, or the agent may further the intent of the living will by providing an opportunity for intensive discourse with the providers prior to final decisions. If an agent and a living will contradict one another, leading health-law scholars generally agree that the actual presence of an appointed individual should take precedence over a more general document such as a living will.

Should a person have both a living will and a durable power of attorney for health care? The question is debated. It is true that overlap exists. Nevertheless, attorneys frequently recommend both because the agent can consider a broader array of situations and alternatives than can the living will. The agent can also serve to make certain that the principal's wishes are carried out as intended. The existence of both documents allows the greatest recognition of the principal's autonomy in decision making.

DUTY   The responsibility or obligation of one person to another. Duty may be familial, legal, medical, or societal. In health care, the physician has the duty of care. This entails providing services to the patient at the prevailing clinical standard, which must equal the national standard of quality for physicians. Alternatively, the physician has the duty not to conduct a medical procedure that is known to be deleterious (harmful) and not therapeutic for the patient.

A variation of duty also encompasses the duty of a person to forbear from doing something. Under a model duty of care, physicians must wait a minimum of six hours and conduct specific clinical tests before declaring a person brain dead. Questions concerning this duty to forebear arise in cases such as that of a sixteen-year-old girl, critically ill, who needs an organ. Without a transplant, she could die at any moment. The individual possibly brain dead is her donor. Can the physician declare the person brain dead at four hours if all the clinical tests indicate death? The test used to determine whether this declaration would be a breach of duty is the reasonable person test, which asks whether or not the physician acted reasonably under the circumstances. The decision in this case would be very difficult.

Duty is also a factor in determining medical negligence. Under the law, the avoidance of negligence requires physicians to conduct themselves in such a fashion that an injury or consequence to a patient does not occur where they had a duty to do something or not to do something.

The duty to warn is also a key professional obligation for physicians. It has two aspects. First, the physician has a duty to warn the patient of the problems associated with the medications the physician prescribes. This aspect of duty is covered by informed consent. Second, the courts have identified a duty to warn others in cases where a patient informs the physician of her intent to harm another. If the physicians and other therapists believe that she will seriously harm the other person, the therapist is under a duty to warn the potential victim. Should the therapist fail to take active steps to warn the potential victim and injury or death results, the therapist may be held liable for the damage. The basis for determining liability would be that the therapist failed to act reasonably under such circumstances.

DYING PERSON'S BILL OF RIGHTS   When a person is dying, the others involved are understandably emotional. Those touched exhibit a wide range of feelings that frequently places unnecessary hardship upon the dying person. To help the dying person, the Dying Person's Bill of Rights was developed in 1978 at a workshop "The

Terminally Ill Patient and the Helping Person" sponsored by the South Western Michigan Inservice Education Council. The purpose of the document is to keep the dying active in their world for as long as is reasonable and, by doing so, to enhance their quality of life.

The Dying Person's Bill of Rights

I have the right to be treated as a living human being until I die.

I have the right to maintain a sense of hopefulness, however changing its focus may be.

I have the right to be cared for by those who can maintain a sense of hopefulness, however changing this may be.

I have the right to express my feelings and emotions about my approaching death, in my own way.

I have the right to participate in decisions concerning my case.

I have the right to expect continuing medical and nursing attention even though "cure" goals must be changed to "comfort" goals.

I have the right not to die alone.

I have the right to be free from pain.

I have the right to have my questions answered honestly.

I have the right not to be deceived.

I have the right to have help from and for my family in accepting my death.

I have the right to die in peace and dignity.

I have the right to retain my individuality and not be judged for my decisions, which may be contrary to the beliefs of others.

I have the right to discuss and enlarge my religious and/or spiritual experiences, regardless of what they may mean to others.

I have the right to expect that the sanctity of the human body will be respected after death.

I have the right to be cared for by sensitive, knowledgeable people who will attempt to understand my needs and will be able to gain some satisfaction in helping me face my death (*Oakland Tribune*, September 30, 1978).

E

EMBRYO CUSTODY   The issue has arisen in a Tennessee domestic relations case. The sperm and egg were combined and the resulting embryos were frozen to be used for in vitro fertilization at a later time. The couple divorced. The issue of who should receive control over the frozen embryos was presented to the courts. (See **Artificial Insemination** for a full discussion.)

EMERGENCY MEDICAL TREATMENT AND ACTIVE LABOR ACT (EMTALA)   This legislation was drafted in response to the problem of patient dumping. Patient dumping occurs when a person in need of emergency care is transferred to another hospital because he or she does not have health insurance or the financial wherewithal to pay for care. Private and proprietary hospitals were found to be the greatest violators, and research indicated that the patients most often transferred were the poor or underinsured in need of emergency or obstetrical care. Because they could not pay, the private hospitals transferred them to the charity or community hospital, which is required to treat all comers.

EMTALA, which was incorporated into the Consolidated Omnibus Budget Reconciliation Act of 1985, requires the hospital's emergency department (ED) to evaluate the person's emergency needs by meeting four basic requirements: (1) a medical screening must be performed to determine the presence of an emergency; (2) if an emergency exists, the facility and doctors must stabilize the patient using the hospital's capabilities; (3) if the ED physician indicates the need for an attending physician, the attending physician must appear within a reasonable time; and (4) the hospital can transfer appropriately if the hospital where the patient is being transferred is able to and agrees to provide appropriate treatment.

An allowable transfer occurs when the first hospital cannot stabilize the patient and transfers the patient for medical reasons. In this case, the patient is transferred to a regional trauma center for care without

EMTALA violation. However, when the incentive for the transfer is the patient's inability to pay, EMTALA has been violated. In either circumstance, extensive documentation is required to provide a complete description and explanation of the occurrence.

The hospital identified to receive the transferred patient cannot refuse to accept the individual unless it does not have the capacity to treat the patient. It must meet the same four admission requirements as the original hospital, but if it is incapable of providing the necessary services, it may deny the transfer without penalty.

If a hospital is reported for patient dumping, the person doing the reporting (called a whistleblower) may not be penalized. To penalize the whistleblower would be to penalize someone for adhering to public policy. If the hospital is determined to have violated EMTALA, the government may impose civil fines and terminate Medicare agreements, and the hospital may face private litigation from the patient. If the violation constitutes "immediate and serious jeopardy to the health and safety of individuals presenting themselves to the hospital for emergency services," the Health Care Financing Administration (HCFA) may notify the hospital on the first day of preliminary termination. Corrective action must occur immediately. If correction does not follow, termination (of Medicare agreements) occurs. At the time of final notice, the public is notified. The maximum fine for EMTALA violation is $50,000 per violation for a hospital with more than 100 beds (fines are readjusted through Congress periodically). For a hospital with less than 100 beds, the maximum fine per violation is $25,000. The hospital would then face the potentially more severe penalty of damage to its clinical reputation, which is not easy to correct.

Physicians are also potentially subject to fines and exclusion from federal health programs. The physician is at risk if he or she misrepresents the patient's condition or falsely certifies that the benefits of the transfer outweigh the risks. The sanctions will come from HCFA, and the maximum fine is $50,000 for each EMTALA violation. They are not subject to private claims.

EMTALA does not apply to health maintenance organizations, private clinics, or private physicians' offices.

EQUAL PROTECTION OF THE LAWS (CONSTITUTIONAL) According to the Fourteenth Amendment to the U.S. Constitution, "*No state shall . . . deny to any person . . . equal protection of the laws*" (italics added). This clause is called the equal protection clause. Applicable only to the states, it forbids a state from denying equal protection to any person, and it requires that similar people be given equal protection of their rights and redress for being wronged.

When a state law is passed, the courts will presume its validity if there is a rational basis for it. This criterion is called the rational basis test. When speed limits are imposed on the state population, for example, the rational basis is the safety of the driver, other drivers, and passengers. The protection is applied to all under similar circumstances.

In other situations, the law may be subjected to strict scrutiny rather than the rational basis test. Strict scrutiny presumes that the law violates the equal protection clause unless the state can prove a compelling interest that can be furthered only by enactment of the law in question. Issues that would challenge or remove basic constitutional rights, such as freedom of speech, are subjected to the standard of strict scrutiny. Legislators are aware that the chances of a law successfully passing strict scrutiny are exceptionally slim, yet some laws do prevail.

One application of equal protection in a health care setting that would not pass strict scrutiny is the right of a person to refuse curative procedures on the basis of religious principles. The physicians, nurses, and other members of the helping profession will be powerless to assist if the patient refuses intervention. The right to practice religion free of governmental involvement and the principle of autonomy constitutionally protect these decisions when made by a competent adult.

A variation of this circumstances involves the child of religious parents. The child is dying. The parents' religious beliefs do not permit medical intervention. The state can intercede, despite the parents' right to practice religion without interference, because it has a compelling interest to protect those who cannot make decisions for themselves. Interventions such as these have been subjected to the strict scrutiny standard, and the state's protection of the innocent has justified the intrusion into religious practices.

The goal of the equal protection clause is to ensure that people are protected by the law in the same manner. If the law is intended to treat people differently, then equal protection does not occur.

ETHICS The societal characterization of its recognized morally guiding concepts. Society recognizes and promotes certain ideas as the ones that should guide our moral behavior. Examples of these concepts are truthfulness, justice, and freedom. These principles are ideals to live by. They are selected as ethical principles because they are universally recognized and valued for their contribution to humanness. Most professions express these values as they apply to the context of their work in codes of ethics. These codes are used by members of that profession as guides for their professional actions.

How these principles apply to specific situations is not always clear.

Often they must be prioritized, which requires adherence to one ethical principle and a violation of another. When we are confronted with such a conflict, we are encountering a moral dilemma. Which ethical principle should be adhered to? In other words, which is more important? Behaving as well as possible by properly weighing the factors in the situation is the goal. For example, telling a patient the truth is a moral obligation, a required ethical principle to which we adhere. But what should we do when telling a patient the truth does more harm than good? When withholding some fact or telling a little lie might serve the patient better? Many argue that it is better to help the patient and sacrifice the principle, because helping a person is more significant than adhering to a principle. Others argue that the patient has a right to know the complete truth. The informer is not in a position to judge how the person will accept the information, and the receiver is the only person who rightfully can judge the situation. It is a very tough choice.

Ethical violations are receiving more analysis and comment. With increasing frequency, ethicists are given the responsibility of confronting these moral and ethical dilemmas and providing insights to help us minimize our human frailties and move more towards acts that would be consistent with ethical principles.

ETHICS COMMITTEES   Hospitals and other health care organizations create these committees to discuss ethics issues that arise in the regular practice of health care. For hospitals accredited by the Joint Commission on Accreditation of Health Care Organizations (Joint Commission), ethics committees are required. Committee members are generally selected on the basis of the organizationally recognized purpose. If, for example, the purpose of the committee is to confront a patient situation where legal liability might occur, the people serving on the committee are an administrator, attorney, bioethicist, nurse, physician, and social worker. These people are trained to consider the variety of ways that the patient situation can be analyzed. This committee is frequently on an "on-call" status: rather than (or in addition to) regularly scheduled meetings, it is on call to respond to a patient situation that might be a legal issue.

Some ethics committees serve as "think tanks." Many health care professional associations, such as the American College of Obstetricians and Gynecologists (ACOG), have ethics committees to provide responses to hypothetical situations or guidance in situations that have been encountered and are likely to be encountered again. These committees meet to consider the practices of health care workers in specific situations. What kinds of issues would the ethics committee of the ACOG discuss? If an anencephalic child is born, is it permissible to transplant its viable organs to other infants who need them, since an anencephalic child (born without its upper brain) cannot survive longer than a month? If amniocentesis reveals that the fetus will be mentally retarded when it is born, should the mother be encouraged to have an abortion? Should the abortion be performed if the finding is late in the pregnancy? The committee will give model answers to these questions.

Other health care think tanks exist to consider the implications of health care policies. They discuss such issues as whether or not a person who is HIV-positive is really handicapped. Is AIDS a handicapping condition? Physically and mentally, most would say it is not. It is, however, a socially handicapping condition because people are afraid of diseases without cures and will go to great lengths to avoid victims of these diseases. These lengths include not giving them jobs even though they are qualified. As a result of ethical deliberations like these, this condition is protected under the Americans with Disabilities Act.

Ethics committees have their equivalents in research institutions and universities, where they are called institutional review boards. (See **Institutional Review Boards.**) The IRB is mandated by federal law, and regulations promulgated by the Department of Health and Human Services direct its actions within the organizations.

EUGENICS   The study of human genetics and its application to human problems. The term gained a negative connotation when the eugenic medical experiments of Hitler's Third Reich studied how to genetically improve the population by breeding only its best specimens. The Nazis' eugenic program was called "racial hygiene." Races were to be made pure, and pure genetic structures were to be created. The concept is similar to that of breeding purebred animals. Our dog and cat shows attempt to select the best and purest animal in a breed—the champion. The goal for the owner is for one champion to mate with another champion, so that the purity of the breed is maintained and strengthened, and better animals are produced. In the Nazis' experiments, people of the Jewish faith were used as experimental animals to test how to ascertain the best genes.

In the United States, eugenics has also occurred. People with mental retardation were involuntarily sterilized beginning in the late 1800s and continuing until the mid-1900s. In *Buck v. Bell* (274 U.S. 200 [1927]) the U.S. Supreme Court upheld eugenics. Carrie Buck was a mentally handicapped woman living at the Virginia State Colony for Epileptics and the

Feeble Minded. She had engaged in sexual activity, and the consequences of these acts scared many. The unfounded belief was that her sexual activity would lead to the birth of "feeble minded" children. Justice Holmes noted that involuntary sterilization was appropriate because "society can prevent those who are manifestly unfit from continuing their kind."

The attempt to maintain the purity of a race or group of people through eugenic procedures is not acceptable. Genetics studies are increasing today, although their aim is not purification but identification and early eradication of diseases by recognizing them in DNA or through other genetic analyses. (See **Human Genome Project**.)

EUTHANASIA   Literally translated from the Greek, the term means good or easy death. Modern usage defines the term as the taking of another's life under the claimed moral authority of prohibiting unnecessary suffering. The element that differentiates euthanasia from physician-assisted suicide as practiced by Dr. Jack Kevorkian is that a second party, someone other than the dying person, takes the life. (See **Physician-Assisted Suicide**.) Dr. Kevorkian sets up a machine operated by a switch. The dying person pushes the switch and causes the introduction of deadly elements into her own body. In euthanasia, the dying person does not cause her death; instead, a second party actively or passively accelerates the victim's death.

Euthanasia is broadly practiced in the United States, but not on humans. We euthanize our pets when they are in the final stages of life or are in chronic, incurable pain. We put our pets "to sleep" when they are struck by a car and cannot recover. Because we do not want to see our beloved animals suffer, we have legally authorized our veterinarians to practice euthanasia. Here is the irony: If we refuse to allow our pets to suffer when they are dying, why do we allow our relatives?

The answer to such a question is not clear. Many perspectives are brought forth. Christians argue that God brings a person into the world and therefore God should dictate the time of a person's death. Others maintain that the reason not to euthanize a person is that we don't know the appropriate time for euthanasia. The body has unique ways to mask the hurt of death. When would it be justified? Or, by a slippery slope argument, if we allowed older people to be euthanized, we would have to decide what is old. Perhaps then we might decide that euthanizing younger and younger people would be better for the society. This issue is the theme of the science fiction book *Logan's Run*, by William F. Nolan and George C. Johnson. In the book, society decides to rid itself of elders, regardless of whether they volunteered for death, through compulsory euthanasia—that is, everyone over 30 was ordered to be terminated. Critics of euthanasia are scared of the potential for this type of outcome, and because of legal conservatism, this side is supported. If one administers a lethal dose to a dying person, even if death is absolutely imminent, the initial charge will be murder. Because of the high emotions involved in such cases, the perpetrator may be convicted of manslaughter, even if love was the motive.

The classic example of such a "mercy killing" occurred in 1995 when an elderly husband took the life of his wife, who had been stricken with Alzheimer's disease. This disease first destroys a person's memory, leaving her confused, then progresses until the victim can no longer care for herself. Such was this situation. The wife was becoming incapable of caring for her basic needs (eating, bathing, toileting), and the husband was becoming physically incapable of caring for himself and her. Years before, they had made mutual promises that each would care for the other until death. The husband, in his eyes, kept that promise. He took the life of his wife so that she would not have to suffer from the disease or suffer the indignity of being cared for by someone other than him. The underlying intent of the husband's action was mercy. But the act was also the premeditated, intentional taking of the life of another, otherwise known as murder. In this instance, the husband was arrested and convicted of voluntary manslaughter, that is, of intentionally taking his wife's life. However, as the husband of a deteriorating person, he was emotionally overwrought, racked by guilt, and thus not completely responsible for his actions.

Proponents of euthanasia acknowledge the potential for uncertainty. They argue that we have extensive medical knowledge about when diseases are incurable and, further, that we know when interventions are inappropriate. We already withdraw active clinical support. What we do not do is administer the lethal dose to end the life. As a result, even though we administer medications to take the pain away from the dying, we unnecessarily allow continued pain and suffering of the family, thus postponing their healing. Furthermore, the costs associated with this time period are high and unnecessary, it is argued, because they only sustain a deteriorating situation.

Clearly, there are strong emotional arguments on both sides. Even if we base our consideration on the physician's most basic rule, "First, do no harm," the course of action is unclear. Is there harm in administering the lethal dose eliminating extended, unnecessary suffering? Or, is there harm by refusing to administer a lethal dose, thus allowing extended suffering? Because these positions are so difficult, bioethicists have further differentiated euthanasia into subcategories based upon outsider participation.

ACTIVE EUTHANASIA

Involves the second party directly introducing a lethal dose into the dying person. This action accelerates the death and intentionally causes it. It is this intentional acceleration of death that causes social discomfort. Most people do not recognize the right of one person to take the life of another, even if the dying person wishes it (called voluntary euthanasia). The belief that humans do not have the right to take a life is fundamental in most religious and in most developed societies.

PASSIVE EUTHANASIA

Involves the withholding of medical interventions that would otherwise serve only to sustain the life. The dying individual is medicated to be pain free, but no lethal doses are administered and the process of dying is neither inhibited nor accelerated. Many people do not classify this passive method of ending a life as a form of euthanasia. Instead, the death is "natural" because biological processes are taking their course without interference from medical science.

VOLUNTARY EUTHANASIA

Occurs when a dying person requests the administration of a lethal dose by another. The initial ethical issue concerns the question of competency: Do competent people ever request their own death? Many believe that a competent person cannot make such a request. In *Bouvia v. Superior Court (Glenshur)*, a very intelligent person, Elizabeth Bouvia, requested that her life support be withdrawn, and in a very controversial Supreme Court decision, her request was denied. She attempted starvation, but this approach was interrupted. Each of Bouvia's personal decisions was denied because people believed her to be incompetent at the time the decision to die was made. (See **Bouvia, Elizabeth.**)

Others believe that voluntary euthanasia should be legalized and allowed under selected circumstances, such as a dying process that is excruciatingly painful and cruelly long. Medical providers will have indicated there is no cure. Under these extreme circumstances, to protect the quality of life of the individual as well as the quality of the person's death, supporters of voluntary euthanasia advocate for the right to be euthanized. The principle involved is that of the right to personal choice and private decision making, in other words, the principle of autonomy in its highest form—a person's control over his or her own destiny.

INVOLUNTARY EUTHANASIA

The taking of lives at certain stages based upon the external individual's belief that death would be the lesser of evils. Here the issue is that the external person is making the decision. Most ethicists do not give this approach much credence. Few advocate that people have the right to make decisions on death for others.

EXTRAORDINARY MEDICAL INTERVENTION   Medical treatments ordered by physicians that move beyond the common course of medical therapy. Dr. Paul Ramsey defined this treatment as one intended to extend an individual's life through excessive therapy at high cost but which will not have a curative result. In other words, extraordinary medical intervention prolongs the life without improving quality. It is, therefore, treatment that is a departure from the normal standard of care.

This definition is best understood by an example. Karen Ann Quinlan was a young New Jersey woman placed on life support after taking a lethal combination of alcohol and Valium™ (a drug prescribed for controlling anxiety, panic attacks, and other related conditions). Terminally ill, she was placed on breathing assistance machinery (a mechanical ventilator) and was given artificial nutrition. The ventilator was subsequently withdrawn, yet she lived for approximately nine years. The extraordinary medical intervention in this case was the ventilator and the artificial nutrition, measures not within the regular course of treatment for a terminally ill person.

The ethical question at issue in extraordinary medical treatment is the underlying motivation for the treatment. If a physician orders extraordinary treatment to avoid liability, the treatment is ethically wrong. Given a litigious society, steps have been taken to avoid this scenario. Patient autonomy is being encouraged through living wills and the durable power of attorney for health care, and inside the hospital, ethics committees guide physicians in dealing with this type of dilemma. The decision to provide or to withdraw treatment will be developed through the committee.

F

FAITH HEALING   Healing based upon the belief in divine intervention into the natural course of a disease. Medical intervention is not attempted and is usually refused. Some religious denominations have healers who conduct religious ceremonies and treat the sick through exhibition of faith. The best-known religion using this approach is the Church of Christian Science.

Some Christian fundamentalist religions do not permit any form of clinical intervention. They believe that illness is the result of sin and that patients must recognize their sinfulness to regain their health and spiritual redemption. In some faiths, parents believe that their sin, not that of the child, is responsible for a child's illness. The innocent child will be protected by God in the hereafter, and the parents must correct their sinful activities or repent of their sin.

Non-Christian religions also practice faith healing. Studies on health care in undeveloped countries report the continued use of witch doctor–priests. These individuals proceed through an elaborate ceremony incorporating a variety of healing actions. They may include herbal treatments, chanting, music, and dancing, yet rely primarily upon faith. Medical anthropologists and trained physicians report that these doctor-priests have had some very impressive successes.

In the United States, unborn fetuses and children present, perhaps, the major legal controversy for health care in coping with faith-healing religions. A classic scenario involves a woman encountering problems during childbirth. The facts indicate that without medical intervention, both mother and child will die. Yet the woman denies herself and her fetus the medical care that would enable them to survive. What should the health care provider do? First, the provider must recognize that adults are presumed competent and have the constitutional right to select and adhere to their religious beliefs. Therefore, if they wish to deny themselves clinical interventions, that denial is based upon their personal choice. However, this same voluntary choice is not available to the soon-to-be-born or the infant. Therefore, the state recognizes a moral imperative to protect the fetus or young child, and court decisions in many states have recognized the child's rights as superior to those of the parent. The state must prove a compelling state interest in the protection of the child. The complex issues that surface in questions such as these blend religious rights, parental rights, and children's rights. Among these, the child's rights are recognized as paramount.

FEDERAL TORT CLAIMS ACT (FTCA)   This 1946 legislation (28 U.S.C. § 1346) indicates the federal government's general consent to be sued for civil and property wrongs committed by its employees. Federal employees may be individually liable for violating certain civil rights as long as they are working within their job description or scope of employment.

Government employees are not protected from liability associated with their administrative or operational actions. For example, if the Veteran's Administration hospital admits a patient, the hospital has a responsibility to provide services in the correct manner. To do otherwise would be to subject it to suits over liability. The FTCA does give immunity to policy-planning actions by government employees, however. Under this exception, if Medicare planning includes an inadvertent harm to an individual, the federal employee is immune from suit.

An action against government health providers for negligence or malpractice must be derived from the Federal Tort Claims Act, and it must be filed in the federal district court. State law guides the amount of damages allowed, with one major exception: punitive damages. The government is immune from the imposition of punitive damages.

In considering a tort (civil wrong) against the federal government, one must make sure that the person being sued is an employee of the federal government. The federal government contracts with many people (called independent contractors) to carry out governmental responsibility. If a federal employee, the FTCA applies. If an independent contractor, then state tort law applies.

The other major exemption concerns federal employees and active duty personnel in the military. Members of these groups are not permitted to bring actions under FTCA, unless the injury occurs while on furlough or leave. In other words, they may file suit only if the injury is not received in the line of active duty (*Feres v. United States* 340 US 135 [1950]).

Many states have a statute equivalent to this act that allows state-employed health care providers to be sued for civil wrongs. The reason that these laws focus upon civil wrongs is that individuals can be negligent or can commit malpractice in the scope of their governmental duties. A criminal act, however, is never within the scope of one's duties. A government employee who commits a criminal act may be prosecuted. Even President Richard M. Nixon, a sitting president, was found not to be above the reach of the criminal investigation.

FETAL REDUCTION   An obstetric-surgical procedure in a pregnancy involving multiple fetuses whereby the physician removes some of the developing fetuses so that the remaining fetuses have a greater chance of survival.

A 1996 case brought this obstetric procedure to the attention of the public. In Great Britain, a woman taking excessive fertility medication became pregnant with eight embryos (she was not following her physician's directions for using the medication). Physicians made it clear to the woman that she would not be able to deliver all eight successfully. Several of the embryos would die in the womb, and their death would likely cause the other embryos to die. The physicians said that their best chance for survival was a fetal reduction technique whereby the physician would surgically enter the womb and remove several embryos. This reduction would allow the others a greater chance of survival. The woman refused fetal reduction, but her body performed its own natural fetal reduction in response to the presence of these multiple embryos. All eight embryos were spontaneously aborted.

This procedure was the subject of bioethical concern because of the conflicting interaction between the health providers and interested onlookers. The health providers believed that some of the embryos could survive, though all eight could not. The interested outsiders were people with sensational interests. They wanted to see a record number of births, or to see how many fetuses could be carried by one mother. These outsiders placed financial pressure upon this mother, encouraging her to attempt to deliver all eight babies. One group apparently offered the mother $1 million if she would deliver all eight successfully and reduced amounts for fewer deliveries. The mother was not a wealthy person, and these forms of financial pressure were seriously inappropriate, according to health care professionals.

The ethical question of whether some of the fetuses should be aborted so that others could survive was also considered. With this many fetuses, there was a greater risk of birth defects and death for all the fetuses. Medical researchers believed that eight fetuses could not become viable and that the woman's body might spontaneously abort them (a natural abortion used by the body to protect itself). Therefore, in order for some of the fetuses to survive, the weakest (those most likely not to survive) would be removed.

▥ **FETAL RIGHTS**   A fetus has the right to begin life with a sound mind and body as biologically defined by the pregnant woman. This right is initially a moral right, not a legal right. There is no legal duty to guarantee the mental and physical health of a fetus until the fetus reaches the stage of viability. At that biological time, also called *quickening,* the state gains an interest in protecting the life of the unborn child. Most issues surrounding fetal rights involve the relationship between the fetus and its mother, such as abortion, maternal behavior causing fetal injury, and maternal medical decision making. The state also has the responsibility to protect the rights of the fetus in the situation of criminal acts.

ABORTION AND FETAL RIGHTS

The unborn have a unique set of rights, depending on their stage of development. Paraphrasing Justice Blackmun in *Roe v. Wade,* the fetus may be terminated at the discretion of the mother's attending physician during the first trimester. Abortions may be regulated by the state during the second trimester as they relate to maternal health. During the third trimester, the state may regulate abortions because of its interest in the potential human life. During this period, abortions may be proscribed except when the life or health of the mother is at serious risk. The third trimester recognizes fetal movement and the medical reality that premature babies can be sustained in a prenatal intensive care unit (PICU). A fetus in the third trimester has limited rights. The fetus is now protected and identified as subject to the state's interest, akin to living people, but the fetus is not accorded full legal rights.

Most issues concerning abortion have focused upon controlling maternal behavior. For example, some states require a 24-hour waiting period after contacting a physician for an abortion. The initial visit is for counseling, to ensure that the procedure is desired and not coerced, and the consequences of the procedure are described for informed consent. Fetal rights and the moral issues associated with abortion are not discussed. Fetal legal rights are on the periphery of the abortion discussion until the third trimester. During this period, all jurisdictions have made elective abortions illegal.

See also **Abortion**.

FETAL INJURIOUS MATERNAL BEHAVIOR

Biologically, the first trimester of gestation is the most hazardous to fetal development. If the mother has measles during the initial weeks of the pregnancy, there is a strong chance that she will give birth to a child with mental retardation. If the mother drinks alcoholic beverages, the baby may be born with disfigurations and fetal alcohol syndrome. If the mother smokes, the child may be born at a low birth weight, resulting in delayed development. Most pregnant women will not place their fetuses at developmental risk voluntarily, so generally the problem arises when the mother does not know she is pregnant. Therefore, there is no cause of action against the mother for unintentional infliction of prenatal injuries stemming from her activities during the first trimester.

When these self-injurious behaviors occur in a woman who is not pregnant, they are considered unhealthy, and most if not all physicians counsel against drinking and smoking. If the woman is participating in sexual activity, many health professionals are more adamant in encouraging her to avoid drinking and smoking because of the possibility of an unanticipated pregnancy. This issue becomes more clouded when the woman knows she is pregnant and continues to participate in self-injurious behaviors that affect the unborn.

Pregnant women who are heavy users of illegal drugs may give birth to an addicted child. Is this a moral dilemma or a legal dilemma? One Ohio case suggests judicially identified alternatives. The woman in this case had multiple children from different fathers and a long history of substance abuse. She was on welfare and supported her drug habit through prostitution. She was arrested multiple times. Several of her children had been addicted at birth and were residing with foster parents. A Cincinnati judge offered the woman a choice: she could commit herself to drug counseling or undergo sterilization. A Youngstown judge offered a woman in a similar situation the options of drug counseling or implanted contraceptives. These judges have tried to address the moral issues through giving the women a choice.

In dealing with pregnancies, health care providers recognize that they have two patients, the pregnant woman and the fetus. In terms of health care, the fetus may be exposed to risks from amniocentesis or from cesarean section. These situations differ from self-injurious behavior because the health of the fetus is the reason for the procedures. As medical science progresses, the number of procedures that fall into this category continues to increase and now includes a variety of fetal surgeries (surgeries on the fetus while it remains in the womb).

Who looks out for the rights of the unborn? The rights of the fetus are indicated by a surrogate, the mother. Under most conditions, the bond between the woman and the fetus is extraordinary—biological, personal, and special. In some instances the mother has denied personal treatment, resulting in her death, in order that her fetus would be born and live. The mother should not be prohibited from being the decision maker simply because she is carrying the fetus. Presuming mental competency, who could be more closely aligned with the unborn child than the mother in this biologically supportive relationship?

Unfortunately, circumstances sometimes dictate that a viable fetus must be aborted if the mother is to survive. There is no law requiring the sacrifice of one person for another. The mother is not required to sacrifice her life for the life of her unborn, but she may decide to do so. In this case, the principle of autonomy appears most significant, allowing the mother to make her own decisions about her and her unborn child's future.

FETAL RIGHTS AND THE STATE

In a few jurisdictions, fetal protection laws, called feticide statutes, attempt to equate the death of a fetus with the death of a living person. Under these laws, criminal charges of double homicide could be filed by the state if a person killed a woman and her fetus. These laws encounter difficulty, however, because they are filled with ambiguous and vague statements about fetuses, when life begins, and other complicated issues.

A civil tort law doctrine requires that you take people as you find them. For example, if you get into a fight with someone and that person is a hemophiliac (a hemophiliac's blood does not clot, which makes bleeding very difficult to stop), you may get into great legal difficulty. If you cause the hemophiliac to bleed to death, you may be found guilty of murder or, at a minimum, manslaughter. Regardless of your intentions, you will be held responsible for that individual's frailties—you take people as you find them. Likewise, if you strike a pregnant woman and you cause her fetus to die, you may be subjected to a wrongful death suit by the mother. The issue of when a fetus becomes a person in these cases is also debated. Is viability, the ability to live outside of the womb, the critical factor?

Fetal rights are problematic for all involved. We are faced with a conflicting set of values within the law, societal morality, and religion. To deal with the conflict, the courts have reached legal decisions that reflect more of an accommodation between legal, societal, and religious doctrines. Because abortion is legal, and social and religious doctrines are not congruent, the courts have not made a definitive statement on fetal rights. The appellate or higher courts often elect not to decide a specific case because the foundation of knowledge is not available and its implications are not clear. The appellate courts do not hesitate to resolve difficult issues, but the courts are exceptionally aware that their decisions will be used to guide other decisions. Therefore, the judges consider how their decisions may be used in similar situations.

FOOD AND DRUG ADMINISTRATION (FDA)   The federal agency responsible for enforcing laws and promulgating regulations concerning medical devices and prescription medications, as well as standards of quality for cosmetics and foods. The FDA is responsible for assuring that proposed medical devices and medications do what they are intended to do. An experimental drug, for example, is evaluated over a seven-year period in terms of its appropriateness, the need for it, and its adverse conditions (side effects). After this extensive evaluation, if the data confirm the use of the drug for the specified condition, the FDA gives its approval.

The authority of the FDA is derived from the Food, Drug, and Cosmetic Act (21 U.S.C. §§ 301–392 [1938]). This law was designed to give the FDA the power to protect the public from unhealthy and harmful foods and drugs, but it has been amended to give the agency control over brand information (information put out under brand names, such as Tylenol® for acetaminophen) provided to the public as well.

The FDA is often the object of criticism, most notably for the length of time it requires to approve new medicines or procedures. Despite the criticism, the agency plays a necessary role in protecting the public charlatan claims of cure-alls and ineffective or poisonous medicines.

The desire for an effective medicine or treatment is substantial. Those who are ill, especially the terminally ill, are crying for answers, and their willingness to try a drug that someone touts as a cure is strong. This desire was exemplified by actor Steve McQueen, who was diagnosed with cancer. After conventional treatment failed, he was reported to have pursued a cancer-fighting drug called Laetrile in Mexico, because this treatment was not FDA-approved and was thus not available in the United States. The FDA had found the drug ineffective in the treatment of cancer—that is, it did not perform as its developer claimed. Laetrile did not cure McQueen. He died a short time after the reported treatments.

Similar stories abound. People want to believe in the existence of alternative cures. Some turn out to be not only ineffective but harmful–the patient's condition is worsened or death is accelerated by the treatment. The FDA faces the enormous challenge of making these situations avoidable.

FOOD AND DRUG ADMINISTRATION APPROVAL PROCESS
The formal process usually takes approximately seven years. The initial research, which attempts to prove that the drug is safe and effective, is submitted to the FDA from the private company. The FDA then undertakes its own analysis to substantiate the data and determine the effectiveness of the drug. Animal studies and eventually human studies are used. (However, experiments on living creatures are not considered until the researchers are able to document the probability of effectiveness). Throughout the process, the agency further defines the warnings and instructions to be included with the drug at the time of sale. The agency also gives the drug with the generic name that must be placed on the

label (for example, ibuprofen is the generic name for the key ingredient in the trademark drugs of Motrin® and Advil®).

The process can be accelerated if the results are exceptional. One such example was found in the treatment of cerebrovascular accidents (strokes) in children with sickle cell anemia. The treatment advance involved frequent (weekly) blood transfusions into the children identified at risk of stroke. The two-year-old experimental study has been so successful that the process is already being introduced to mainstream physicians. Concern for the long-term effects of the procedure remains, but the reduction of children's strokes has warranted the FDA's action. The FDA will monitor the outcomes of the children and the success of the procedure, making changes if required.

The FDA can also withdraw approval. An effective weight-reducing drug called Fen-Phen (fenfluramine-phentermine) had its approval withdrawn in September 1997. The use of the drug in practice indicated a previously unknown side effect—it caused permanent damage to heart valves. After these consequences were identified, the manufacturers of this drug withdrew it from the market at the FDA's request almost immediately.

EXPERIMENTAL DRUGS

In the United States, approximately 60,000 new drugs are identified annually. Many are slight variations on existing drugs. Several are new responses to an identified need. For example, there are drugs currently very effective drugs in use for the treatment of tuberculosis. However, a problem has recently arisen: the disease has become drug resistant, and existing drugs are not as effective as they once were. As a result, new alternatives must be developed. Derivatives are often not a successful substitute because their effectiveness comes from the same chemical that the disease is resistant to. Totally new drugs may require the full time period for testing.

Drugs are FDA approved for specific purposes, but they may also have desirable side effects. For example, Tagamet®, a well-known FDA-approved drug for controlling stomach acidity and stomach ulcers, accomplishes its task by reducing the patient's anxiety. Physicians may decide, with the assistance of their pharmacy and therapeutics committees, to prescribe the drug for its side effect, reduced anxiety. This use is not considered experimentation, since the effect was identified through the FDA process.

In 1997 the FDA began to undergo a broad overhaul following passage of the Food and Drug Administration Modernization Act. The bill received bypartisan support in both houses of Congress. The act provides for a faster review system for medical devices, provisions for the desperately ill to have access to experimental drugs, wider circulation of information about unapproved uses of already licensed drugs, and relaxed label requirements. The goal, according to Senator James Jeffords of Vermont, Senate sponsor of the bill, is to make the FDA more efficient and stronger in its focus upon saving people's lives.

G

GENE THERAPY   The process by which a normal gene is inserted into cells to replace a malfunctioning gene that is causing some genetic disease. This therapy consists of medical procedures designed to change the genetic composition of cells. The intended outcome of these procedures is to remove genes that would result in disease and to avoid passing genetic disorders to offspring.

Gene therapy is important both at the level of the individual patient and at the level of the health system as a whole. To determine whether an individual has a problem gene, a genetic map of the individual may be developed (see **Genetic Screening**). The map will indicate the presence of a disease-causing gene that either predetermines the individual's future or will be passed to the individual's children, causing them to become victims of the disease. Clearly, this information is helpful to people who want to know their risks. If handled incorrectly, however, the information could be emotionally damaging.

At the health system level, genetic information could be used to identify abnormal genes that could be located, then supplemented or replaced by normal genes. The added normal genes supply increased information to facilitate proper cellular function and may be able to minimize the negative impact of the disease.

A long-range goal for researchers is to be able to use gene therapy as a treatment for diseases such as cancer. Cancer is characterized as abnormal cellular growth. Conceivably, genes with enough information to stop and correct the aberrant cellular activity could be inserted, bringing the cells back to normal replication.

However, this genetic knowledge is also potentially damaging. Though the information gained from genetic screening could be used positively by employers, insurers, and the courts, it could also be used to discriminate against people with problem genes. Hiring an individual with a gene indicting a high probability of an early heart attack, for example, might raise a company's health insurance premiums. As a result, the employer might deny the individual a position for which he or she is well qualified.

GENETIC SCREENING   The medical identification or mapping of a person's genetic structure. In the genetic screening process, an individual's DNA is evaluated to discover whether or not certain genes are present, indicating that a disease is likely to develop. For the known genes, genetic screening is very accurate. Unfortunately, only a few genes are known. Identifying additional genes is the purpose of the Human Genome Project.

Screening for disease is an important tool in preventive medicine. The goal for secondary prevention is to identify a disease before it is symptomatic, because it can then be more effectively eliminated. Genetic screening takes secondary prevention to a new level of diagnosis. The identification of a gene that would lead to the occurrence of a deadly disease could assist in preventing the disease's onset.

There are several negative aspects to this knowledge, however. First among them is its impact on the individual. Do you want to know that you will eventually suffer from an incurable, disabling disorder? What might this knowledge do to your emotional state? Your willingness to marry and have children? Would it influence your motivation on the job?

A second problem concerns access to genetic screening information. An individual's medical records are confidential. However, we normally agree to allow certain people to review our medical information. Your insurance company and your employer, for example, may have access to your records. Many insurance or managed care policies require a review of the treatment rendered to their beneficiary in order to ensure quality and the provision of necessary services. At the same time, however, they read very personal details. A review of a policy holder's genetic screening would not be inappropriate under current practices.

Another issue deals with ethnic discrimination. Several diseases are specifically associated with a person's ethnic background. African-Americans are at greater risk than other Americans for sickle cell anemia. Tay-Sachs is found only in Jewish people from Eastern Europe. American Indians are believed to have a predisposition to alcoholism. Several of these disorders are very serious. Can the government require that a certain ethnic group be screened for the presence or absence of a bad gene? Or is it appropriate only to screen entire populations for genes, such as the gene for cystic fibrosis or amyotrophic lateral sclerosis (commonly called Lou Gehrig's disease)? The problem of discrimination in the name of the public's health must receive extensive scrutiny.

GOOD SAMARITAN ACT   Common law does not require that a person stop and assist an accident victim, and many people do not stop because of the potential for charges of malpractice or negligence. In order to increase the assistance of qualified people at an accident, many states have written legislation to protect a person who helps an injured victim during an emergency from civil legal action by the victim. The emergency is one that occurs "at the scene of the accident." If the helper is a medical provider, he or she must undertake this service without expectation of any form of payment. Under the Ohio Revised Code, for example, people who attempt to provide medical services in an emergency are immune from civil action if the care is rendered outside of the health care facility and without the expectation of payment—unless the person engages in willful or wanton misconduct. Ohio further extends the protection to emergency medical technicians on ambulance calls (ORC 2305.23).

This protection has its limits, which vary extensively from state to state. Should a lawsuit be filed, the court would evaluate the helper's actions in order to ascertain whether or not the helper acted in good faith. If the helper acted but was guilty of ordinary negligence, the person would be protected from lawsuit. If the helper acted in a grossly negligent manner, the legislative protection would be withdrawn and the lawsuit allowed. Gross negligence means that the helper is acting in a way that a reasonable person would know would probably harm the victim. Therefore, if a person stopped to help an injured person and gave reasonable care but the injured was further harmed, the helper's efforts would be legally protected.

Consider a situation where a helper was appropriately administering cardiopulmonary resuscitation (CPR) to an elderly person. CPR requires chest compressions by the helper to make the heart pump. Elderly people may have bones that are easily broken. During the compressions, the helper accidentally breaks the ribs of the victim and the rib punctures the lung. The victim survives, but the healing process is slower because of the helper's actions. Under these circumstances, the helper would be protected from civil action. The actions were consistent with the need of the victim, and the damage was not a result of wanton acts.

The definition of those protected varies by state. The degree of negligence also depends upon the qualifications of the person accused. A medical specialist will be held to a higher standard than a lay person who has taken a course in first aid. A statute of limitations on filing these types of case applies, and the time period usually begins when the injury occurs or is identified.

H

HEALTH   From a general perspective, health is the condition of biological, psychological, spiritual, and social well-being wherein one is able to carry out basic activities of life. Health is also defined very personally: it is the personal perception that one is mentally and physically able to pursue those aspects of life that make one satisfied with one's capabilities.

Health is also a personal biological, mental and physical state that individuals can influence and, to some extent, control. We can take a great degree of control over our personal health by our choices concerning appropriate diet, exercise, and stress control. A low-fat diet has been identified as preventing heart disease and high blood pressure. Both aerobic exercise (jogging, bicycling, and other exercise that enhances the body's use of oxygen and the heart's physical capability) and anaerobic exercise (exercise focused on building muscle, such as weight lifting) are important for human performance. Effective stress control involves recognizing both good stress and bad stress. Good stress (eu-stress) enables individuals to challenge or motivate their own performance. Uncontrolled bad stress (dys-stress) leads to anxiety, panic attacks, heart disease, and stroke.

Certain aspects of health are genetically determined. Some of us are genetically predisposed towards developing a particular disease. One of the greatest predictors of early breast cancer in women is the age when the mother or grandmother had breast cancer. The same is true of heart disease. Many men should be concerned if their fathers had early heart disease or high blood pressure. Optimal health under these conditions involves taking steps to correct any unnecessary risks in our behavior that might cause these conditions to manifest themselves. If heart disease runs in the family, consider aerobic exercise to build up the heart (after checking with your doctor, of course). But even those of use with have genetic problems can often positively influence by changing those adverse health conditions we can influence and minimizing the problems we create through our behavior.

111

Good health does not mean that an individual is a perfect biological specimen or that the person is completely free of disease (or pathological conditions such as paralysis). A person who has a physical handicap may still be very healthy. Paraplegics (people paralyzed below the waist) may be found wheelchair racing or playing wheelchair basketball using extraordinary arm and stomach muscles. People who are blind, deaf, or otherwise handicapped may be very healthy individuals. They maximize their emotional, mental, and physical capabilities, and the handicap simply constitutes another hurdle to overcome in life.

HEALTH INSURANCE   Health insurance is a financing mechanism intended to protect an individual or family from financial devastation in the event of expensive medical care.

Health is a unique form of insurance. Traditional insurance policies, such as car, fire, or theft, are offered for sale by either proprietary or not-for-profit companies. Their purpose is to spread the financial costs of one person's catastrophe across many people so that the individual is not financially devastated by the unexpected situation. The risk of the disaster that each person carries determines the monthly cost (premium) that he or she is required to pay. The greater the risk, the higher the premium. If the risk too great, the individual will not be sold a policy. Because such disastrous events are infrequent, the insurance company can invest the funds it receives from policy holders, which grow until the time they are needed.

Car and fire insurance provide coverage for the unexpected. Health insurance covers both expected treatments and unexpected situations. The coverage for routine care, informally called "health assurance," addresses insurance situations that will happen. Because coverage deals with health care, insurers do not wish to deal with the social outcry if they attempt to cut costs by restricting coverage. If a health insurance company dropped customers just because they were frequently ill, that company might be accused of not caring for human life. Bad public relations can destroy companies. Yet insurers must investigate those who make frequent claims on health insurance to make sure that their use of medical services is not frivolous, raising overall costs unnecessarily. Naturally insurers constantly look for ways to minimize their costs. One option is to increase their coverage of preventive services in order to lower the frequency and cost of future serious conditions.

Thus health insurance covers a variety of diagnostic services and medical procedures. The purchaser, usually an employer, has many options in deciding which services are covered and which are not, since an insurance contract provides many negotiating points. One important area is that of pre-existing conditions. A pre-existing condition is a chronic or debilitating (that is, expensive) condition that existed prior to the person's obtaining insurance. The insurance company does not have to cover the medical procedures and treatments associated with that disorder and informs the policy holder of that fact via its policy statement. The statement identifies the pre-existing conditions and advises the policy holder to investigate other available coverages, if any.

Pre-existing conditions are a problem confronting everyone involved in the health care industry. These conditions are almost always expensive to treat and require long-term treatment. A classic example is insulin-dependent diabetes. This condition strikes young people, often in their teenage years. The consequences of diabetes, some of which are quite serious, will occur over the next 50 to 60 years. These people will have to pay for the treatment from their personal resources, since this condition is almost always considered a pre-existing condition. As employees, they will be able to obtain insurance coverage only for those procedures and services unrelated their diabetic condition. If, however, this condition is first diagnosed after they have insurance, it is not a pre-existing condition. Then, they have insurance coverage.

Insurance carriers are regulated by the states, usually by the state department of insurance. In most states, insurance companies must initially prove they have a minimum financial worth to cover the services for the insured. States further regulate insurance policy forms, marketing, and claims procedures. Many also have consumer complaint departments. To achieve some continuity and uniformity of supervision over the insurance companies, the National Organization of Insurance Commissioners was founded. This organization has issued several model codes and regulations.

The federal government has also become increasingly involved with insurance supervision, even though the U.S. Supreme Court has indicated that insurance is not an interstate transaction. Through the Consolidated Omnibus Budget Reconciliation Act of 1986 (COBRA), group insurance coverage was mandated for continuation for six months after an employee resigns. The employee will be responsible for paying the company rate for the insurance coverage. COBRA's authors hoped that the six-month window would decrease the number of people who are uninsured because they are between jobs. Several other pieces of federal legislation influence insurance activities, such as the prohibition of discrimination through Title VII of the Civil Rights Act of 1964, the Americans with Disabilities Act (ADA), and the Age Discrimination in Employment Act (ADEA).

The newest law modifying health insurance concerns group health insurance. Specifically, COBRA stipulates that employees with pre-existing conditions can take their group health insurance with them when they leave their jobs. The legislation defines pre-existing conditions and specifies when an exclusion of a pre-existing condition may be imposed. This new legislation indicates stringent conditions on portability and provides a guaranteed renewability of group health insurance under certain conditions.

The need for health insurance began during the Great Depression of the 1930s, when people found they could not afford hospital and physician care. The first health coverage, the Baylor University Hospital plan, was for hospitalization. It enrolled Texas teachers in the surrounding area and for 50 cents per month guaranteed 21 days of hospital care. With the advent of World War II and restraints on employee wages, employers were encouraged to offer assistance to help employees cover the costs of health services. Health insurance was the response.

Nongovernmental health insurance is currently the principle payer source for health care costs. As a result, the interaction between the insurance carriers and the health care industry has influenced the decisions on the delivery of health services in the United States. Only two industrialized countries, the United States and South Africa, offer no form of universal minimum health care. The current private organization and structure of the health system is well entrenched. Several universal plans have been proposed, some inspired by Canada's apparently successful governmental plan. Nevertheless, the universal governmental programs set forth by several presidents have encountered tremendous resistance and the proposals have failed. Consequently, many policy authors are looking for ways to work within the existing private structure to provide some form of coverage for the approximately 40 million Americans with inadequate coverage or no health insurance at all.

HEALTH MAINTENANCE ORGANIZATION (HMO)

A form of managed care organization that is responsible for both financing and delivering comprehensive health services to a defined group of members for a capitated or flat fee. Today, it has two principal characteristics: it uses a physician as primary care provider to control the enrolled person's medical care; and it places some of the primary providers at financial risk for excessive medical expenses. These two characteristics reflect the modern activities of managed care and the managed care philosophy of controlling costs by controlling utilization. (See **Managed Care** for complete discussion of payment.)

The HMO concept is not new. It was the approach used in 1938 by the Kaiser-Permanente Health Care System of California. Originally, an HMO was defined as a prepaid organization that provided health care to voluntarily enrolled members in return for a preset amount of money on a per member per month basis. This description is still accurate, but the modern HMO has evolved into a more complex arrangement between consumers, providers, and health care organizations.

HMOs take many forms. The staff model HMO employs physicians to be the primary care providers and provides the physicians' offices and basic support services (for example, laboratories, pharmacy). Specialty medical services are contracted, although the physician specialist is not usually an HMO employee. A complete outpatient setting is provided. When inpatient services are required, the HMO will contract with hospitals or other inpatient facilities. Significantly, the person enrolled in the HMO usually cannot select a physician outside of the employed physicians.

Following the 1973 HMO Act, the individual practice association (IPA) form of HMO was developed. IPAs are organizations of physicians that contract to provide services to HMO enrollees. The physicians may be in solo or group practices. The major benefit of this structure is the ability of the HMO to offer a broader array of primary care physicians for the enrollees to select from. For the physician, negotiating a contract and knowing the true costs of treating the HMO's enrollees is the most complex challenge.

Many other forms of managed care companies are being rapidly developed, since this approach is currently the fastest growing health reimbursement organizational arrangement.

HEALTH MAINTENANCE ORGANIZATION ACT OF 1974

This act was passed to increase the number of HMOs so that insurance and delivery of services were combined. Its premise was that the HMO was more efficient than the present health structure. With efficiency, costs would decline and services would be more available.

The act mandated that companies with 25 or more employees offering an HMO, if available. It also gave the HMO the opportunity to be "federally qualified." A federally qualified HMO provided a set of mandated services, including those characteristic of traditional insurance such as hospitalization and emergency services. It also required physician services along with mental health, home health, family planning, and health education. It focused upon providing comprehensive health services (insurance and providers as one entity) at one cost per month. The only extra cost was the copayment, which was not mandated. The copayment was a small amount that the enrollee would pay at each visit, usually less than $15.

HEMLOCK SOCIETY   A voluntary society formed in 1980 advocating the right of voluntary euthanasia for the terminally ill and physician-assisted suicide. Its motto is "Good Life, Good Death." Its purpose is to campaign for rights for the terminally ill. It publishes a variety of informational resources, including newsletters and books. Perhaps its most notable publication was the model statute, "The Death with Dignity Act." Promoted in the various states, its purpose was to provide a model for legislation permitting physician-assisted suicide for the terminally ill.

The executive director of the society, Derek Humphry, wrote a book entitled *Final Exit*. On its back cover, the author's intentions are made clear: "*Final Exit* is intended to be read by a mature adult who is suffering from a terminal illness and is considering the option of rational suicide if and when suffering becomes unbearable. It also gives guidance to those who might be supportive of this option." To accomplish these intentions, the author provides detailed information on how to take your own life. He indicates how to accumulate medications, the desirable types of medications, and the other steps required to successfully bring about your own death. Because of the level of detail and its explicit "how to" nature, the book was highly controversial.

The society is also controversial. Their promotion of the model legislation was widely discussed, and publication of *Final Exit* caused opponents to call for a review of the constitutional right of free speech and demand that publication be prevented. The prepublication press coverage resulted in tremendous book sales during the first days.

Many ethical issues are raised in the publications of the Hemlock Society, but the fundamental issue is whether rational people have the right to take their own lives. The rights of autonomy and personal nonmaleficence as a guiding principle are brought squarely into the limelight of discussion. Regardless of the correctness or incorrectness of the society's actions and beliefs, it has inspired extensive analysis of the process of dying and the concept of a "quality death."

HIPPOCRATIC OATH   A traditional oath of ethical conduct taken by physicians upon entering into the practice of medicine. Its principal purpose is to ensure benefit to the patient by indicating the extent of the physician-patient relationship. Its most important contribution is putting into application the key ethical constructs of autonomy, nonmaleficence, beneficence, justice, and guides for the physician-patient relationship. Several versions exist. The following is one recognized version:

I swear by Apollo the physician, and Aesculapius and Health, and All-heal, and all the gods and goddesses, that, according to my ability and judgment, I will keep this Oath and this stipulation—to reckon him who taught me this Art equally dear to me as my parents, to share my substance with him, and relieve his necessities if required; to look upon his offspring in the same footing as my own brothers, and to teach them this Art, if they shall wish to learn it, without fee or stipulation; and that by precept, lecture, and every other mode of instruction, I will impart a knowledge of the Art to my own sons, and those of my teachers, and to disciples bound by a stipulation and oath according to the law of medicine, but to none other. I will follow that system of regimen which, according to my ability and judgment, I consider for the benefit of my patients, and abstain from whatever is deleterious and mischievous. I will give no deadly medicine to anyone if asked, nor suggest any such counsel; and in like manner I will not give to a woman a pessary to produce abortion. With purity and with holiness I will pass my life and practice my Art. I will not cut persons laboring under the stone, but will leave this to be done by men who are practitioners of this work. Into whatever houses I enter, I will go into them for the benefit of the sick, and will abstain from every voluntary act of mischief and corruption; and, further, from the seduction of females, or males, of freemen or slaves. Whatever, in connection with it, I see or hear, in the live of men, which not to be spoken of abroad, I will not divulge, as reckoning that all such should be kept secret. While I continue to keep this Oath unviolated, may it be granted to me to enjoy life and the practice of the Art, respected by all men, in all times. But, should I trespass and violate this Oath, may the reverse be my lot.

This oath has been criticized, primarily because it was developed over 2,000 years ago and times and technologies have radically changed. It does not deal with the desires of the patient's proxy (e.g., power of attorney making recommendations for the patient) nor with human experimentation. Today's current clinical demands also conflict with the oath. Abortion, euthanasia, and physician-assisted suicide are specifically disallowed, but contemporary challenges refute these directives. As a result, some medical schools have developed their own physician code and take the Hippocratic Oath only because it symbolizes tradition.

HUMAN GENOME PROJECT   A U.S. government project whose purpose is to map and understand the entire human genome. It is an extraordinary biological task expected to take fifteen years and cost over three billion dollars. The result will assist in preventing genetic disorders and allow influence over human genetic change. Not all of the genome information is important, however. Scientists suggest that as much as 90 percent of the information is unnecessary because it has no genetic purpose.

The human genome consists of 46 chromosomes in 23 pairs. Each chromosome consists of DNA (deoxyribonucleic acid). These chromosomes contain approximately 4,000 genes, each made up of basic chemical groups called "base pairs." A person's genetic endowment or genetic traits are indicated by the structure of the base pairs. A person has both dominant and recessive genes. For example, brown hair and brown eyes are dominant genes. For a recessive genetic trait to become evident, there must be a matching DNA sequence. People with blue and green eyes have these matching sequences because blue and green eyes are the products of recessive genes.

Approximately 4,000 inherited disorders have been identified to date. The information from the genome project will be used to correct these diseases or better yet, to prevent the diseases from ever happening. Once gene pairs that indicate the future occurrence of a disease have been identified, they can be removed or new genes can be inserted to redirect the bad or aberrant genes.

As positive as this information appears, not everyone supports the project. Many express the fear that the information will be used inappropriately to influence the progress or deterioration of a genetic group. Scientists will be able to reshape human beings from what they are naturally to what we want or think is desired. Some critics view this process as similar to Nazi eugenics, where the optimal Aryan was to be created.

Difficult social and moral decisions arise when technology is perceived as capable of influencing the building blocks of human life (DNA). At the same time scientists are singing about the benefits to humans, others fear the potential for abuse from that same knowledge.

I

IATROGENIC DISORDERS   Disorders caused by the physician's practices and treatments, either as result of the process of diagnosis or the physician's acts. These disorders may range in severity from the very mild to life threatening, depending upon the clinical situation. One example of an iatrogenic disorder is an infection transmitted by the physician to the patient during surgery. Such an infection places the patient under unnecessary physiologic stress. Another example occurred when a pair of hemostats (surgical steel clips that prevent blood vessels from bleeding unnecessarily during surgery) was left inside the patient's body by mistake. The patient complained of pain soon afterward, and x-rays indicated the hemostat. This disorder was caused by the actions of the physician.

Iatrogenic disorders are increasingly being brought to the public's attention as a result of the power of the medical interventions now at the physician's disposal. Pharmaceuticals (prescription drugs) have the potential to interact with one another and mute or neutralize the action of another drug (antagonism). Or one drug may interact with another and intensify the effects of the drugs (synergism) to the point they may be life threatening or actually cause death.

Because of the constant production of new drugs, today's physician, pharmacist, and pharmacologist are all extraordinarily conscious of the possibility of these interactions. However, there are too many possible interactions for any one person to know. To protect patients, many pharmacies purchase software that reviews the prescriptions of the patient and checks for drug interactions. Should an interaction or problem be noted, the physician is notified and the patient is protected.

IN VITRO FERTILIZATION   This is just one of several methods of artificial insemination currently in use. In this process, the egg and sperm are joined together (into a zygote) in a laboratory rather than the womb. The zygote is then implanted into the

119

woman. The hoped-for result is the development of a fetus into a healthy infant. (See **Artificial Insemination**.)

INCOMPETENT PATIENTS   A person is judged incompetent when she does not know or understand the nature and consequences of the decision under consideration. A person is presumed competent unless she is an "unemancipated minor," that is, a person under the age of 18 who is under the direction of parents or guardians. Such a person is considered "unfree" for purposes of decision making. However, an individual under the age of 18 who is living away from the parents or guardians, married or otherwise independent, may be considered competent for decision making.

In some situations, adults may have their competence questioned. In this process, qualified individuals document the person's thought difficulties and then prove them within the legal system. If the person is legally determined to be incompetent, decision-making responsibilities are turned over to a guardian. Three types of people frequently fall into this category: the elderly, people with developmental disabilities, and people with mental illness.

TREATMENT OF INCOMPETENT PERSONS

The permission of the parent or guardian is required before a minor's treatment can proceed. The process is usually simple. The same is generally true for persons with developmental disabilities. The parents of these people are responsible for their health care. In some situations, however, the costs of raising a developmentally disabled child become too high, and the parents turn to their state for assistance. In this case, the state officially becomes the guardian, responsible for the welfare of the person. If possible, the parents are assigned guardianship responsibilities. If not, the state assigns an individual to be guardian to make the necessary survival decisions. The guideline most commonly used for these decisions is the "best interest" of the person coupled with a subjective evaluation of the person's circumstances.

Situations involving mentally ill people are more difficult, since their conditions rarely result in a constant state of mental confusion. However, their thoughts may be unclear or disoriented for an extended period of time. For the period of this thought inadequacy, the individual will be appointed a guardian. The legal issue is the process of determining whether the person's thoughts are, in fact, disoriented and out of touch with reality.

One of the crucial issues in all of these cases, and especially for the mentally ill, is variable capacity. Sometimes the person can make certain decisions and cannot make others. For example, a person with the ability to understand the nature of her property and know what she desires to do with it is considered competent to make a will. This same person may not be able to make health decisions for herself because she does not understand the nature of the actions. In these instances, the courts remove the rights of decision-making in the area where the person is incompetent from the individual and give that responsibility to another person. All of these decisions are premised upon allowing incompetent people the greatest autonomy possible while preventing them from allowing their incompetency to hurt themselves of others.

INFORMED CONSENT   When people preparing to receive medications or undergoing medical procedures understand the purpose of the proposed therapies, their decision to undergo them is considered informed consent. The purpose of informed consent is the recognition that all people have the right to make informed decisions about activities or practices that will affect their health. Informed consent is also intended to ensure that the patient is aware of possible side effects as well as other possible treatments.

Health care providers are responsible for making sure that the information they provide is clear and understandable to the patient. Very often, the patient is under emotional strain and may require extra information to make a decision. Another component of understanding is the patient's educational level. Physicians are exceptionally educated, and medicine also uses its own terminology. A lay person may not understand the medical jargon and may also be intimidated by the provider. Therefore, the physician or nurse must take whatever steps are necessary to "translate" the clinical language into language that communicates to that individual. If communication does not occur, the provider may be found negligent.

Informed consent may be verbal or it may be in writing, both being voluntary. Many physicians have patients sign their name under the informed consent paragraph indicating that they understood the description of the procedure and were given the opportunity to ask questions. The provider must make sure that the patient does not simply sign the document just because the provider indicated "sign here." The goal of informed consent is to protect the patients' rights to decide issues about their own health future. (See **Consent [Informed]**.)

INSANITY   A legal term indicating that a person is unfit to enjoy freedom of actions because his or her behavior may pose a threat to himself or others. Insanity is not a medical term, although it is often used as a synonym for psychotic mental illness; instead, it reflects an individual's legal mental capacity. A person who has been declared insane is viewed as incompetent and incapable of being found responsible for his or her own acts. Often we associate the designation of insanity with criminal actions, but it also affects many other actions, such as making a will, personal health care treatment, the ability to enter into a contract, and the ability to enter into marriage.

Determining whether or not a person is legally insane is difficult. In this matter, law and medicine are intertwined, because the person is almost always suffering from a mental illness. If the court finds him insane, he is excused from the consequences of his actions. This does not mean that he is allowed to go free; rather, he is usually committed to a forensic psychiatric unit for a time period determined by the psychiatrists.

A person can be sane at the time of the crime and go insane while waiting for trial. In this situation, the person is treated for the mental illness. When she regains her competency, she is legally tried for the crime. If convicted, she goes to jail to serve her sentence. If she has committed homicide, she will be treated to help her regain competency. Then, if convicted and sentenced to death, she can be put to death only if she retains her competence. The logic is that a person cannot "pay her debt to society" if she doesn't understand her crime.

Three major legal standards are considered in determining whether a person is legally insane. According to the M'Naghten rule, the person is not criminally responsible at the time of the act if he or she was mentally ill to the extent that he could not tell whether he was doing right or wrong. If the individual had sufficient mental ability to understand the rightness or wrongness of his acts, the individual is considered competent. This rule was the first of the three and was originally written in England in the year 1843 (M'Naghten's Case, 8 Eng. Rep. 718 (1843]).

The second test is the Durham rule, also called the irresistible impulse test of criminal responsibility. It regards an individual as insane if he or she is incapable of resisting a compulsion to carry out an unlawful action. The person may have been aware of right and wrong, but the impulse was so controlling that the unlawful act could not be avoided. The act was the product of a mental abnormality.

The M'Naghten and Durham rules were incorporated into the third legal rule, the American Law Institute's Model Penal Code (MPC), § 4.01. The MPC suggests that "a person is not responsible for criminal conduct if at the time of such conduct as a result or mental disease or defect he lacks substantial capacity either to appreciate the criminality (wrongfulness) of his conduct or to conform his conduct to the requirements of law." Under this model, the individual has a mental condition that either causes or prevents lawful actions. This approach is used by most federal courts and, with some modifications, by several states.

The criminal plea of insanity is not a simple one. To make the plea, the accused must admit to the court that he carried out the unlawful act at the same time he files the insanity plea. Then the defense has the burden of proving that the accused was insane. The prosecution, on the other hand, attempts to prove that the accused knew and understood his actions.

TEMPORARY INSANITY

People may lose their ability for rational thought and understanding of their actions for a short period of time, due to the emotional strain of the circumstances. In such a situation, the person is not held responsible and is usually acquitted or found guilty of a lesser crime. Highly emotional circumstances characterize these situations, and occasionally homicide charges are reduced to involuntary manslaughter. In voluntary manslaughter, a killing is intended but the emotions so clouded rational thinking that the person did not realize the true nature of his or her acts. One example is the father who shot and killed the man who had involved his daughter in pornography. Another similar example is the mother who killed her son's rapist. The intense anger and hatred felt by these parents overcame any normal thought. Once the anger was gone, the accused would return to normal thought and action processing. These sorts of conditions indicate possible temporary insanity.

INSTITUTIONAL REVIEW BOARDS (IRBs) The

IRB is a product of law passed in the 1970s, and federal regulations guide its actions. The purpose of the IRB is to protect research subjects, both humans and animals, from being subjected to unjustified exposures or treatments. A secondary purpose is to consider the legal implications of a research proposal in order to protect the organization from subsequent legal action. The federal Department of Health Education and Welfare (DHEW) was originally the agency responsible for reviewing and promulgating IRB guidelines. The Department of Health and Human Services (DHHS) is now the agency responsible.

The organizations required to have an IRB are research universities and research organizations. The primary function of an IRB is to analyze any research proposal with human beings as research subjects. For research involving human subjects, very detailed scientific rationales and justifications are required. The board determines the subjects' risks and benefits, the extent of human rights violation, and the informed consent necessary prior to becoming a subject. The potential for damage to the physical, psychological, and social well-being of the participants is considered, and if the board finds the research problematic, it has substantial organizational authority to deny the researcher the right to proceed.

At the University of Kentucky, for example, the IRB must be informed of all research using human subjects. It then evaluates the study, even if the only human involvement is answering a questionnaire. Even though risk to the subject from answering a questionnaire is minimal, the possibility does exist, and the IRB will review the proposal.

INTEGRATED HEALTH SYSTEM (IHS)

Under this organizational system, hospitals and physicians join together to form a single organization intended to provide complete health services for their community. Legally, the providers are no longer individual entities but merge into one. The resulting organization is intended to eliminate uncoordinated health care for the patient.

Becoming an IHS requires many structural changes. Integration requires the new organization to assume the responsibility for general management of services and long-term planning for economic success. The hospitals and physicians invest their assets into the new company and share the resulting rewards or risks.

The formation of a single organization where several existed before has sparked controversy. The new organization may result in the elimination of competition, raising antitrust questions. An antitrust question asks whether the new organization severely restricts or eliminates competition by price discrimination or price fixing (or other measures). Once competition is removed, there is no incentive to keep costs down. Federal and state laws have been passed to protect consumers from losing their rights to the lower costs. Violating organizations may have their merger disallowed. This antitrust issue is a major concern for people considering the development of an IHS.

(For complete discussion, see **Managed Care**.)

J

JOINT COMMISSION ON ACCREDITATION OF HEALTHCARE ORGANIZATIONS

The Joint Commission was formed in 1952 under the name Joint Commission on Accreditation of Hospitals (JCAH) when the American College of Physicians, the American Medical Association, the American Hospital Association, and the Canadian Medical Association formed a consensus on the need for quality assurance, that is, minimum standards of quality, in health care. The growth of hospitals was reaching its peak after the 1946 Hospital Survey and Construction Act (called the Hill-Burton Act after its authors). In order to ensure quality, the JCAH, an independent evaluative group, was formed. Hospitals were requested to comply with a recognized set of standards published by the JCAH and in return would receive accreditation. Accreditation was approved for different lengths of time, with three years reflecting JCAH's best endorsement.

The importance of accreditation was significantly increased when the Health Care Financing Administration and Medicare decided to essentially equate accreditation with compliance with Medicare conditions of participation—a difficult set of standards to meet. Originally, surveys approving hospitals for Medicare were carried out by federal employees, but the JCAH accreditation approach was preferred, though the loss of accreditation also results in the loss of Medicare.

During the late 1970s and 1980s, multi-institutional organizations increased. Organizations diversified in health care (called vertical integration by management scholars). These organizations were made up of the top organization (usually the hospital) and contributors to that organization, such as a nursing facility, laundry, pharmacy, doctor's office complexes, etc. These facilities were in need of qualitative standards, and the JCAH became the Joint Commission on Healthcare Organizations—the Joint Commission for short.

The Joint Commission has attempted several approaches to ensuring quality of care. Recently it attempted to use accreditation to encourage the application of ideas based upon the precepts of Total Quality Management (TQM), but many critics surfaced. Since then, the Joint Commission has reworked its emphasis, returning to the demand for compliance with standards and outcome measures, an approach formerly called "quality assurance."

JUSTICE   The meanings of this term vary. Lawyers typically consider justice to be the appropriate and fair administration of society's laws. Citizens may expand the definition to include the administration of moral correctness. The third definition is that of title for judge, for example, a Justice of the Supreme Court.

Justice, when defined as the administration of society's laws, is principally concerned with the application of laws to factual situations. In the classic jury trial, the jury is the finder of fact and the judge is the trier of the law, meaning that the judge tests and evaluates the application of the law. This means that the jury will ascertain the facts of the case, the judge will instruct the jury in the applicable law, and the jury will apply the law to the facts they have identified. These actions are interwoven with the social ideals of moral correctness, and many want absolute justice applied. The defendant is tried by a jury of her peers. Via due process, the defendant is allowed to confront her accuser and prove whether she is innocent or guilty of the charge. The acquittal or conviction by peers indicates society's contribution to justice and reflects the goal of absolute justice, the undeviating enforcement of correct principles.

Moral correctness and justice extend beyond the courtroom. Concerns for compassionate justice frequently enter into the decision of medical clinicians in carrying out their medical responsibilities. This form of justice recognizes that there is merit on both sides, but the weaker side of the argument is allowed some degree of preference. For example, Dr. Jack Kevorkian has recognized and radically promoted physician-assisted suicide. However, it is unclear whether it is just or morally correct to help a person die, even when he or she requests the assistance. The issue is a moral one. Does the physician's basic rule, "Do No Harm," mean helping or not helping a person die? Kevorkian believes that society should be compassionate and allow people with training in promoting life to assist the competent dying individual in terminating life. He argues for compassion for the dying. This position does not have widespread appeal at the current time. Whether or not this will change is not known.

The concept of justice also has a classic, authoritarian definition. Justice may also be an instrument of social power. Justice may demand the death penalty for some heinous crimes. In these instances, justice becomes the implementation of social power. Under this situation, analysts ask whether the result was just and should be used as a model for future decisions. This approach is exemplified by the critics of governmental rationing of health care. They claim that governmental power would decide how goods and benefits are distributed rather than having the distribution based upon the population's needs.

In conciliatory justice, the decision maker recognizes that there are good points in the presented arguments and adopts a midpoint between the arguments with an outcome that is equally divided according to need. The Bible's King Solomon was put into extraordinarily difficult positions. His decisions were "just" because they were fair and impartial. Their consequences were the best under the circumstances.

In practice, justice does not mean society is always right. All people use or encounter these forms of justice. It is involved in our decisions no matter what role, whether we are negotiators, parents, judges, or physicians. Justice is an evolving concept whose development parallels the development of society. As human beings increase their sensitivity to the ethical administration of society, justice should be enhanced and more correctly applied.

K

KEVORKIAN, JACK   Dr. Jack Kevorkian is recognized for his fight for a person's right to physician-assisted suicide (see **Physician-Assisted Suicide**.) Assisted suicide means enabling a person to take his or her own life; it does not include introducing a lethal substance into another person.

Kevorkian was a licensed physician in Michigan specializing in pathology. His medical license was revoked by the Michigan Board of Medicine after he indirectly assisted people to take their own lives. This involved creating the machines that allowed people to kill themselves by pushing a button, which would begin a sequence of events resulting in the person's death.

Kevorkian did not help everyone who wanted to commit suicide. He only accepted people with a terminal disease who wanted to die before they suffered extensive personal indignities. He counseled them for an extended period of time, and if they decided to go ahead with the procedure, he used his medical training to assist them in committing suicide and made sure the process was as pain-free as possible.

Kevorkian has been arrested and charged with murder a number of times over the past several years. On March 26, 1999, he was convicted of murder for the first time. In this case, Kevorkian deviated from his suicide assistance to actually becoming the death-causing agent. He videotaped his actions and mailed the tape to the CBS television network. The tape was aired nationally and charges of murder followed.

Legislation has been passed in Michigan and other states in an attempt to prevent these assisted-suicide activities from spreading. Oregon, however, passed a Death with Dignity Act, which was approved by a public vote but is being constitutionally challenged in the courts. The law has not inspired a rash of assisted suicides in Oregon, as critics predicted; nor have people moved to the state so they can commit suicide. Assisted suicide has, to this date, been a relatively quiet, "personalized" set of actions.

The influence of Dr. Kevorkian has been extensive, and the assisted-suicide debate he sparked remains volatile. Critics call him "Dr. Death" and claim he is murdering people who cannot think rationally. But his supporters claim he is responding to a need that medical practices currently ignore. He provides support during the most personal time of a person's life and gives the person with a terminal disease control. This area and its collateral topics will be subject to many years of debate.

L

LIFE An attribute of animals and plants characterized by the ability to grow, reproduce, and respond to internal and external conditions.

There are many ways to define life. For humans, life is often thought to exist when the heart is beating and cognitive functioning occurs. However, a definition of human life must also include the performance of natural functions and motions. Life may also be called vitality, reflecting an individual's aggregate of vital phenomena. According to *Dorland's Medical Dictionary*, it is "that obscure principle whereby organized beings are peculiarly endowed with certain powers and functions not associated with inorganic [nonliving] matter."

However, a simple definition of life does not exist. Many argue that we do not truly know when life begins and when it truly ends; we simply know what our instruments record. The growth of science has repeated confirmed this belief. Once we defined birth as the start of life and the ending of a heartbeat as the end of life. But today modern technology allows us to remove a fetus from the womb before birth and help it to develop into a viable individual. We also have the ability to restart the heart. Furthermore, our definition of life has expanded to include more than biological functioning. Thus, brain death is an issue even though the heart may be functioning. Therefore, because we cannot define life clearly, for pragmatic reasons we must use an operational definition of life (a definition that expresses the concept by the actions or behaviors it encompasses).

START OF LIFE

Operationally, life may be said to begin when the fetus is capable of living autonomously outside the womb of the mother, which may or may not require an artificially supportive environment. This operational definition is selected because at this point the fetus is no longer parasitic and biologically dependent upon the mother for life but has autonomy and vitality on its own.

However, many criticize this definition. Scientific evidence indicates that the fetus has a heartbeat and brain activity before it is capable of living outside the womb. Religious arguments also promote the idea that life begins at conception. Both positions have merit and many supporters. Yet, both lack the recognition of individual autonomy as a fundamental requirement, and it is this characteristic that separates humans from other living beings. The principle of autonomy means that each person is in individual control of his or her own body, mind, and person. It is a recognizable, operational attribute that also separates humans from living plants, and it recognizes that science may change this attribute as gains are made in newborn survival.

Judicial opinions tend to follow this approach to defining life. In the landmark case of *Roe v. Wade*, the Supreme Court stated that life begins at "quickening," or when the baby is viable outside the womb if the fetus had to be removed. This example is an application of an operational definition. With this type of formulation, new knowledge and clinical advances can be incorporated into the definition.

END OF LIFE

It is equally difficult to define the end of life. It, too, requires an operational definition. Death is the cessation of humanness. It is not simply the stopping of the heartbeat, although death occurs there, too. The complete loss of humanness by the loss of one's ability to think (or to be human) is a form of death called "living death." Thus, when one is found to be brain dead, the body may still be alive and capable of sustaining itself with artificial support, even though the brain has ceased to function. The Uniform Definition of Death Act recognizes the unique qualities associated with human life along with biological characteristics. (See **Death, Uniform Determination of Death Act**.)

LIFE SUPPORT SYSTEMS   Modern technology used to substitute for or assist normal physiological capabilities. The frequently encountered types of life support are respirators that help people breathe, artificial kidneys (called hemodialyzers) and hemodialysis (hemodialysis: hemo—blood; dialysis: cleaning or removal of waste from blood that the kidneys can no longer remove), blood transfusions, and other life-sustaining technological interventions.

Most commonly, life supportive technology is encountered in emergency departments and surgical suites. It is made available to a person who is hurt or undergoing a potentially hazardous surgical procedure. Many times these supportive technologies are part of the complete procedure to protect the individual should an unexpected condition arise. The use of life support here is a normal procedure, and rarely do major bioethical issues arise.

Issues surrounding life support systems are most commonly found in life-threatening situations associated with impending death. The relatively straightforward situations occur with the competent individual. A legally competent person has the absolute right to direct what happens to her; thus she can decide whether or not to accept the life support mechanisms and inform others of these decisions by advance directives (living wills, durable power of attorney for health care). The legally competent individual also has the right, for whatever reason, to decide not to accept the device. She may decide not to accept life support because it will increase the cost of her care. She may not wish to end her life on a machine. Or she may also not wish to be hooked up to machines or accept an organ donation or blood transfusion for religious reasons. Regardless of her reasons, the health professions are bound to follow these decisions.

The incompetent person or the person incapable of communication, on the other hand, may not be able to make decisions for herself and may not have provided any form of advance directive. Decisions about life support for a person in this situation raise difficult questions. The standard of care is to presume that the person would want all opportunities to continue her life, and life support is provided.

The most difficult issue concerns the decision to withdraw life support, which will result in the person's death. Ideally, the issue will be addressed before the situation arises. Otherwise, the family or guardian may be called upon to authorize the cessation of life support. The withdrawal from life support machinery occurs when the therapeutic benefit has ended, alternatives are not available, and death is imminent. Many families want their loved ones to have every second of life. Others want to allow the person the right to die naturally without the technology. The decision is a very difficult one.

LIVE DONORS   Living persons who donate organs or parts of organs from their own bodies. The most common organ donations from live donors are blood, blood components (plasma, platelets), and bone marrow. Blood transfusions and blood components are very important and donors are invaluable. Bone marrow is donated for people suffering from leukemia, and the need for these donors is increasing.

The donation of complete organs by living donors is rare, since there is only one of each organ in the body, with the exception of the kidneys.

Humans are usually born with two kidneys. Medical studies have consistently indicated that an individual can live with only one kidney. Donations are therefore possible, although they are uncommon. Recently, a brother donated a kidney to his younger sister. The risk was that he would need a transplant should his kidney fail, as his sister's kidneys had done. He acknowledged the health threat but wanted to donate anyway. Otherwise, his sister would die unless another donor could be found. The donation occurred, and both brother and sister are alive and apparently healthy.

Another type of donation, still experimental, is the donation of a part of a liver from a living donor, first achieved in humans in 1996. The whole organ is not transplanted, since a person cannot live without a liver. Part of the donor's liver is implanted into the recipient (usually the donor's child). Experiments have shown that the liver grows into the recipient's body and assumes the classic liver functions. It is too early to determine whether this "partial" organ transplant is a viable option. If the partial transplant is successful, many new opportunities will arise for live donors to make new contributions.

LIVING WILL   A living will is a legal document made in advance of a situation where the person is incompetent to make health care decisions. It results from the fact that the refusal of medical treatment is a personal right of autonomy and a right guaranteed to U.S. citizens by the federal Constitution. It contains directives for the patient's care in the event of catastrophic circumstances. The variety of possible catastrophic circumstances makes this type of document difficult to draft. The classic situation for which it is intended would occur after an accident, when the victim is being kept alive only by machines. Under this circumstance, the document makes the patient's wishes clear and takes the burden of responsibility off of the family.

Ohio follows the Modified Uniform Rights of the Terminally Ill Act, which identifies the conditions required for implementation of the directives encountered in the living will. The person must be terminally ill and/or in a permanently unconscious state. In other words, the person must be in a dying condition that is irreversible, incurable, and untreatable. Death is relatively imminent. The person is also permanently unconscious; that is, psychically unaware of the condition and unable to experience pain or suffering. (The patient may be in either or both clinical conditions.) The physicians must ensure that the patient meets these guidelines before complying with the document.

Under the best circumstances, an individual creates this document after careful thought, before any medical condition exists. It may be a standard form (as it is in many states). If so, because of the comprehensive nature of the form, the individual needs to give careful attention to the writing, including consulting an attorney if there are questions. Once the document is completed, the person should make sure that his or her signature is witnessed by at least two people or notarized. In most states, having the signature notarized is preferred, and most attorneys' offices have notaries, as do most banks. The completed document is then added to the person's medical charts to guide the health providers, should a catastrophe occur. Many states require that a patient complete the living will document upon admission to the hospital, regardless of the reason for the admission.

Access for health care providers to the document is extremely important. If the hospital admission follows an accident, the family must provide a copy of the living will to the hospital for its records. (The original should be maintained by the attorney or by the family in their safety deposit box.) The patient's personal physician should also have a copy, but in a sudden emergency situations, another doctor may be treating the patient. For that reason, depositing the document with an attorney is recommended. Since attorneys maintain many special documents to which access is necessary, they are prepared for such access emergencies.

The living will is often used in combination with the durable power of attorney for health care. Both documents and their respective uses are important to investigate. (See **Advance Directives; Appendix** for a sample living will.)

M

MALPRACTICE, MEDICAL Medical acts of professional misconduct, improper discharge of professional duties, or failure to meet professional standards of care, resulting in harm to another. The acts may be unskillful or qualitatively poorer than minimally accepted standard practice. The professional misconduct may be that of a physician, nurse, pharmacist, or other health care practitioner. Medical malpractice does not occur frequently. Yet physicians are acutely aware that they are considered to have "deep pockets," which means that they have the money (or insurance) to pay damages should malpractice occur. They work closely with their insurance underwriters to make sure they don't commit malpractice (called defensive medicine). The amount of money that is paid in medical insurance premiums depends upon the type of physician practice or specialty. Obstetrics, for example, has one of the highest malpractice premiums (around $130,000 per year). Why? If an infant is harmed through the obstetrician's malpractice, the damage may influence the quality of life (for both the parents and the child) for many years to come. With U.S. citizens having an average life expectancy of more than 70 years, the infant could be damaged for an entire 70-year lifespan. Therefore, the compensation must be enough to cover a full lifetime.

Defensive medicine is problematic. It makes physicians reluctant to attempt some of the more risky, yet potentially effective procedures. This conservative approach may result in a worsening of the patient's condition or even death, but the physician is less likely to be sued for malpractice. Defensive medicine is sometimes considered responsible for contributing to rising health care costs, as physicians may order tests and procedures primarily to reduce their risk of malpractice lawsuits.

In the United States physicians and most licensed or registered health practitioners are held to a national standard of care. In other words, a practitioner in one location will be as competent as a peer in another location. This high level of practice and "standard" is considered to be the minimum acceptable. The availability of national educational opportunities and continuing professional education has allowed the professions to

137

be held to this standard. When a practitioner breaches that standard without acceptable reasons, malpractice is considered to have occurred.

A classic case of medical malpractice occurred when x-rays showed a patient's stomach pain was due to the presence of a surgical tool in her stomach. The patient had had surgery approximately six months prior to her stomach pain. A pair of hemostats (a tool used to stop bleeding) was left inside of the patient.

Most cases of medical malpractice are not so clear. Malpractice does not occur, for example, when a physician attempts a procedure that is normally beneficial but in a particular instance does not have the expected results. The family is upset, the patient is upset, and the physician is upset. But because each patient is unique and may not react the same way as the majority, in this case the physician would not be held to be at fault.

Medical malpractice is also not typically considered to occur when the practitioner is attempting to provide emergency care. Under the Good Samaritan Acts found in all fifty states, providers may attempt therapeutic care for a person within the limits of their professional expertise in emergencies. Because emergencies frequently occur in a location other than a health setting, lawmakers have recognized that the same strict hospital (or other health organization) standards cannot be applied "in the field." As long as the acts of the provider are within the expected capability and the limitations of the location, they will not result in malpractice.

ASSAULT AND BATTERY

This form of medical malpractice typically occurs when the physician makes inappropriate contact with a patient. A basic example may be found in surgery. The physician has the patient sign a statement of informed consent indicating the extent of the surgical procedure. The surgeon, during the intended procedure, identifies a non-life-threatening condition that is outside the scope of the intended surgery. The surgeon, with all good intentions, corrects the condition during the surgery. This act by the surgeon is battery. The physician had not been authorized to correct the non-life-threatening problem by the patient, and the act is, therefore, inappropriate touching by the doctor. To avoid the battery, the physician should complete the intended surgery and then discuss the new situation with the patient. Once the surgeon has the patient's permission, the condition can be corrected without concern for battery.

Had the condition been life threatening, then the physician could have corrected the situation and been protected by the Good Samaritan Act. Unconsented and nonemergency procedures are batteries, even though the intentions of the physician/surgeon are honorable.

NEGLIGENCE

In cases of negligence (also known as medical negligence), the physician has violated a duty to act or not to act toward a patient, directly causing a compensable injury. This claim is perhaps the most commonly claimed cause of medical malpractice. The complainant (the plaintiff) argues that the provider violated (breached) their responsibility (duty) to the patient, thereby causing an injury. This definition allows legal analysis to encompass the entire medical procedure if there is an unexpected clinical outcome. The defense by the physician is that the practices used are within the guidelines of acceptable national practices (the national standard of care). It is when they are not within this standard that negligence may be ascertained.

MANAGED CARE
A generic (nonspecific) term that has recently evolved and encompasses a variety of forms of prepaid and managed fee-for-service health care. It is characterized by the structuring of the delivery of health care around the principles associated with effective administration.

Under managed care programs, the fundamental incentive structure of traditional fee-for-service medicine is dramatically altered to encourage greater control over the uses and costs of health services.

Managed care can be defined as the process of structuring or restructuring the health care system in terms of financing, purchasing, delivering, measuring, and documenting a broad range of health care services and products. The best description of managed care is an operational one. Managed care restructures the delivery system by providing appropriate incentives and barriers for providers and consumers to contain costs; imposing an administrative structure with components related to managing the enrolled population and its use of services; and facilitating the paperwork required on the part of consumers.

Managed care proponents indicate that their organizations have the goal of offering health services at lower costs and curbing unnecessary medical procedures. These companies usually operate under the auspices of an insurance company. Policies are instituted requiring medical procedures (except emergency care) to be approved in advance by the insurance company. A second opinion is required for identified medical procedures, and a utilization review to determine how long patients can stay in the hospital is mandated.

CAPITATION AS A METHOD OF PROVIDER REIMBURSEMENT

Managed care organizations use a prospective form of reimbursement to their providers entitled capitation payment. Capitation payment through managed care programs is presented as an alternative to diagnosis-related groups (DRGs) and other forms of cost-containing reimbursement approaches. These capitation systems are simple in concept. The contract developers prospectively determine the probable amount of services/money that their consumers (called enrollees) will use given the types of services offered. The company then negotiates with the clinical providers (hospitals and physicians) for the provision of services on a lump-sum-payment basis. In a hospital, for example, once negotiations are completed, a large percentage of the reimbursement is provided to the hospital to do with as it will. The only requirement is that the hospital must provide to the health maintenance organization (HMO) members as many of the covered services as are necessary. A portion of the money, called a withhold, is set aside for patients who have serious illnesses for which the routine reimbursement would be inadequate.

This advance payment is believed to encourage the use of preventive services. Organizations would prefer to see managed care enrollees for regular checkups to enable the provider to identify and correct any health problems. Early diagnosis and treatment is more beneficial for the patient, and it is less expensive. According to proponents of this system, greater numbers of basic services are rendered, healthier habits are taught, and overall costs are lower.

If the managed care enrollees do not use the contracted services, the funds are the organization's profit. Another possible "profit" results from the withhold. If the services are rendered efficiently and the patients do not need it, many contracts allow for the withhold to be distributed to the health care providers as a form of "economic bonus" for provided financially solid health care.

CAPITATION PAYMENT (TECHNICAL BASIS)

In prepayment or capitation, the person served, rather than the medical act, is the unit of remuneration. The capitation payment takes care of reimbursement for a contractually stipulated length of time. It is prepayment for services on a per-member per-month basis (PMPM). The physician, called a primary care provider (PCP) or a gatekeeper, is paid the same amount of money every stipulated period for a member of a capitated plan regardless of whether that member receives services or not and regardless of how expensive those services are (the services that must be provided will be identified by contract).

These capitation payments may vary according to the characteristics of the member, as age and gender influence the frequency and quantity of the services rendered. Other factors may be considered, for example, experience with the member population indicating a high-risk group, such as smokers working in an asbestos factory, who are known to be at exceptionally high risk of serious lung disorders.

Reimbursement for physicians often involves the development of withholds (discussed above) and risk/bonus arrangements. The withhold may be increased in the event of unusual cost excesses beyond what the withhold currently deals with. The risk/bonus arrangement occurs as risk is shared with all physicians in the plan. Residual funds from the withhold are divided among the physicians; thus the amount of the bonus is the result of effective diagnoses (early diagnoses), preventive care, and administrative efficiency (which together result in lower use of the withhold amounts). When physicians are administratively and clinically efficient, they receive a greater bonus at the end of the year (or at the contractually specified time).

The advantages to prepayment and the associated bonuses are that the system is administratively simple; it facilitates advance global budgeting; and it gives physicians an incentive to control the cost of medical treatments. The bonus arrangement, however, is also the subject of great social criticism. Some critics believe that having hospitals and physicians working for financial incentives is contrary to the social good. If the bonus promotes a reduction in health care tests, physicians may misdiagnose the disorder and cause the patient to receive inadequate or inappropriate care. Another criticism is that physicians who do spend more money on tests will be financially penalized because their increased costs cut into the financial bonus. The fear is that if a physician cuts into the bonus, that physician will be dismissed from the managed care contract, being perceived as, for example, an inadequate diagnostician. This topic is being heatedly discussed at the time of this writing.

MANAGED COMPETITION
Created by a think tank of health care policy makers at Jackson Hole (called the Jackson Hole Group), managed competition is simply an extension of managed care. It uses consumers, health plans, and sponsors to promote cost-conscious consumer choice for a universal coverage. Managed care organizations and networks play a central role in this model. The foundation of the managed care model is accountable health partnerships that integrate financing and delivery of health care, in addition to the health care networks of HMOs. Such plans, integrating physicians, hospitals, and insurers, would compete for patients, and patients would have the right to take their health care coverage with them should they transfer employment. The plans would also have consumer choice, tax-free employer contributions, vouchers for the needy to be used as their insurance premium, and other devices to make consumers cost sensitive. This plan would also have public sponsors such as a state agency to guarantee health coverage and to act as collective purchasing agents for smaller employment groups. Such plans would be paid on a capitated

basis and would extend the managed care model into all areas of the country.

See also **Cost Containment**

MATERNAL RIGHTS   Questions of maternal rights surround a woman's ability to procreate, particularly her decisions concerning conception or contraception.

The rights of a mother and the extent of these rights has been the subject of recent debate, particularly concerning abortion. In all states, the woman's decision to undertake an abortion is respected (*Planned Parenthood of SE Pa v. Casey,* 112 S. Ct. 2791 [1992]) and the role of the father in decision making is minimized. The courts have recognized the underlying principles of the right of autonomy and the right of privacy. The right to accept or reject medical treatment to one's own person has also been recognized as a fundamental right. These rights are further supported by the Court's opinion expressed in dicta (a dictum refers to the discussion the Court uses to make its decision; it is not the holding, which is the rule that future courts will follow under stare decisis) that the male partner should not have the power to dictate what happens to the female medically. The balance of rights is aligned with the pregnant woman under these circumstances.

BRAIN DEATH

An unusual situation regarding maternal rights has arisen due to advancing medical technology. In Europe and the United States, medical technology is now capable of sustaining a person's body, even after brain death. This achievement has proven controversial in certain bioethical situations concerning pregnant women. In several situations, a pregnant woman has been declared brain dead yet the fetus is alive and, with support, apparently capable of progressing through the pregnancy. Despite the declaration of death, several women's physiological activity has been continued by means of life support machines and physical movement accomplished by clinicians in order to give the unborn the opportunity to survive. The fetus is provided an environment in which to grow and is only taken from the womb when physicians believe it can survive outside the womb with assistance. The fetus is removed by cesarean section and placed into a neonatal intensive care unit. The baby is often supported by an artificial womb until capable of surviving with regular newborn support.

One woman in Germany suffered a head injury in an automobile accident and was declared brain dead. She was thirteen weeks pregnant. Another woman in Rochester, New York, was four months pregnant when she suffered a cerebral hemorrhage (serious bleeding from vessels in the brain within the skull) and was determined brain dead. Both women were placed upon special life support that was enriched to sustain the body and promote fetal development. Both babies were successfully delivered by cesarean section at the earliest time possible and have survived with no ill effects identified.

Some of the issues that arise, however, include the possibility of problems with fetal development. When the mother is brain dead and placed on machine support, the body deteriorates. Fetal damage is possible in terms of both mental and physical development. Perhaps more importantly, psychologically the child will be without a mother and will be the "product of a dead person." Where does a "right to life fit?" Are the possibilities of maldevelopment overwhelming? In both of these situations, the mothers died within the legal period for abortion. The fetus could not survive in any other way. The issue is one of great debate.

JUDICIAL ORDERS NOT TO CONCEIVE

What is the maternal right to have a child? Are there circumstances when it is in the best interests of the child not to be born? This issue has become increasing controversial, because one judge has recently ordered a drug-abusing woman not to conceive children after she had had several children born addicted to drugs and with sexually transmitted diseases.

This woman had multiple children as a result of her prostitution, which was forced upon her by a drug habit. She had had several children born addicted to crack cocaine and other drugs, and had been diagnosed with a variety of sexually transmitted diseases. She had been arrested and ordered into drug treatment on multiple occasions. Her children were placed into foster care. Despite the health care (or jail sentence), she always returned to her former way of life and continued to have children. The state children's protective services remained active, and the children were regularly taken from the mother and placed in foster care. Finally, after having exhausted the traditional punishments and means of assistance, the judge ordered her not to conceive. He indicated that this woman's activities were a form of child abuse. To prevent the abuse in the future, she was ordered to have a contraceptive implanted or to undergo a tubal ligation (sterilization). The judge acknowledged in his sentence his frustration about his failure to make her change. He justified his decision by noting that his intention was in the best interests of her unborn children.

Whether or not this judge's sentence will stand is uncertain at this time. It is currently in the appeal process and being reviewed. Bioethically, the situation is a difficult one. The woman has the right to have children. Since this right is fundamental, overcoming it requires a compelling state interest. Is the best interest of the child a compelling state interest in these circumstances? The children also have a right to be born free of drugs and sexually transmitted diseases. They have a right to be raised by their biological mother rather than multiple foster parents. On the other hand, allowing this type of dysfunctional mother to bring children into the world creates a wealth of problems.

Social support for the judge has been tremendous. At the same time, an uproar has arisen over judicial activism—judges going where the law has not really gone before. Is the judge working within his legal guidelines in this case, or has be gone beyond them? A similar issue has also arisen in cases where a judge has ordered men to undergo a vasectomy as part of a sentencing plan. The final question is whether the judge has identified a compelling state interest that justifies such exceptional state actions.

MATURE MINOR DOCTRINE   This doctrine, which is not found in all states, is a set of practices that allows a person under the age of 18 (a minor) to consent to certain medical treatments. In all states, the parent or guardian is the person who will give consent to medical procedures and treatment. However, under certain conditions parental consent is not required. A minor may be allowed to consent to treatment for sexually transmitted diseases, sexual abuse, drug treatment (including alcohol), and AIDS testing. With some tests, there may be an age requirement. For example, in Ohio the age is 14 to give consent for mental health treatment and 17 to give blood.

Under this doctrine, physicians are not liable for unconsented touching (battery) when the minor has given permission for the therapeutic act under these limited circumstances. They are liable only if they exceed these boundaries. There is also a substantial public policy justification for each of these selected exceptions to the parental consent rule. Many minors who might have contracted a sexually related disease would be hesitant to request permission for treatment from their parents. In the case of sexual abuse, the parent may be suspect. The permission from the abused to be examined is important, since an abusive parent may try to cover the abuse and prevent it from being discovered. For the protection of the individual and the protection of society, the mature minor doctrine is set into practice.

MEDICAID/TITLE XIX   Medicaid is medical welfare. It was enacted into law on July 30, 1965, as Title XIX of the Social Security Act. The model for the Medicaid Act was the Kerr-Mills Act of 1960—Medical Assistance for the Aged. Under federal guidelines, states set income and asset levels for case assistance and medical eligibility. Problematically, Medicaid is the fastest growing component of aggregate state spending. In 1990, Medicaid spent 71.3 billion of federal and state funds for personal health care.

Two important considerations for reviewing Medicaid programs are: states participate in the Medicaid program at their option, and the state, not the federal government, administers Medicaid programs. However, the state is required to work within broad federal requirements and guidelines, so the program is a cooperative state-federal program to provide medical assistance to the poor. Federal requirements allow states considerable discretion in determining not only eligibility but covered benefits and provider payment mechanisms as well. (These are the programs that Oregon and Hawaii have modified to make attempts at rationing [Oregon] or universal coverage [Hawaii]). States with approved programs are entitled to federal matching funds for their expenditures.

In its most fundamental form, Medicaid is limited to specific groups of low-income individuals and families called the categorically needy. It was designed to cover those groups who are eligible to receive cash payments under one of the two existing welfare programs established under Social Security—Aid to Families with Dependent Children (AFDC) and Supplemental Security Income (SSI)—as well as certain low-income pregnant woman and children not receiving welfare payments. Receipt of a welfare payments under one of these programs usually means automatic eligibility for Medicaid. AFDC families are the largest group of recipients (about 70 percent). Due largely to nursing home services, 34 percent of total Medicare outlay was attributable to the elderly.

States have the option of providing Medicaid to other categorically needy groups as well. This option includes increasing the income levels for eligibility to the aged, blind, or disabled. It also includes the medically needy, those persons who, due to medical bills, spend their income and wealth down to the medically needy standard.

MEDICAID BENEFITS

Title XIX of the Social Security Act mandates that every state Medicaid program provide specific basic health services:

- hospital inpatient care
- hospital outpatient services
- prenatal care
- laboratory and x-ray services
- skilled nursing facility (SNF) services for those 21 and over
- some health services for those eligible for SNF services
- physician's services

- family planning services and supplies (excluding abortion)
- rural health clinic services
- early and periodic screening, diagnosis, and treatment for children under 21
- nurse-midwife services
- certain other federally qualified ambulatory and health center services

Within these service areas, the states may determine the scope of the service offered. They may limit, for example, the days of hospital care or number of physician visits covered. The state also has the option to provide additional services or offer optional services. Some that have been considered are:

- clinic services
- intermediate care facility services for the aged, blind, disabled, and mentally handicapped
- optometrist services and eyeglasses
- prescribed drugs
- prosthetic devices
- dental care

MEDICAID IN LONG-TERM CARE FACILITIES

In long-term care (LTC) facilities, individuals are required to use their own excess income (that in excess of their personal needs and maintenance needs of their spouses) to help pay for their care. In other words, they are required to use their own resources for health care before Medicaid will be used. Since this rule can impoverish the spouse, several states have instituted protections for the spouse of the one needing Medicaid. The couple can effectively separate their assets so that the spending down to qualify for Medicaid assistance is not devastating for both parties.

There are several forms of payment under Medicaid. Some states use a daily rate, called a per diem. This rate varies, depending on the level of care required by the resident—personal, intermediate, or skilled care, with skilled care demanding the highest level of service. More registered nurses and skilled clinicians are required in a skilled care environment areas than in personal or intermediate care.

Other states use prospective payment. Here, the amount to be received is known in advance. The reimbursement is based on the amount of services required rather than on diagnoses. Similar in principle to Medicare's diagnosis-related groups, the long-term care facility can project the amount of its expected income by knowing what resources its residents require. The prospective payment reimburses the nursing facility on the basis of the amount of resources required to optimize a patient's care. A registered nurse is responsible for evaluating the clinical status of each resident, and residents are then categorized according to their individual needs. These needs are incorporated into a therapeutic treatment plan, and the resident receives funding based upon the amount of resources needed. Some of the tools to be considered would be the Minimum Data Set+ (MDS+)© or the Resource Utilization Groups III (RUGS III) ©. These tools evaluate the unique therapeutic needs of the patient/resident. They identify the resources that are required by that person; then the costs associated with those needs can be determined. Reimbursement can follow based upon that resource use. Managed care techniques are also being tested for incorporation into the Medicaid cost containment effort.

Because of the large federal and state expenditures, other approaches are also used in Medicaid long-term care. Governments are currently highly flexible as they search for ways to reduce the costs of care across the country.

MEDICAL SAVINGS ACCOUNTS   A new approach to cost containment that shifts the responsibility for initial health care to the individual. It has been used by a few industries, notably Forbes, Inc., publishers of *Forbes Magazine* and others, and is now being considered for Medicare. As of October 1, 1996, the Ohio state legislature had passed a law to allow medical savings accounts.

In this system, as promoted by 1996 presidential candidate Steven Forbes, the employer provides the employee with an initial outlay of money (so far the discussions have considered $1,000 to $1,500 per person). The employee spends money from this account for her personal health care. Once she has expended this initial outlay, she is then responsible for spending the same amount from her own pocket. Then, after these expenditures, a standardized medical catastrophic insurance program comes into action. If the employee does not spend the allocation, she gets to keep what was not spent as an inducement to spend wisely; alternatively, the money is rolled over into the program for the next year. Each year an additional sum is added by the employer so that the amount in the account increases—hence the name medical savings account. What was spent would be deductible from annual income tax.

A second approach has been legislated in Ohio. A medical savings account is an individual consumer's savings account containing funds for eligible health care expenses. It would be available in either a single or family amount. Funds would be deposited by the account holder (the consumer) into an MSA throughout the year. During that year, the funds could be withdrawn only for health care expenses. Any interest generated by the MSA would be the property of the MSA account holder. After that first year, the individual can withdraw the previous year's funds (and other accumulation except for the current year's allocation) for any purpose. However, if the funds are withdrawn for a purpose other than health care, an Ohio income tax liability would be incurred. The amount withdrawn for purchases other than health care is added to the account holder's federal adjusted gross income and would then be considered taxable income. In other words, the account holder is discouraged from withdrawing these funds for purposes other that for health expenses.

In the Ohio plan, the money for the MSA comes from either the individual or a sponsoring employer. The deposited amount is deducted from the individual's Ohio tax liability, a pretax deduction. To be eligible to establish a medical savings account, the individual must be a participant in a qualifying health insurance plan, a health maintenance organization (HMO), a self-funded employer-sponsored health benefit plan, or other eligible party. The account holder pays health care deductibles from the funds in the MSA account. After the insurance deductible is paid, the health care plan from the insurance company or HMO would cover the remaining eligible medical expenses. The amount deposited is limited to a maximum of $3,000 per tax year with future adjustments to reflect increases in inflation. The plan encourages the individual to reserve the interest generated for health care services by allowing her to claim it as a deduction from Ohio income tax liability to the extent that the earnings had been reported as federal gross income.

Advocates of this approach claim that giving people control of those initial funds effectively gives them greater control over their treatment. They are not as willing to spend the funds frivolously. Critics argue that people will avoid preventive and necessary health care so that they can have the funds for personal spending in the next year. Also, it would be particularly beneficial to the healthy, leaving too many sick people needing expensive care in a smaller and less economically solvent regular insurance pool (the current Medicare-type arrangement).

MEDICARE   Social health insurance for the elderly and other restrictively eligible groups. The Social Security Amendments of 1965 (Public Law 89–97) established Title XVIII (18) of the Social Security Act authorizing Medicare and the payment of costs for health services to eligible beneficiaries. Medicare is the principal social health insurance program in the United States, providing a variety of hospital, physician, and other medical services for three groups of people: (1) persons 65 and over, (2) disabled individuals entitled to Social Security benefits or Railroad Retirement benefits, and (3) end-stage renal disease victims, who qualify immediately, regardless of age, if they have worked enough time to qualify as fully insured under Social Security. Younger individuals who are receiving Social Security payments because of a disability qualify for Medicare after a two-year waiting period.

Medicare began operating on July 1, 1966. Recently it has become a political point of focus because observers have predicted that it will be bankrupt by the year 2001. Beginning in 1997, new strategies are being created to prevent bankruptcy from occurring, including premiums based upon beneficiary income.

Medicare is statutory law and can be found in the Code of Federal Regulations at 42 Code of Federal Regulations (C.F.R.) or 42 United States Code (U.S.C.). The Social Security Administration is charged with administering determinations of eligibility for Medicare. The Health Care Financing Administration (HCFA), the agency charged with controlling the costs of medical care, administers the Medicare program. It employs several different kinds of cost containment strategies, currently a prospective payment system and fee for service based upon usual and customary charges.

Medicare initially followed the designs of the 1965 Blue Cross–Blue Shield plans with the development of Medicare A and Medicare B. Medicare A deals with inpatient care and outpatient services equal to those needed by inpatients. Medicare B deals with physician services and outpatient care. Medicare contracts with private health insurance companies, called carriers (under Part B) or intermediaries (under Part A), to process Medicare claims. Hospitals and other agencies desiring to become health care providers under Medicare must comply with the conditions of participation (COP) in order to receive Medicare payments. These conditions are federal requirements intended to insure the quality of the medical services provided. The provider must satisfy the COP and execute a provider participation agreement with HCFA. Survey and certification teams inspect providers and determine whether they comply. Accreditation from the Joint Commission on Accreditation of Healthcare Organizations (JCAHO) can substitute for this survey process. Both of these survey groups evaluate the governing body, quality assurance programs, medical staff, nursing services, medical records services, pharmaceutical services, radiology services, laboratory services, food and dietary services, utilization review, physical environment, and infection control (42 C.F.R. Part 42).

Hospitals are required to sign provider agreements to participate in Medicare. The statute lists rules governing hospital practices included in the provider agreement. If the hospital accepts and qualifies for Medicare payments, it has an assignment. An assignment refers to an agreement by the hospital or physician to accept Medicare payment as payment in full, i.e., without billing the patient for the balance. Assignment is mandatory with respect to all Part A services, including inpatient hospital services. Assignment is also mandatory for laboratory and ambulatory surgery center services under Part B.

Physicians are automatically eligible to render services if they agree to participate, but they do not have to accept Medicare patients. When physicians do accept assignment, they are referred to as participating physicians or suppliers. Participating physicians are listed in a directory published annually by the Medicare program and are eligible for certain claims processing advantages (they get paid more quickly). Nonparticipating physicians and suppliers are paid 5 percent less than participating physicians.

MEDICARE COVERAGE

Medicare coverage under usual and customary reimbursement approaches is provided under two programs: Part A (Hospital Insurance) and Part B (Supplementary medical insurance). Part A covers inpatient hospital and skilled nursing facility care (100 days per year), home health care, and hospice care. Beneficiaries are given Medicare cards and are assigned claim numbers. Part A is funded by payroll taxes paid by employers, employees, and the self-employed. The tax revenue is credited to a trust fund that ordinarily invests its funds in a special interest-bearing debt obligation issued by the Treasury.

Part B covers physician services, ambulatory surgical services, outpatient services, and certain other miscellaneous services. Part B is a voluntary program funded primarily by general Treasury revenues and borrowing, and to some extent by premiums paid by the insured. All individuals eligible for Part A coverage may elect to enroll in Part B and are automatically enrolled in Part B when they become eligible for Part A unless they opt out. Persons age 65 or older can enroll in Part B regardless of their eligibility for Part A. For beneficiaries eligible for Medicaid, state Medicaid agencies often buy in to Part B by paying the Part B premiums (which saves the states money by transferring costs from Medicaid).

According to the HCFA Provider Reimbursement Manual, cost-based reimbursement follows these rules regarding the costs that Medicare will pay, called allowable costs. To be considered an allowable cost, (1) the cost must be related to patient care; (2) the financial loss is allowed only if the provider has acted as a prudent manager; (3) the cost cannot be substantially out of line with other institutions in the same area similar in size, scope of services, utilization, and other relevant factors; and (4) costs must reflect the provider's action as a prudent provider or buyer of clinical services. In other words, all claims must be supported by adequate cost data that will withstand an audit.

The manual defines reasonable costs as the costs actually incurred minus any portion found to be unnecessary in the efficient delivery of needed health services. In addition, costs attributable to the Medicare program are not to be borne by non-Medicare patients and vice versa (no cost shifting is allowed). Furthermore, in determining its allowable costs, a provider must exclude costs related to the provision of services that are not covered by Medicare. Medicare does not cover luxury or personal comfort items such as telephones, TV, and radios solely furnished for patient comfort.

To ensure that excessive costs were not claimed by the hospital, Congress passed PL 92–603 in 1972, which placed limits on the reasonable inpatient cost of providing routine hospital services. These rules are commonly known as section 223 limits, named for the section of the law in which the limits are found. This law also created per diem limits and labor and non-labor components.

MEDICARE A—INPATIENT INSURANCE   Medicare Part A—Hospital Insurance is social health insurance. It uses an indirect pattern of finance and delivery wherein the Health Care Financing Administration (HCFA) contracts with independent insurance providers. HCFA sees to it that the provider is paid, but the actual health care providers are neither owned nor hired by the government. Ninety-five percent of the aged population in the United States is enrolled in Medicare Part A.

Beneficiary Payments: The beneficiary is responsible for a portion of the payment for inpatient hospital services for each eligible benefit period. This deductible equals the nationally determined average cost of one day of hospital care. Coinsurance is applicable after the 61st day of hospitalization (called an extended stay). The beneficiary (or co-insurer) is responsible for $190 (1997) per day for the 61st through the 90th day (the benefit decreases by 25 percent). For stays between the 91st and 150th day (1997), the patient is responsible for $380 a day (the benefit decreases another 25 percent).

The patient participates in cost sharing. He is required to pay an inpatient hospital deductible in each benefit period that approximates the cost of one day of hospital care ($652 in 1992, $696 in 1995, $760 in 1997). (A benefit period is a spell of illness beginning with hospitalization and ending when a beneficiary has not been an inpatient in a hospital or skilled nursing facility for 60 continuous days. There is no limit to the number of benefit periods a beneficiary can use.)

For care in a skilled nursing facility, Medicare will pay all covered expenses for the first 20 days. For the 21st through 100th day, the beneficiary or coinsurance is responsible for $95 per day (1997). The beneficiary is responsible for his or her own care beyond the 150th day, although this situation is rare—the average hospital stay for a Medicare patient is 8.8 days.

The beneficiary is also responsible for blood transfusion deductibles, equal to the cost of the first three pints of blood received. If the beneficiary arranges for the three pints to be replaced, the beneficiary is not charged.

Coinsurance: A form of private insurance that pays those costs not covered by the beneficiary's primary insurance payer. Nearly 70 percent of Medicare enrollees have private Medigap policies that cover some or all of the deductibles and coinsurance listed under Medicare. These policies are also increasing in price. In 1996, they were expected to increase an average of 30 percent, according to the American Association of Retired Persons. Average premiums for Prudential Medicare supplement insurance policies range from $51 to $151.75 a month. (The increase is attributed to increased use of outpatient services, since Medicare beneficiaries pay approximately 20 percent of outpatient services, which is part of the deductibles/coinsurance indicated.) The increases began in the second half of 1994.

PART A BENEFITS

Part A provides four basic benefits for the covered population: (1) Ninety days of inpatient hospital care in a benefit period; (2) a lifetime reserve of 60 days of inpatient care, once the 90 days are exhausted; (3) one hundred days of post-hospitalization care in a skilled nursing facility; (4) home health agency visits.

Hospital Inpatient Benefits: Hospital room and board (including private accommodations if medically necessary); nursing and related services (excluding private duty); use of hospital facilities; medical social services; ancillary services (radiology, laboratory, surgery, etc.); drugs, biologicals, supplies, appliances, and equipment; other diagnostic or therapeutic items or services; medical services provided by an intern or resident in training.

Skilled Nursing Facility (SNF) Benefits: First, the nursing facility must provide skilled levels of care and be certified to participate in the Medicare program; it cannot simply agree to admit people needing this level of care. The nursing facility is required to comply with requirements dealing with resident rights; admission, transfer and discharge rights; quality of care; nursing service; dietary service; physician services; dental services; pharmacy services; and infection control. In addition, the nursing facility must be licensed in the state in which it operates. If the conditions of participation (COP) are met, the facility may participate in

Medicare if it submits an executed participation agreement to the Department of Health and Human Services and is accepted by the secretary. The provider must also be found to be in compliance with Title VI of the Civil Rights Act of 1964.

Up to 100 SNF days are covered per year: 1–20 days at no cost; in 1997, days 21–100 require $95 per day copayment (up from $89.50 per day in 1995), and requires 3-day prior hospitalization during the prior 30 days. If 31 days since the hospitalization, the hospitalization does not count.

A patient may move between levels of care within the nursing facility if the person has a new spell of illness. If this condition requires hospitalization (again, 3 days), the person can move from the intermediate or personal levels of care back to the skilled treatment area. If the person is moved to an intermediate level of care and then gets sicker but is not hospitalized, Medicare will not pay except for the remaining days from the initial 100 days.

Benefits include SNF room and board (semiprivate accommodations usually, private only if medically necessary); nursing (excluding private duty); physical, occupational, or speech therapy; medical social services; drugs, biologicals, supplies, appliances, and equipment; medical services provided by interns or residents from hospital with agreement from SNF; diagnostic or therapeutic services provided by hospital with agreement with SNF; other services required for patient care.

In addition to skilled care, the nursing facility may provide other levels of care: intermediate and personal care. These levels of care are not eligible for Medicare reimbursement because they are not considered medical care.

Nursing Facility Reimbursement: The Medicare program reimburses nursing facilities for routine service costs on a reasonable cost basis, subject to cost limits.

Home Health Agency Benefits: Home health services are provided in a patient's home or on a visiting basis by a participating home health agency. The beneficiary must be confined to home, in need of skill nursing care on an intermittent basis, or in need of physical therapy, speech therapy, or occupational therapy. There is however an overall limit: 62 days in the benefit period. The patient may receive a normal maximum of 28 hours per week unless special documentation is presented. If it is accepted, the patient may receive a maximum of 35 hours per week. The beneficiary does not pay a deductible or coinsurance (HCFA encourages people to use this service, since it is less costly).

Covered Services in Home Health: Part-time or intermittent nursing care provided by or under the supervision of a registered nurse; physical, speech, or occupational therapy; medical social work; medical supplies other than drugs and biologicals, and durable medical equipment; medical services by interns and residents in training under an approved teaching program of a hospital affiliated with home health agency.

Hospice Care: The hospice must enter into a provider agreement with HCFA to receive payment from Medicare. Hospice care is an elective benefit. Enrollees can elect the hospice benefit for two 90-day periods and one 30-day period, with one subsequent extension period during the individual's lifetime. If hospice care is elected, the beneficiary gives up the right to receive most other Medicare benefits. The election is revocable, however.

Hospice Benefits: Nursing care provided by or under the supervision of RN; medical social services; physician services; short-term inpatient care; medical appliances and supplies, drugs, and biologicals; home health agency (HHA) services; and physical, occupational, and speech therapy.

The beneficiary is responsible for coinsurance payments for drugs furnished while not an inpatient and for respite care (short-term care giving the primary care giver some time away from the patient).

The Medicare program reimburses hospices for covered hospice services based on a cost-related prospective payment method subject to a cap amount per beneficiary. There are four basic payment categories used for reimbursing hospices: routine home care day, continuous home care day, inpatient respite care day, and general inpatient care day. These rates are adjusted to account for wage variation geographically. The 1993 cap was $12,248.

MEDICARE B—PHYSICIAN AND OUTPATIENT SERVICES

Ninety-seven percent of Medicare Part A beneficiaries are enrolled in Part B. It provides payments for physicians, physician-ordered supplies and services, outpatient hospital services, rural health clinic visits, and home health visits for people without Part A (Part A also covers home health visits). Part B is supplementary medical insurance and is neither compulsory nor funded by a trust fund. Seventy-two percent of the funds for Part B comes from Medicare Part A recipients who elect to have Part B premiums deducted from their monthly Social Security check.

Under the charge-based payment system, Medicare pays what the statute calls "reasonable" charges and what Health Care Financing Administration (HCFA) now usually calls the "allowed or approved" charges. The basic rule is that the Medicare-allowed charge is the lowest of (1) the actual charge, (2) the physician's own customary charge for the service, or (3) the prevailing charge in the locality for the service. Charges greater than these amounts are allowed only in unusual circumstances requiring extra effort, and only if the local practice is to charge extra in those circumstances.

Beneficiary Payments: In 1995, Part B requires the beneficiary to pay an annual deductible (about $100) as well as a monthly premium of $43.80 in 1997 (up from $31.80 in 1992). After the deductible is satisfied, Medicare will ordinarily pay 80 percent of the Medicare-approved payment amount; the beneficiary is responsible for the remaining 20 percent.

Services Received: physician services such as diagnosis, therapy, surgery, and consultation; services incident to physician services; ambulatory surgical services; rural health clinic services; outpatient hospitals services such as diagnostic services, physical, occupational, and speech therapy, emergency services, supplies, and prosthetic devices; rental or purchase of durable medical equipment (wheelchairs, etc.); renal dialysis services; ambulance services; some inpatient ancillary services when beneficiary is not eligible under Part A.

Under Part B, physicians may elect one of two reimbursement strategies: first, to accept the Medicare fee determination as payment in full, billing Medicare directly, and receiving 80 percent payment from the Medicare intermediary—a practice called "accepting the assignment." The beneficiary is liable for the remaining 20 percent coinsurance. The second is called an "unassigned claim." The patient is charged the physician's customary charge, which may be considerably higher than the Medicare allowance for that service. Medicare pays its normal allowance for that covered service, and the patient is then responsible for the difference between the physician's charge and the Medicare payment.

In order to encourage physicians to take claims on assignment and thus agree to accept the Medicare payment as payment in full, the medical statute creates a participating physician program under which physicians can agree on an annual basis to accept assignment for all services furnished to Medicare beneficiaries during the year. The Medicare payment for participating physicians is higher than for nonparticipating physicians. Medicare also promotes the use of participating physicians through publications of directories listing them, toll-free telephone numbers through which beneficiaries can obtain names of participating physicians, and statements in notices to beneficiaries in connection with unassigned claims reminding them that they are not subject to balance billing if they use participating physicians.

Medicare uses pecuniary incentives to get physicians to participate. A nonparticipating physician can continue to treat Medicare patients, accepting assignments or not on a claim-by-claim basis, but Medicare will reimburse only 96 percent of the Medicare fee schedule amount. This amount is less than the normal Medicare assignment.

📖 **MEDICARE C**   Also called Medicare + Choice, this new, optional program was implemented in 1999. It is available to Medicare-eligible people when a managed care organization provides the services of Medicare A and B (at minimum). A gatekeeper physician is in control and coordinates the person's entire medical treatment. Many believe this unified approach is an improvement over the (allegedly) fragmented services provided under earlier programs.

The federal government will also benefit from this program, since it will contract with local managed care companies and hold those companies responsible for providing the necessary services. The managed care companies must compete for the Medicare C contracts, and this competition, coupled with managed care's claimed efficiency, will lower health care costs for the elderly. With the large baby boom population soon to be in need of costly health care, many avenues to reduce costs are being actively pursued.

📖 **MEDICARE PROSPECTIVE PAYMENT SYSTEM**   When it passed the Tax Equity and Fiscal Responsibility Act (TEFRA) in 1982, Congress allowed the establishment of prospective payment systems. This action set the stage for Title VI of the Social Security Amendment of 1983, commonly known as the prospective payment system (PPS). A prospective payment system identifies the amounts that will be reimbursed so that the provider knows how much will be received for each service. The Health Care Financing Administration (HCFA) was charged with coordinating and administering the system; its plan of action was to implement diagnosis-related groups (DRGs).

DRGs were developed by the Yale School of Organization and Management and tested in the state of New Jersey. The New Jersey Medicare discharges were analyzed. Results showed that the main or primary diagnosis of the patient, secondary diagnoses, age, and/or surgical procedures performed predicted costs for the majority of patients. The university statistically collapsed the variety of diagnoses to 23 major diagnostic categories (MDCs) containing 467 diagnosis-related groups (actually 470 DRGs; the added three deal with the patients who are exceptionally difficult to classify). Within each MDC, cases are initially classified as either medical or surgical, depending on whether an operating room procedure was reported. If the case is medical, it is generally classified into a particular DRG based on the patient's diagnosis, age, and the presence or absence of complications and comorbidities. If it is surgical and more than one surgical procedure is involved, classification also depends on a "surgical hierarchy," a ranking of surgical procedures designed to direct a case into a DRG based on the surgical procedure with the greatest resource use.

Current DRGs are listed in HCFA's annual notice of PPS rates published annually on September 1. In 1990 there were 477 DRGs; in 1993 there were 489 DRGs. With increasing medical advances in diagnosis, the number of DRGs will continue to grow.

The purpose of the DRG classification system is to group together cases that are similar in consumption of hospital resources so that payment rates can be established for a few hundred types of cases rather than for the many thousands that would have to be priced if each patient's condition and treatment had to be considered individually. However, as the term *diagnosis-related group* indicates, cases are ordinarily grouped by diagnosis as well as by their use of resources.

Commencing in 1983, payment rates were prospectively determined on a case-averaging basis that was to be phased in over four years. The Medicare hospital prospective payment system (PPS) uses diagnosis-related groups (DRGs) to classify cases for payment. All providers must bill Medicare directly in order to qualify for reimbursement.

The hospital does not initially classify a case directly into a DRG. Instead, it reports a series of codes reflecting the patient's principal and secondary diagnoses and the procedures performed on the patient during the hospital stay. The requisite clinical information is based on the ICD-CM (International Classification of Diseases—9th Edition—Clinical Modifications) coding scheme. The Medicare billing form currently has space for the principal diagnosis, four additional diagnoses, and three surgical procedures. These entries, together with information on age, sex, and whether the patient was alive, dead, or transferred at discharge, are the factors used for classifying cases into particular DRGs.

To avoid erroneous initial assignments, the patient is first assigned a DRG at discharge. The following variables are used in combination by the GROUPER program to assign Medicare patients to DRGs: the principal diagnosis or principal operating room procedure, other diagnoses and procedures, patient's age at admission, patient's sex, discharge status. The principal diagnosis is the diagnosis established after study to be chiefly responsible for occasioning the admission of the patient to the hospital for care. "After study" means that erroneous diagnoses made at the time of admission do not control the classification.

The DRG statute requires the HCFA to adjust the DRG classifications and to weight each procedure by its medical complexity (the more complex the procedure the greater the reimbursement) at least annually to reflect changes in treatment patterns, technology, and other factors that may change the relative use of hospital resources. This process is called recalibration.

Physician Payment Reform (PPR) under Medicare Part B: Refers to provisions of Omnibus Budget Reconciliation Act of 1989 (OBRA 89) passed by Congress to make changes in the way payment for physician services is determined by Medicare Part B. It has two general components:

1. Payment for physician services will be based on a fee schedule using a resource-based relative value scale (RBRVS). Beginning January 1, 1992, this fee schedule replaced the charge-based reimbursement system. The fee schedule is based upon the following calculations and principles:

- the amount of work necessary to render the service.
- physician costs incurred in rendering a service, not the charges they have typically billed.
- recognition of variations in practice costs according to the geographic practice cost indices.
- no payment differentials for services based on the specialty of rendering physician.
- nationally established resource-based relative value units (RBRVU) of work for each service that will not vary between carriers. (Note the similarity in principle with DRGs.) The RBRVU is the sum of the relative value units associated with the physician work required for the service, practice overhead (rent, salaries supplies, etc.), and malpractice premiums.
- the RVUs for practice costs are established for each procedure.
- a single national conversion figure (CF) is used by all carriers in calculating payments under the Medicare fee schedule.
- fee schedule amount = RBRVU x GPCI x CF.

2. Medicare volume performance standards (MVPS) are established to monitor annual increases in Medicare Part B benefit payments for physician services and future adjustments as necessary. The MVPS is an estimate or projection of a reasonable percentage increase in the volume of physician services for the coming fiscal year. The projection deals with items or services commonly performed by a physician or in a physician's office. Two MVPSs are established: surgical and nonsurgical procedures.

The MVPS is determined pursuant to a congressional directive to the Secretary for Health and Human Services for the upcoming fiscal year.

Beneficiary financial protections have been established. There are caps on charges that would formerly have been passed on to the spouse.

Reimbursement and medical policies used by Medicare are standardized. The "Medicare language" must be used for the various components of the physician payment reform (PPR). The codes for filing must use the same definitions and numerical categories, known in slang as "Medicareese." Narrative descriptors of the visit must be written in more consistent fashion to allow for auditing of diagnosis or procedure determination.

MERCY KILLING   See EUTHANASIA

MILGRAM, STANLEY   A psychologist who gained fame (and notoriety) during the 1970s for conducting experiments on obedience and social conformity that resulted in the recognition of unethical practices.

Dr. Milgram's experiments involved bringing students into the research laboratory to participate in a study that, they were told, focused upon the effects of punishment on learning. This representation was, in fact, false. The goal of the research was actually to determine how far a person would proceed in administering pain to another when ordered to do so. Further, the student-learner was Dr. Milgram's confederate, so that the reactions were prepared.

The research called for the subjects were to work in pairs. One would act as the teacher and the other as a student. The student was strapped to a chair and had electrodes attached to his or her wrists. The student was to learn word pairs. If the student failed to learn, the teacher was to administer electric shocks. The shocks would become stronger as the student made mistakes.

With progressive shocks, the student was observed to be apparently writhing in pain. Nevertheless, the teachers were told to continue to administer painful shocks. Many teachers continued into the "Danger" category. When the subjects attempted to withdraw, the experimenter would encourage them, "in the name of research," to continue. The results indicated that approximately 62 percent of the teachers continued to shock the students even though pain was evident. At the end of the session, Dr. Milgram and his confederate would explain the situation to the subject.

Ethicists reading his work challenged his acts on the basis of lack of informed consent. The potential for truly damaging the psychological wellbeing of these subjects was clear. Dr. Milgram indicated that the response of the participants was not negative. Only 1 percent indicated negativity toward their participation, and 84 percent indicated they were glad to have participated.

Dr. Milgram's general conclusion regarding his compliance with ethical standards was that subjects should be informed that the experiment may involve deception or nondisclosure of all the facts of the research. As long as there is no significant risk of harm to the subjects, this information was acceptable. In response, bioethicists strongly argue that the greater concern is that the subjects can exercise the personal right to make decisions that effect them only with a full understanding of the situation. Dr. Milgram's experiments and ethical suggestion would not comply with that complete understanding. Bioethicists continue to debate these issues.

MINORS AND CAPACITY   In most states, a person under the age of 18 is considered a minor. Eighteen, the age of majority, is the objective measure of when a child becomes an adult for legal purposes. This social policy reflects the belief that after eighteen years of life, the person should have the essential experiences necessary to make decisions and understand their implications.

Capacity essentially means the ability to understand the implications of one's decisions. By entering into a contract, for example, people agree to perform an act or refrain from performing an act. If they do not act as they have agreed, then a penalty arises. Understanding the consequences and the implications of entering into the contract is capacity. Minors often don't have capacity, especially in dealing with health issues. The general adult population is woefully undereducated on health issues, and minors even more so. Public health issues are quite commonly encountered by minors. One example is the current fad of body decoration, including tattoos and body piercing. Parental permission is required because of the obvious health risks and the permanence of the procedure. Tattoos can be removed by modern laser treatments, but scarring still results. More dangerous, the tattoo artist may not follow proper aseptic techniques, putting the recipient at high risk for hepatitis, HIV, or some other infection.

Minors, generally, are perceived as not having the capacity to enter into a contract without an adult's cosignature. The reason for denying minors capacity is to protect them from adult consequences until they are ready and capable of understanding the possible consequences of their actions. Further, society recognizes that by placing a minor in the role of an "innocent," the minor can be protected from unscrupulous adults who might otherwise try to take advantage of someone with less experience and knowledge.

MORAL HAZARD   A moral hazard is a decision made by some that would usurp the rights of others. The basic, unalienable rights are the right to life, the right to make decisions about one's personal actions, and the right not to experience harm at the hands of others. (See **Autonomy, Principle of.**) A moral hazard would be encountered

when decisions were reached that would threaten these basic and fundamental rights. In modern times, many argue that a right to a "good death" or to control one's own death is also a basic and fundamental right. A good death would be a death where the dying person's wishes were followed and the person died pain free and as comfortably as possible, surrounded by loved ones.

N

NATURAL DEATH ACTS A general category of legislation forming the basis for an individual's right to author advance directives. Considering the decision-making complications of encountered by the family of Karen Ann Quinlan, the California legislature took very direct and specific action. The legislators passed the California 1976 Natural Death Act. Its authors mandated that a legally enforceable declaration of a person's wish to "die a natural death" cannot be executed until fourteen days or more after an individual is diagnosed as having a terminal illness. A terminal illness was defined as one that would cause the patient's death imminently, whether or not life sustaining procedures are continued. By 1992, approximately 40 states had followed in the footsteps of the California legislature. By 1999, all the U.S. states and territories have passed variations of this act under living will statutes. Each state has adapted the concepts now categorized as laws guiding advance directives and their alternatives. (See **Advance Directives.**)

NEGATIVE MEDICAL OUTCOME A medical result that was not intended or expected to result from a particular medical/surgical/therapeutic initiatives. These are adverse possibilities that do not happen often but could happen as a result of the clinical intervention. The possibility of a negative medical outcome (and the meaning of the term) should be included in the discussions between the physician and the patient.

NEGLIGENCE The legal claim of negligence occurs in one of two ways: when one person (the plaintiff or complainant) alleges that another has failed to use the requisite care to do something that a reasonable person would do under the same circumstances, or when the plaintiff alleges that another's conduct was inappropriate and a reasonable person would not act in the same way. Damages are the result.

When evaluating a situation for negligence, one looks for a duty to act (to do something) or to forebear from doing something, and the act or forbearance to act essentially causes compensable injury or damages. There are multiple degrees of negligence, depending on whether the negligence was simply an oversight or the omission was willful or reckless. (See **Malpractice, Medical.**)

The reasonable person standard is used in the evaluation of negligence. The court asks what a normal person do in that same situation. Every person is believed to have a duty to conduct his or her actions so that another is not harmed. The harm may occur from doing something or from not doing something within that duty such that the action (or inaction) is the relative cause of the injury.

A person's acts are evaluated from their social position within the activity under consideration. For example, the physician is considered to have a duty to act within the physician's normal competence if the physician is working within the doctor-patient relationship. If the physician is a specialist in the area of the occurrence, the physician is held to the standard of the reasonable specialist. If the physician is a specialist but the situation is different from the area of specialty, the physician would be held to the standard of reasonable knowledge of the normal physician.

The court also considers the circumstances within which the act occurred. If the act or forbearance occurs within the standard clinical area, the standard is applied directly. When the act or forbearance occurs outside of the normal situation, such as on the scene of an automobile accident, the unique conditions where the negligence is alleged to have occurred are considered. (See **Good Samaritan Act.**)

In health care, intentional acts of negligence are not common. Most charges of negligence arise because a patient or the patient's family is dissatisfied with the result of a procedure or treatment, but these are not usually cases of negligence. The physician has a right to use a variety of techniques to treat a patient and may select a technique not used by the majority. The standard applied is that the physician must use a generally accepted clinical technique.

Along with the reasonable person test, the concept of proximate cause is frequently encountered in negligence cases. The proximate cause is the action that resulted in injury. It need not be the immediately preceding action; rather, the proximate cause is that action or forbearance which, without interference, causes the injury. Time and space are not issues unless they intercede in the causal sequence. For example, pain in the abdomen was reported after a surgery. Initially both the medical personnel and the patient believed that the pain was associated with the surgery and medication was prescribed. The complaints continued and phantom pain (a pain reported by the patient that is not medically explained) was believed to be the cause. Finally, in exasperation, the physician ordered x-rays. A surgical instrument was found to have been left in the patient's abdomen. The proximate cause of the pain was the instrument, and the pain had lasted approximately one year! The physician's negligence was in not assuring that the surgical instrument was located at the completion of the surgery. The time period that had elapsed was not an issue in proximate cause (but it was a consideration in the settlement of the case).

To summarize, the health care provider has a duty to provide services with reasonable skill and knowledge, from the initial consultation until the completion of the service, avoiding injury to the extent possible within the scope of the reasonable provider. (Licensure requirements demand that health care providers are further required to maintain their skills through continuing education.)

DEFENSES TO NEGLIGENCE

In general, a defense is the response that a party makes to a complaint filed by another. The responding party claims a legal reason or justification why the allegation of the complaining party should not prevail. The most common defenses in health care are denial of the facts as alleged, releases of liability through informed consent, and the expiration of the statute of limitations.

The denial of the facts is perhaps the most common defense. As an example, a physician may deny having done a certain procedure. As noted, many allegations of negligence occur because the results of the procedure or treatment do not satisfy the complainant. Side effects, although undesirable, are not necessarily the result of negligence. Most informed consent documents and patient preparation interviews between the patient and the health care provider deal with side effects. Patients are reminded that everyone has the potential to respond differently than the "normal" person. Physicians are trained to expect the abnormal, but patients may not handle an abnormal response well. Physicians attempt to protect themselves by effective clinical documentation and by preprocedure or pretreatment informed consent. (See **Consent [Informed]**.) Negligence may result from an inadequate informed consent, though the intent of informed consent is to avoid that exact situation.

The statute of limitations defense protects the health provider by limiting the time period during which a lawsuit can be filed. Negligence encountered in medical malpractice is normally a tort (civil wrong). The time limit for filing a lawsuit for an act of negligence, approximately two years, is expressed in the state's laws, e.g., Kentucky Revised Statutes, Ohio Revised Code, or Montana Code Annotated. However, argument has arisen over when the two years begins. Originally, the time limitation began with the occurrence of the wrongful act, and many states continue to use this time frame. However, as legal and scientific knowledge increased, many states have determined that the two years begins when the reasonable patient should have discovered the injury. This is called the discovery rule. Often, these states make available a maximum time span for filing so that a lawsuit based on the discovery of a problem resulting from a surgery ten years ago may be filed.

The time frame is a factor that has been argued in many courts. Many plaintiff's lawyers argue that exceptionally long periods of time may pass before an injury from a treatment is identified. In some cases, drugs were administered and initially believed safe. Many years later, the treated patients begin to report similar symptoms that were eventually traced to one common experience, the drug treatment. A lawsuit based on this injury recognition may be allowed under the discovery rule, which acknowledges that the reasonable person could not discover the problem until the time had passed and the problem was identified. Upon discovery of the injury, the reasonable person would respond to the problem and file a lawsuit. The statute of limitations begins to run with the discovery of the injury.

Three other defenses to negligence involve the conduct of the complainant (plaintiff): assumption of the risk, comparative negligence, and contributive negligence. Under these conditions, the awards for the injury may totally barred or may be reduced because of the plaintiff's own actions.

Assumption of the Risk: The complainant's behavior reveals that he or she voluntarily assumed the risk that the procedure might cause an injury. This defense may be used with informed consent. The complainant gives consent, in advance, to the possibility of injury associated with the procedure or treatment. As long as the consent is not given under duress or force, this defense is very effective.

Comparative Negligence: Two negligent acts are recognized in this defense. Each party establishes negligence by the other party. The court then holds each party responsible for paying damages for the injury. The plaintiff does not recover the entire amount, but the defendant does not get off the hook. Both pay compensation for the damages they respectively caused. This approach is entitled the pure system.

An alternative to the pure system is called the 50 percent system. If the plaintiff's fault causes 50 percent or more of the injury, then the plaintiff may not recover any damages. The complainant is recognized as being the major reason for the injury. In such circumstances, forcing another person to pay is believed unfair and a breach of social justice.

The wording of the forms of comparative negligence varies from state to state. Readers should consult the laws of their individual states.

Contributory Negligence: This defense indicates that the plaintiff and the defendant proximately caused the injury. The plaintiff is knowledgeable about the risks (or a reasonable person would be knowledgeable) and disregards the dangers associated with the act. The plaintiff places his or her own person at risk, and this inappropriate conduct results in the injury. In some states where this defense is used, contributory negligence of the plaintiff may result in compensation to the plaintiff being completely barred. This defense actually holds plaintiff responsible for personal actions, the reasonable person standard being applied to the patient.

No Duty Rule   In civil law, a person does not normally have a duty to care for another person. The duty arises when a person enters into a relationship with another. In that relationship, each person assumes certain responsibilities, the most basic being that the helper cannot leave the victim worse off.

In health care, the provider enters into a patient-provider relationship that entails the performance of certain duties by the provider, notably the provision of health services with due diligence, knowledge, and skill. Until the health provider enters that relationship, however, he or she is not required to assist the victim. There is no duty to render services. But once the provider begins to render services, the relationship has been initiated and the no-duty rule is no longer applicable. For example, if the provider sees a complete stranger in need of assistance and fails to act, the provider is legally blameless because there was no duty to act. The provider would be morally wrong for bypassing someone in need of help, but he or she is not under a legal duty to help. To encourage these people to help, society has protected them through Good Samaritan statutes.

Noncompliant Patient   A patient who refuses to accept the medical treatment ordered. Noncompliance may occur inside of the health organization or at home.

Noncompliant patients, especially those at home, can be very frustrating for physicians. Anecdotal research indicates that many people do not comply with medical regimens when they begin to recover from the disorder. They stop taking their medication when they feel better. Many save the unused medications for a future bout with that disorder. These patients believe that saving the medications will save money by avoiding future visits to the physician. However, patients who are beginning to feel better may be on the road to recovery, but they are not totally healed. The medication prescribed is intended for the duration of the treatment and recovery. To stop the medication early may result in a resurgence of the disease, and the second onset may make the medication less effective because the disease may become resistant to that drug. (The resistance may not occur if the complete order is followed and the disease is eradicated.) This second visit to the doctor may require stronger medications and a longer recovery period.

Noncompliant persons may also be found in the hospital. Bioethically, many noncompliant people are not problems. If the person is competent, the principle of autonomy and the right of a person to control her own privacy dictate the health care response. The competent person has the right to deny medical treatment even if it means her death. She may even be discharged AMA (against medical advice). Such a patient may be frustrating to the provider, but she is following her own decisions.

The incompetent, noncompliant person presents bioethical and practical problem. This person may not understand the treatment or his entire health situation. (See **Incompetent Patients**.) Society has dictated that a person is legally incompetent when he presents a threat of harm to himself or others. Equally, he may be incapable of understanding the situation. In this context, an emergency medical condition may arise. In this case, the physician submits an emergency application to a judge, who orders an emergency admission, allowing the individual's personal rights to be temporarily set aside. In most states, a formal hearing (due process) must be held within 72 hours. The person's personal condition is evaluated in combination with his loss of personal rights. The priority is placed upon returning him to competency with minimal insult to constitutional rights. At this hearing, a decision is made to keep him in the hospital voluntarily or involuntarily. If the person's frailty is the consequence of noncompliance with the medication (a common finding in repeat psychiatric admissions), he may be involuntarily placed in the least restrictive environment to help him recover. The length of involuntary commitment varies with the patient's prognosis. In most, if not all states, additional hearings are required to determine the continuation of involuntary commitment and to make sure the least restrictive environment is maintained.

NONMALEFICENCE, PRINCIPLE OF   Nonmaleficence, one of the first directives of clinical practice, is expressed by the Latin maxim "Primum non nocere," which means "First, do no harm." It complements the principle of beneficence, which requires the physician to promote good. Physicians are taught the principle of nonmaleficence from the very outset of medical school. It is this directive that raises ethical questions concerning abortion, advance directives, and physician-assisted suicide.

Not inflicting harm, in its simplest form, means not killing, causing pain, or taking away someone's opportunities. But in health care, the application of this principle is anything but simple. For example, the radiation treatment of leukemia involves the administration of toxic dosages of chemotherapy and radiation. In turn, this treatment causes great sickness and leaves the patient's body an ineffectual (immuno-suppressed) immune system. Yet this result is exactly what is intended. The toxic chemotherapy and radiation are intended to destroy the cause of the disease. After the disease is destroyed, bone marrow is injected and, hopefully, takes root and revives the immune system. In this example, the harm is necessary to bring about a good consequence: cancer remission and the preservation of the patient's life. In such instances, then, harm must be conceptualized as action intended to bring about inappropriate or bad results.

Harm may also be brought about by omission—by not doing something one should have done. (See **Negligence.**) Thus the principle of nonmaleficence may also be recognized in actions the practitioner takes to avoid unreasonable risks.

In the contexts of abortion and physician-assisted suicide, the concept of harm is disputed. In a therapeutic abortion, the fetus is removed surgically from the mother, either for personal reasons or medical necessity. When the procedure is elective, is the physician violating the principle of nonmaleficence and doing harm? Bioethically, the issue raises many questions. If abortion helps the mother finish school and avoid being a single "welfare" mother, is harm being done? But abortion kills a fetus that would have grown into a human being (and some argue that a fetus is already human). Is that harm? The debate over these issues has continued for many years.

Physician-assisted suicide is equally controversial. (See **Physician-Assisted Suicide.**) Some physicians believe that if a competent person has contracted an incurable condition and life has become unbearable, she has the right to take her own life. If she is incapable of doing so, then she has the right to have the assistance of a trained individual. Physicians are trained in medications and know when doses become deadly. On the other hand, they also know how to administer medications to minimize pain. Is taking a life under these conditions doing harm? Many do not believe this act is harmful. Others believe this taking of a life is the absolute harm.

Clearly the principle of nonmaleficence is at the heart of many health care controversies and in the forefront of social debate. Since the concept of doing no harm is essential to health care, its definition within a variety of contexts must be agreed upon by society.

▥ **NUREMBERG CODE**   This document is derived from the World War II war crimes tribunal that convicted German medical practitioners, mostly physicians, of experimenting on human beings. It has become the modern basis for the ethical practice of medicine and health care.

The Nuremberg Code recognized that experiments on human beings require adherence to certain basic principles, here paraphrased: (1) informed consent to the experimental procedure must be freely given (see **Consent [Informed]**); (2) the findings of the experiment should yield positive results for the benefit of society unavailable by other means of study; (3) the experiment must be based on results on experiments with animals; (4) unnecessary physical and mental suffering and injury must be avoided; (5) death or serious injury must not be an expected experimental consequence; (6) the degree of risk must never exceed the humanitarian importance of the result; (7) proper precautions and protections must be taken for the subjects of the experiment; (8) the experimenter must be scientifically qualified and exhibit the highest degree of skill and care; (9) the subject can cease participation at any stage of the experiment of his or her own choosing; and (10) the experimenter must be prepared to terminate the experiment if a continuation of the experiment is likely to result in injury, disability, or death to a subject.

This code was a response to the discovery of the atrocities of Nazi medical experimentation. Experiments involved genetic studies on twins, hypothermia, and on the mentally handicapped and mentally ill. These medical studies was described as "racial hygiene," part of the Nazi's attempt to develop a pure race of Aryans.

One of the most infamous Nazi experimenters was Dr. Josef Mengele, known as "The Angel of Death." Mengele's twin experiments provide a sense of the cruelty of his work. Following the genetic recognition that identical twins were completely identical in every biological way, he believed that these twins were ideal subjects for comparative experiments. Often using children, he injected one twin with a germ. The other twin was not infected. The infected twin received little food or water and was forbidden medical intervention. When the infected twin died, the second healthy twin was killed as well. Their bodies were dissected and their organs compared to determine the changes. Mengele believed that any change he found in the diseased twin would be due to the injected infection. Mengele did not stop with these atrocities. He and his criminal cohorts attempted many other experiments, including attempts to change genders, create Siamese (conjoined) twins, and experiment on the genitalia.

Other physicians also carried out experiments. But some experiments were simply ordered by people interested in medicine. One such interested individual was Heinrich Himmler, head of the Nazi Gestapo. Among other topics, Himmler was interested in hypothermia, the condition wherein the body is not warm enough to sustain itself. On Himmler's orders, the physicians at the Dachau concentration camp conducted hypothermia experiments. The claimed underlying purpose was to provide a means to keep German pilots alive when they were shot down over the cold waters of the North Sea. Many subjects were forced to participate, and those not forced were almost always lied to in order to gain their participation. The prisoners were subjected to immersion in freezing water. Sometimes the prisoners were clothed, but more commonly were they were immersed scantily clad or naked into the water in order to rapidly reduce the body temperature to under 80 degrees Fahrenheit. The physicians were attempting to ascertain how long a person could survive in such an extreme condition. Death was the norm.

As a result of these and other experiments, the Nuremberg Code was developed. All recognized that human experimentation is necessary; at the same time, all agreed that adherence to certain principles was absolutely essential. The code was an attempt to provide guidelines for those who wanted to conduct human experiments. The implications of this code may be perceived throughout this dictionary or any other medical research text. The requirement for informed consent, the institutional review board, and the adherence to principles are all emphasized and adhered to because of the Nuremberg Code.

NUTRITION AND HYDRATION   These three words, which mean food and water, represent the principal components necessary for human life. In order to survive in a healthy way, a human must have adequate nutrition and clean water. Many public health officials point to the improved health status in the United States during the early years of the twentieth century as a result of improved nutrition and the development and proliferation of water and sewage treatment plants.

In the 1990s, the words nutrition and hydration have become increasingly associated with the final days of life. Specifically, when a patient is identified as beyond therapeutic intervention, artificial or mechanical life support may be eliminated and the person provided only nutrition and hydration. Or a person may order the removal of hydration and nutrition for himself through written advance directives.

Many people equate the removal of food and water with the discomfort they would feel when they are in their normal physiologic condition. In the natural process of dying, research has found that certain sensitivities, such as the desire for food and water, decrease. They can be further lessened by prescribed medications. Many believe that the dying process is made more natural through the removal of food and water than by attempting to prolong the death through artificial means and mechanical life support.

One of the bioethical issues in decisions concerning hydration and nutrition is the principle of nonmaleficence, or doing no harm. The provision of artificial and mechanical interventions to sustain life can cause substantially more pain than it eliminates. Alternatively, letting someone die by removing the basic life-sustaining elements and without making attempts to intercede is considered by many as causing harm through inaction. The principle seems violated no matter what one chooses.

The means to die and the right to die are very personal, and indeed the principle of autonomy also must be considered. The individual's right to decide what happens to him is fundamental. These issues are being extensively debated among the bioethical, legal, and philosophical communities and will be debated for many years to come.

See also **Artificial Nutrition.**

O

OMNIBUS BUDGET RECONCILIATION ACT (OBRA)
An annual federal tax and budget reconciliation act. The document reconciles incoming taxes with budget expenditures. In other words, it identifies how taxes are to be spent and budgeted. Each act is identified by title and year it was passed: for example, "OBRA" '89 and "OBRA '90."

This annual document frequently contains specific requirements for health care providers. OBRA '87, for example, removed the difference between skilled nursing facilities and intermediate nursing facilities, defining both as "nursing facilities." This definitional change meant that Medicaid pay the same reimbursement for both intermediate and skilled beds, which simultaneously complicated and simplified the reimbursement process. It became more complicated because other funding sources did not make the same change; it became simpler because Medicaid providers only had to deal with two rather than three levels of care.

Many other OBRA-mandated changes have affected the provision of health care. The current cost-containment efforts embodied in OBRA use managed care approaches, and a review of recent OBRAs indicates that sections in the act frequently focus upon managed care activities. Thus it is important for the health care provider to stay up-to-date on OBRA.

OREGON'S DEATH WITH DIGNITY ACT
This law legalizes the request by qualified patients to obtain a medication that will end their lives in a humane and dignified manner. This law is the first of its kind to identify safeguards to legalize physician-assisted suicide. The public vote was extremely close (52 percent to 48 percent). Legal challenges to the law occurred immediately.

Because of the sensitivity of the topic and the potential for abuse of physician-assisted suicides, the law was written very narrowly and explicit requirements incorporated. The safeguards stipulate a process that the patient must follow and criteria that she must meet. The process begins with an oral request by the patient. Following the oral request, there must be clear documentation that the patient is competent, is making these decisions as a competent adult, and has reached these decisions voluntarily, without pressure or duress. Two physicians must have diagnosed the patient as terminally ill, and both must agree that the she is likely to die within six months. A psychiatrist may be required to attest to the patient's competency. At any time, the patient can remove herself from this process. The physician is not required to administer the means of death but would be authorized to provide the means for the patient to take her own life.

The law is applicable only to those who have six months to live. Many ethical questions confront those whose lives may be much longer. A patient with Alzheimer's disease may live for many years, physically healthy but with progressive mental deterioration. This law would not apply to people with this type of condition because they are neither terminal nor will they be competent to make such a decision when they are within six months of their deaths.

In a June 1997 decision, after extensive debate and subsequent to Oregon's Death with Dignity Act, the U.S. Supreme Court left the issue of physician-assisted suicide to the states, based upon *Vacco v. Quill* and *Washington v. Glucksberg*. The Oregon law has not yet been implemented. It has been legally contested, and it appears that the question of the law's constitutionality may reach the U.S. Supreme Court.

ORGAN AND TISSUE DONATION   In the United States, people may voluntarily donate their organs and tissue to others. The intention to donate is indicated by a person's advance directives or, in some states, on their driver's license. The organs and tissues commonly donated are blood, bone marrow, eyes (notably the cornea— the clear part of the eye that looks like a lens), heart, kidneys, and skin. The liver, the long bones (tibia, fibula, femur, humerus, radius and ulna), and the lungs are also transplanted. The donations usually occur after a person has suffered brain death. The process of collecting the organs is called harvesting.

Organs and tissues may also be donated by living persons. The most common are blood, bone marrow, and kidneys. Since the body reproduces blood and bone marrow, these donations are seldom problematic. Kidneys, however, present a greater problem. A healthy person has two kidneys, but that same person can live a full and complete life with only one kidney. The fear, of course, is that the donor will experience some type of kidney disorder making the remaining kidney ineffective. The donor must consider this potential problem and the hazards of major surgery. Full informed consent must be ensured. In a recent example, one of the elite basketball players in the National Basketball Association (NBA) had a sister dying of kidney disease. Despite the risks, he made the donation.

ORGAN SELLING

Organs cannot be bought or sold in the United States. They may be donated, but only under strict conditions (See **Uniform Anatomical Gift Act of 1987** in this entry.)

The demand for organs has increased because of medical successes in transplantation. Kidney transplantation, for example, is no longer considered an experimental procedure. As a result, reports of organs being bought and sold illegally on the black market are also increasing. As recently as October 1998 an American was arrested in Italy for allegedly attempting to purchase organs.

Many legal agencies work to obtain organs from donors and donor families. The only costs to the recipient are the costs associated with obtaining the organ and its implantation. Most, if not all, bioethicists believe that making an organ a "marketable commodity" to be sold on the open market should not be allowed.

PRESUMED CONSENT

The local medical examiner may presume an individual's consent to donation if the body is within that official's custody. The official must not know of any unwillingness of the victim or the victim's family to not allow the donation. If the donation is allowed, the official must make sure that the donation does not interfere with any criminal or medical investigation. Reasonable efforts must be made to contact the family to obtain their consent. The determination must be clearly documented.

PROHIBITION AGAINST ORGAN PURCHASES

A federal law (42 U.S.C.A. §274(E]) made organ purchases unlawful. No one can knowingly acquire, receive, or transfer any human organ for valuable consideration for use in human transplantation. Valuable consideration is money paid for the organ itself. It is not the reasonable payment of money for the medical services necessary to remove, transport, implant, process, and preserve the organ.

UNIFORM ANATOMICAL GIFT ACT OF 1987 (UAGA)

This act has set the stage and strategy for locating organ donors. It identifies how cadaver organs are identified and obtained, including how a person may make and revoke an anatomical gift. A donor may make an anatomical gift if there is a document of gift signed by the donor with two witnesses. If the donor wishes to revoke or amend the donation, the new document should clearly state the donor's intentions and, again, be signed in the presence of two witnesses.

If no written documents exists, Section 3 of the UAGA indicates the family members who may authorize an organ donation. The anatomical gift may be authorized, in this order, by the decedent's spouse, an adult child of the decedent, either of the decedent's parents, an adult brother or sister of decedent, grandparent of decedent, and the decedent's guardian. Other unlisted persons may make such an authorization if documented evidence exists for the donation.

P

PALLIATIVE CARE   An approach to medical care that is used by hospice agencies. People admitted to hospice are terminally ill. Usually, to qualify for hospice services, the patient's physician must indicate that he or she has a life expectancy of six months or less. With this poor prognosis, the goal for many patients is organizing the end of life and ensuring that the patient is as comfortable and pain free as possible. The goal of palliative care is not to pursue futile curative medical objectives; it is to allow death to occur naturally, with the dying living their lives to the fullest until their time comes.

An important feature of palliative care is that all aspects of life are dealt with. Physicians and nurses support the patient medically. Prescriptions may be given for high dosages of pain medication that would be unusual in other circumstances. Social workers help the patient and the family prepare for the death and maximize the final time with the loved one. They also help tie up loose ends. The fears of a dying person are usually not focused only upon dying. They also concern the family, the pet, and what will happen to their loved ones in the future. These issues are dealt with. More importantly, the dying person is able to participate in the planning of the family's future by helping the family deal directly with the death. Death may not be desired, but unnecessary stresses can be resolved, and a person can die knowing he or she took care of the priorities.

Some people challenge palliative care because it does not cure. Critics argue that medical procedures are developed that may cure the individual. They believe the final months are better spent with a hope that a cure may be found. Proponents of palliative care acknowledge that a cure may be developed but argue that it is unlikely for the patient with a terminal diagnosis. These patients have already received the benefits of modern medicine. It is now time for them to put the final touches on their lives and move to the next level. This move, according to the proponents, should be as free from discomfort as possible and complete with the knowledge that the patient led a full life until the very end.

177

PARENS PATRIAE AUTHORITY   The principle that the state must care for those who cannot care for themselves. This authority is most commonly found when the state takes responsibility from the parents and assumes responsibility for the proper care and custody of minors (those under 18). It is also encountered in situations where a person is mentally incompetent and unable to care for himself. The state has the authority to intercede and act on the person's behalf.

If the person is a minor, two sets of rights must be protected: the rights of the child and the rights of the parents. The state may not simply remove a child and take over for the parents. It must first prove that the parents are neglecting the child or are incapable of providing for the child. A hearing to decide the matter is convened in the juvenile court. The child's and parent's rights of autonomy are protected through this constitutionally ordered due process.

If the person is mentally ill and will be committed to a psychiatric hospital, his legal rights are protected by the state, which provides an attorney for him. The commitment hearing is a formal meeting with a judge or magistrate, a prosecuting attorney for the people arguing that the person needs psychiatric commitment, a defense attorney for the client, and the client. The treatment is discussed by testimony and cross examination of the mental health expert (usually a psychiatrist or physician, psychologist, or social worker). The testimony is intended to prove that the treatment being rendered is the most appropriate and the location that is being recommended for the patient is the "least restrictive environment." Any time an individual's rights and freedoms are being removed, this form of due process protection is constitutionally required.

The incompetence of an individual can also result from an injury accident or disease, for example, a stroke (cerebrovascular accident). In the absence of immediate family, advance directives, or a durable power of attorney for health care, the protection of the individual often becomes the responsibility of the state. To protect the rights of the incompetent person, the state will appoint an individual to a guardianship or a protectorship. That individual is required that individual to act in the best interests of the incompetent. Here again, the appointment of a guardian requires a formal hearing, since the incompetent's right to make personal and private decisions is being removed. The proof required is that the incompetent person is incapable of making the decisions about his person and/or estate. A guardian is therefore appointed.

The range of this parens patriae authority is broad, but it is constrained by the constitutional protections required. Therefore, through constitutional protections of due process, this authority is supervised.

PARENTAL RIGHTS   These are the rights of the parents to raise and teach their children. (See **Child Protective Laws**.) Although the concept is simple, the identification of the extent of these rights is much more difficult.

Parental rights concerning a child or an infant needing medical care can raise classic bioethical issues. The child's physician advises that without treatment, its condition is life threatening. The parents, however, do not believe in medical treatment but that God will intervene if their belief is strong enough. Should the parents lose their rights because of this religious choice for their child? Because the government believes in the medical establishment and the parents don't? What about the Bill of Rights and religious practice? Who has the decision-making authority when the child could be cured and the parents do not allow medical intervention but turn to prayer instead? If the child dies because the parents followed their religious practices, are they guilty of homicide or manslaughter?

The courts have consistently held that the child should not suffer nor lose its life because of the choices of its parents. Judicial decisions restricting parents' rights have been sustained for acts concerning mandatory childhood immunizations and for life-saving medical interventions. If the individual victim is incapable of making her own personal choice, even though the parents of the victim differ with the decision, then the state may and will likely intercede with medical treatment. If, however, the victim is fully capable of making her own informed choice, then medical intervention will not be started. Rather than parental rights then, the right of the individual appears to be dominant. This area is being disputed constitutionally and ethically.

Another question on the extent of parental rights might be, when does a person stop being a father's child? Once a child becomes "emancipated," the parents are no longer responsible for making decisions for their children. When the emancipated child becomes incapable of decision making due to accident, disease, or other traumatic experience, are the parent's rights available to be reintroduced? The answer: not really. The family may still be consulted, but the state will often invoke its parens patriae authority to ensure that all avenues of individual protections are introduced. There may be other indications of the victim's wishes with which the family is unfamiliar.

PATIENT DUMPING   Slang term for transferring an emergency patient from the receiving hospital to another hospital because the patient is unable to pay for the services and treatments received. This activity was prohibited by Congress in the Emergency

Medical Treatment and Active Labor Act (EMTALA) in 1984. The prohibition against patient dumping is even recognized by the Internal Revenue Service. An organization that is attempting to become a not for profit, charitable (501(c)(3) organization is prohibited from any form of patient dumping.

PATIENT SELF-DETERMINATION ACT   Became law as part of the Omnibus Budget Reconciliation Act (OBRA) of 1990. This legislation may be found at 42 U.S.C.A. § 1395. It provided, among other things, increased weight to decisions made and acknowledged within advance directives. (See **Advance Directives**.) Living wills and health care durable powers of attorney were most heavily emphasized.

PATIENT'S BILL OF RIGHTS   This phrase has been used in several contexts. The current Patient's Bill of Rights has been presented by the American Hospital Association (See **American Hospital Association**.) The AHA version of the bill was identified as a goal for the Clinton administration in 1999. In President Bill Clinton's proposal, the bill of rights ensures a minimum standard of care for all people. It is an underlying philosophy of the rights of all patients that providers of all types (hospitals, physicians, etc.) will recognize. It has not been adequately developed for complete representation at the time of this writing.

PERSISTENT VEGETATIVE STATE   Coined by Dr. Fred Plum, this term describes a body that is functioning entirely in terms of its internal controls. It maintains temperature, heartbeat, and pulmonary ventilation (breathing). It maintains digestion, muscle reflex activity and nerves for low level conditioned responses. However, there are no behavioral indications of either self-awareness or awareness of surroundings. This state is also called persistent unconscious state (PUS) because some legislators do not like the "vegetative" term.

A person in this state are recognized as alive, but it is a life without human existence. The person in a persistent vegetative state has only a biological existence. Many courts have permitted life support to be discontinued for these people. The ethical issues surrounding this situation involve the definition of human existence. What does it mean to be human? One must consider the human thought, human emotions, and human interactive capabilities. Is there more? What is the bright line that will advise us when a person loses her humanness?

STANDARD FOR DISCONTINUING CARE

The bright line that guides us in making such difficult determinations is called the standard for discontinuing care. Many states use the standard set forth in the Uniform Determination of Death Act (UDDA). This is a model act that state legislatures are encouraged to analyze and incorporated into the laws of their state. Frequently the act has been adopted without change. The UDDA emphasizes brain death as the true absence of or loss of life. This emphasis replaces the traditional definition of the end of life: the cessation of heartbeat and respiration. When a person is brain dead as defined by the act, life support may be discontinued. (See **Death, Uniform Determination of Death Act.**)

PHYSICIAN-ASSISTED SUICIDE   A form of suicide
where a physician prescribes a lethal dose of medication and the patient is the active "deliverer" of the deadly dose. Proponents of physician-assisted suicide argue that a person should have the right to control his own destiny. That future includes, according to proponents, the right to control how he dies. People who die suddenly from accidents or sudden cardiac death have no control, but these people die quickly and with a minimum of suffering. People who are terminally ill with many forms of cancer or with other long-term (chronic) debilitating diseases may suffer for months or years with pain and anguish. Physician-assisted suicide is considered desirable for these long-suffering people. The goal is to allow a death with dignity rather than a long and painful process of passing from life.

The key bioethical principle argued to support physician-assisted suicide is the right to personal autonomy or personal decision making. The individual can control how she will die based upon her own perception of "a good death." This decision is exceptionally individual and personal. Society, therefore, should not be allowed to curtail this intimate decision.

Opponents of physician-assisted suicide often argue religious themes. Judeo-Christian religious phrases indicate themes of life. For example, "God gave you life and it is up to God to decide when you die." Also, "Life is holy and a gift from God." The Ten Commandments order that "thou shalt not kill." Those who hold these philosophical perspectives object to physician-assisted suicide. Because of our country's philosophical foundation, many of these beliefs have been transposed into laws. The laws against murder, "the intentional taking of the life of a human being with malice aforethought," is one of our strictest laws and potentially carries the death penalty (the application of another religion-based philosophy, "an eye for an eye").

Opponents also argue that allowing physician-assisted suicide would broaden the array of situations in which we are willing to take life. This argument is best described by example. A child is born with the disease progeria (more technically Hutchinson-Gilford Progeria Syndrome). The child becomes physically old very prematurely, often between the ages of 5 and 10. Children afflicted with this disease do not grow to their full height or develop to their biological potential. They are small, their faces are wizened. Externally, they have the characteristics of a person in their 70s and 80s, but in children's size. These children often develop early atherosclerosis (plaque in the arteries) and die of heart or cerebrovascular (stroke) disease between the ages of 7 and 27. Because of this premature death and the unusual problems encountered with this disease, opponents arguing the slippery slope contend that physician-assisted suicide could be expanded to include these and other similarly afflicted people. In other words, once you allow one exception to the rule of not taking a human life, you open the door for other reasons to take lives.

Bioethically, great dispute surrounds the concept of "doing no harm" or the principle of nonmaleficence. Two opposite positions are espoused. Opponents of physician-assisted suicide promote the belief that taking a life is harmful, as death is the result. Therefore, physicians cannot assist because harm is the result violating the principle. Proponents of physician-assisted suicide argue that allowing a patient to live in agonizing pain, a patient whose quality of life is limited to wasting away, is the true harm. Death, under these circumstances, is a relief. Many argue that the patient's face is the greatest proof of this truth. When people are coping with serious pain, their faces are contorted and distorted. Once they have expired, calm and a relaxed expressions take over. They are free of the pain.

Arguments over physician-assisted suicide, passive euthanasia, and other forms of medically influenced death will rage for many years to come. In an attempt to bring this matter to a conclusion, Dr. Jack Kevorkian acted dramatically. He administered a deadly dose of drugs to a terminally ill man, at the man's request. The doctor admitted administering the deadly dose directly, and therefore was involved in active euthanasia and not physician-assisted suicide. The CBS television program *60 Minutes* televised a videotape of the September 7, 1998, death. Importantly, it was not the patient who was not administering the deadly dose but rather the physician. By fundamental definition, the doctor wasn't committing physician-assisted suicide but *was* doing harm.

PHYSICIAN-PATIENT RELATIONSHIP   The unique clinical and personal interaction between the person seeking assistance and the physician; also known as the doctor-patient relationship.

The social roles of the patient as student, worker, mother, or father are excused by sickness when diagnosed under the authority of the physician. The mantle of personal responsibility is also shifted to the physician. The physician is allowed to probe into the most sensitive of topics with each person. The diagnosis-related information discussed is considered confidential and protected by absolute privilege, the highest legal protection of communication available. Violations of this relationship are sanctionable by professional and state medical licensing boards.

This very special relationship between the patient and physician was first described by medical sociologist Talcott Parsons. He described how a person takes his perceptions of deviance from normal health to a specially trained person, the physician. She revises the character of the deviance and gives it social credibility. She uses her unique knowledge to legitimize the social deviance, converting the individual into a patient. She offers the cure or treatment. The patient follows the doctor's orders and is excused from expectations of social contributions (e.g., work, school). Upon completion of the medical regimen, the patient regains his "person" status and returns to society.

The intensely personal relationship between the patient and physician is required, because the physician must be allowed to clinically explore parts of the individual's anatomy and psyche that are not available to any other under normal social conditions. The "doctor" has undertaken extensive scientific training and is clinically detached from the immensely personal examinations and procedures. To make this arrangement work, the patient is obligated to reveal everything that might be irregular in his health and the physician to interpret clinical findings.

The communications between the two must be complete, and the privilege of confidentiality is very significant, since trust is a critical part of the healing process. But today's societal issues put this relationship to a test. First, if the patient or physician has an incurable disease, should the other be informed at the outset of the relationship? Second, under managed care, physicians are being increasingly perceived as putting financial gain in front of quality patient care, eroding the necessary trust. The bioethical issues associated with both issues are significant.

When does a patient tell the clinical provider he has AIDS, a contagious and potentially fatal disease? The practitioner is expected to take standard safety precautions against any exchange of bodily fluids, and these precautions reduce disease communicability. Even so, some clinicians do not wish to treat people with this disease because of the risk. They will not enter into the clinical relationship and refer the people elsewhere. Many people believe these actions to be forms of discrimination, and the Americans with Disabilities Act does cover these types of issues in employment situations. One way to avoid the possibility of discrimination in treatment is not to tell the physician until the last moment that the patient has the disease. Most clinicians and bioethicists believe this action to destroy the physician-patient trust-based relationship.

Alternatively, does the physician advise her patients that she is HIV-positive? Using standard precautions, body fluids are not passed in most medical care. Clearly HIV-positive surgeons and other persons practicing invasive procedures would place the patient at greatest risk. Some clinicians believe that if they were HIV-positive, they would not tell their patients because by informing the patients, their medical practice would be destroyed. They would have no other way to support themselves and their families. The physician would be discriminated against, as would her family, and her privacy would be unprotected. Gossip such as news of an HIV-positive physician spreads quickly. Others believe that patients have an absolute right to know that their physician is HIV-positive. Some proponents desire clinical provider testing on a regular basis. Virtually all medical providers believe that HIV-positive surgeons should not carry out the surgical procedures but should step back into a consultative practice or select another form of clinical practice that does not involve invasive procedures.

The physician-patient relationship is critical to the successful healing of the patient. But under managed care, that relationship is eroding. Managed care introduces considerations of cost-effectiveness into the provision of medical care. Theoretically, the physician becomes more skilled in diagnosis rather than wasting resources by using tests and procedures unnecessarily. From the cost savings, the physicians are paid a financial dividend or bonus. Some critics of managed care arrangements say that the financial bonus encourages physicians to practice medicine with an eye on the size of their bonus. If they order more tests than the managed care company allows, their bonus is reduced. The critics point out that cost-conscious clinical behavior reduces the quality of care that the patient receives. Proponents of managed care deny these charges and point out that unnecessary waste is rampant throughout health care. They contend that they are making the system better and more affordable and thus available to more people.

Regardless of who is right—the proponents or the critics of managed care—the trust required for an effective physician patient relationship is threatened under this system. Patients may wonder, Is my doctor refusing to order the test because of its cost? How will I know if the doctor does a poor job in order to make more money? These issues present a major challenge to the physician-patient relationship. They will not be resolved for several years to come.

PLACEBO   A substance that is without medicinal value yet is prescribed for use, usually in research situations. The placebo is often used in experimental research to test whether or not a medicine is causing a therapeutic consequence. It is given to a portion of the experimental subjects, and the others are given the actual treatment. The subjects do not know whether they are receiving the placebo or the actual drug. If other conditions are equal, and the experimental group receiving the actual drug is helped more quickly than those receiving the nontherapeutic placebo, then any therapeutic responses are considered to be the result of the drug being tested.

PLACEBO EFFECT

The placebo effect occurs when the patient believes she is receiving treatment when she is actually receiving a placebo. Research has indicated that the power of belief is often a strong and effective healer.

Physicians may use this placebo effect to help treat people likely to use or over use medications. For example, a patient called for the doctor to give her a sleeping medication. Knowing that the patient was already on a strong medication, the doctor made up a liquid "sleeping potion" of orange juice and soda. He poured a small amount into a liquid medicine cup and took it to the patient. He advised the patient that this was an extremely powerful drug and she would be asleep in minutes if she drank it. She took the medication and was asleep within minutes. This is an example of the therapeutic use of the placebo. It avoided unnecessary medication and the patient was not harmed. To avoid encouraging the patient to request this medication, the physician also advised her that this medication could not be taken again because it would not be effective. The power of belief was actually the tool that worked.

PRODUCTS LIABILITY   The health care issue involving products liability is the responsibility for medical therapies' side effects. A medicine virtually always causes side effects. The common aspirin, for example, has several side effects: thinning the blood, possibly harming the stomach, and if taken by a child it can cause Reye's Syndrome. Yet this medication is used extensively. Another example would be when implants used in plastic surgery leak or rupture.

When a medication causes extensive harm, drug companies may be found liable for the harm incurred, even though the side effects may not show up for an extensive period of time after the medication was prescribed. Some prescription drugs have been found to cause cancer. The most recent highly publicized example of harmful side effects was

Fen-Phen, a weight-loss drug usually prescribed for extremely over-weight people. It was quite effective, but the side effect, unknown at the outset of the drug's use, was heart problems. Several people died because they used this drug. The drug manufacturers responsible for its development and sale have been sued by former users of the drug.

The logic behind products liability is the recognition that the manufacturer is responsible for the consequences that result from the use its products and for warning the public of dangers associated with its products. If problems arise that the company should have foreseen and did not, then it is negligent. If it finds a problem and fails to warn the user, then the company is also liable.

Manufacturers now spend considerable time and money attempting to warn people of the potential side effects of their products. Consumers see the influence of products liability when they purchase over-the-counter medication. In the box is a piece of paper with instructions and a list of identified side effects. The information is there to warn the consumer so that he or she is intelligently taking the risk. The company has warned the buyer and is therefore not liable for failing to warn.

THALIDOMIDE

This drug, first developed as a sedative, has recently been reintroduced to the health care drug formulary for the treatment of cancer. When first introduced in the 1950s, it caused many children to be born with developmental abnormalities. As a result, many people today are strongly opposed to its reintroduction.

Thalidomide was initially prescribed for the control of morning sickness during pregnancy and as a sleeping pill for nonpregnant women. It was very effective for controlling morning sickness and was widely used throughout Europe. Fortunately, it was used on an extremely limited basis in the United States because it was never approved by the Food and Drug Administration. The drug caused fetal malformation, and the child was often born with incompletely developed arms and legs that somewhat resembled a dolphin's fins. This physical resemblance resulted in the side effect's name: dolphin syndrome (technically, phocomelia). Approximately 12,000 babies were afflicted with this syndrome and other adverse side effects. The drug was banned worldwide in the early 1960s. Many of the people, now adults, who were adversely affected by this medication retain their fear of the drug and do not want thalidomide made available for any purpose.

Thalidomide has recently been revisited as a treatment for leprosy (also known as Hansen's disease). Rare in the United States today, it is a slowly progressive, long-term, contagious disease. Ugly lesions develop on the skin, inside the nose, in the body on nerves and bones, making the person appear mutilated. Thalidomide has been found to be an effective treatment because it has a therapeutic effect on inflammation. Its effectiveness as an anti-inflammatory has made the drug eligible for FDA approval. Because of the drug's action, it is also being studied for use with AIDS victims, arthritis, and several other chronic or long-term, debilitating disorders. It remains unlawful for use with pregnant women.

PROSPECTIVE PAYMENT SYSTEM (PPS) The

prospective payment system of health care reimbursement is intended to curb the continuous increase in health care costs. Under the PPS, providers know how much they will be reimbursed for a diagnosis or a treatment for a patient ahead of time, that is, prospectively. The prospective amount is rigidly set, and it is intended to require the providers to provide efficient and effective care. If the care is very efficient and effective, then the patient may be discharged early or may respond to treatment more rapidly. The cost of treating the patient will be less, and the profit is given to the provider. Alternatively, if the provider is inefficient and the costs exceed the prospective rate, the provider loses money.

If the patient's case is unique and extraordinary costs or lengths of stay are incurred despite the best practices of the provider, then special arrangements can often be made to treat these unusual patients. The provider is required, under these circumstances, to provide the necessary documentation to prove that the case was exceptional and special reimbursement is necessary.

TAX EQUITY AND FISCAL RESPONSIBILITY ACT OF 1982 (TEFRA)

Often called by its abbreviation, TEFRA, this congressional act authorized the federal Health Care Financing Administration to develop a reimbursement in which reimbursement rates were known ahead of time. This authorization has allowed the development of Medicare's diagnosis-related groups and capitated/managed care programs that use a prospective approach to reimbursement. (See **Medicare Prospective Payment System.**)

AMBULATORY PATIENT CLASSIFICATION (APC)

Congress has mandated the Department of Health and Human Services to search for a way to pay for hospital outpatient care under a prospective payment system similar to that used for inpatient services. This new payment system, the Ambulatory Patient Classification system, is similar to diagnosis-related groups (DRGs) and was developed to serve as the basis of payment for visit-based outpatient PPS. The new system was authorized by the Balanced Budget Act of 1997, and the initial implementation date has been set to occur as soon as possible after January 1, 2000.

With the APC system, greater financial incentives will exist to keep outpatient Medicare patient costs down. Payments are set in advance so that providers are sharing the risk of treating the patients. If costs exceed the predetermined payment, the provider will suffer the loss. If services are delivered at a lower cost than the predetermined payment, the provider will profit.

The APCs serves as a patient classification scheme that reflects the amount and type of resources used in an ambulatory patient visit. Patients in each APC exhibit similar clinical characteristics regarding resource utilization and costs. These characteristics and their associated health services are bundled together to form one APC (just like a DRG). The APC rate then covers the entire set of bundled services.

More than one APC may be billed if more than one procedure is performed, but there is significant discounting of reimbursement for added APCs.

In 1999 there were approximately 347 APCs that describe the complete range of services provided in the outpatient setting. The APCs were developed in 1990 by 3M Health Systems as Ambulatory Patient Groups under a contract with the Health Care Financing Administration (HCFA), primarily for use with Medicare.

The APCs are divided into surgical, medical, and ancillary only groups. Therapies (physical [PT], occupational [OT], speech), laboratory services, screening mammography, DMEs (durable medical equipment), partial hospitalization, and end-stage renal disease are paid on a fee schedule.

The benefits for Medicare providers will be the increase in efficiency through an improved data structure and improved knowledge for negotiations with other providers. Other benefits include the ability to spot and correct practice problems (incorrect coding, incomplete documentation, excessive services); comparing costs; and predictability of income.

MEDICARE RESOURCE-BASED RELATIVE VALUE SCALE (RBRVS)

This system was established by the Omnibus Budget Reconciliation Act, 1989, and implemented in 1992. This program was enacted following the relative success of DRGs, the Health Care Financing Administration implemented a prospective reimbursement system that would modify Medicare Part B as DRGs modified Medicare Part A. Part of the issue that this approach was intended to remedy was the high cost payments to physician specialists. This prospective approach would pay the same reimbursement amount to the physician whether performed by a generalist or a specialist. (See **Medicare B—Physician and Outpatient Services**.)

Q

QUALITY OF LIFE A subjective, relative measure of a person's experience while living. Quality of life is perceptual rather than absolute or quantitatively measurable. However, a good quality of life, from a medical point of view, might be described as a condition in which the person has all their normal capabilities. A poor quality of life could be experienced during the process of dying, if the person is sustained only through medical technology and lacks the ability to communicate and think.

Many argue that the mere existence of life allows for a good quality of life. Others argue that quality means positive and beneficial for the individual. This concept is used in the context of physician-assisted suicide, euthanasia, and life support issues, even though it is not clearly defined.

QUINLAN, KAREN ANN Quinlan was a 22-year-old woman whose tragedy brought forth the issue of the rights of incompetent patients and the need for advance directives. She was in a persistent vegetative state, and her "life" could be sustained indefinitely with mechanical assistance (ventilator and artificial feeding) and physical assistance (being turned over and helping with hygiene). However, her physicians recognized that she would never regain consciousness and would die if they removed the life support. Quinlan's parents wanted her life support discontinued. Because she was an adult and her parents were appointed her guardian, an extensive courtroom drama followed (*In Re Quinlan* (355 A.2d 647, cert. den. sub. nom, *Garger v. New Jersey,* 429 U.S. 922 [1976]). It was unclear what proof was needed to ascertain the patient's would have wanted; Quinlan had left no written communications of her wishes.

The Court essentially established two procedural requirements for Quinlan's guardian/father. First, he must work through her doctors. Second, a hospital medical committee must confirm the diagnosis of the persistent vegetative state. The court asserted that if the health organization's medical ethics committee (also known as the prognosis committee) determined that the patient was in a persistent vegetative state, discontinuation of treatment could occur and none of the doctors following this review would be subject to lawsuit. If there was a possibility of recovery, even a remote chance, then removal of life support could not be carried out. After nine years in a persistent vegetative state, she died.

This case was the first to truly confront the complexities associated with life-sustaining medical technology. The capability of the medical technology was found to have an unfortunate side—the ability to keep a patient alive without therapeutic benefit. A more significant case soon followed, the case of Nancy Cruzan. (See *Cruzan v. Director, Missouri Department of Health.*)

R

RADIATION EXPERIMENTS   During the 1940s and 50s, when the United States was involved in the Cold War with the Soviet Union and the threat of nuclear disaster loomed, scientists wanted to better understand the consequences of atomic attack. Their desire for knowledge associated with radiation resulted in human radiation experiments sponsored by the federal government. The Atomic Energy Commission (now the Department of Energy) and the Department of Defense conducted secret experiments in which a variety of people were fed foods with radioactive tracers and some subjects were exposed to total body irradiation. Importantly, many other governmental agencies were involved in these radiation experiments as well.

There were four categories of human experiments: bomb material experiments (using plutonium, uranium, polonium); isotope tracer experiments; body irradiation; and prisoner testicular irradiation. Exposures occurred through injection, ingestion, and external administration. The purpose was national defense, space exploration, and biomedical science. These experiments were, however, nontherapeutic—that is, not for the patient's benefit.

In 1994, President Clinton ordered an internal governmental investigation and brought in external citizen groups. A variety of governmental responses were offered depending upon the type of experiment to which the individual was subjected. The governmental responses were predominately civil. Funds were cut and researchers were excluded from applying for future grants. Many responses have not been made public because of the government involvement in the experiments. (For further information see the *Advisory Committee on Human Radiation Experiments, Final Report* [Washington, D.C.: Government Printing Office, 1995]).

RATIONING OF HEALTH CARE   Proponents of health care rationing believe there is a specific amount of health care available and that it should be distributed (rationed) according to recognized need. Health assessments and needs analyses should be conducted on specific locations. These evaluations would determine what services or technologies were needed by that population. If one of the technologies was a duplicate of another close by, an evaluation was conducted to determine if the technology was needed in that location or whether the patients could travel to the nearby health center without significant risk. Nevertheless, the process for assessment of need has not been clearly defined nor has an acceptable definition been offered. One governmental initiative dealing with rationing was the Certificate of Need.

CERTIFICATE OF NEED

This approach actually rationed health care services. The certificate of need (CON) concept began in the mid 1970s and was the primary federal and state regulatory strategy for controlling health care costs. The purported benefit of this planning approach was ensuring cost effectiveness by requiring hospitals to obtain government approval for capital investments. The federal government has now moved to other approaches but CON programs remain in existence in many states.

This cost containment strategy had as its basic premise the idea that demand for medical treatment increases as supply increases. This theory was originated by Milton Roemer, who coined the idea "A bed built is a bed filled is a bed billed." The need for health resources was identified by first discerning the appropriate level of demand for health services and then the amount of health resources needed to meet this demand. The permitted level of health resources supply is then allocated among institutional health providers through the CON program, if CON criteria are met.

This approach was a form of rationing of health resources, that is, restricting services. Studies have shown that a CON can have a positive effect on cost, but the CON-politicized decision making processes can result in erroneous decisions and thus an oversupply of technology. The majority of states have dropped this process, but it continues in several states. (See **Cost Containment.**)

REHABILITATION ACT OF 1973   This 1973 act (29 U.S.C. §§701 et seq./41 C.F.R. §§60–741.54) prohibits employment discrimination towards the handicapped. Section 504 was one area of particular significance because it addressed employers who receive federal funds, including Medicare and Medicaid. The breadth of this act was exceptional. It was also a major influence on the Americans with Disabilities Act of 1991.

The definition of "handicapped" was written very broadly. It included any person who "(i) has a physical or mental impairment which substantially limits one or more of such person's major life activities, (ii) has a record of such an impairment, or (iii) is regarded as having such an impairment." This broad-based definition protected persons with the traditionally recognized handicaps (physical handicaps) and opened many doors for persons with other, formerly unrecognized handicaps (many psychiatric disorders). Of greater importance, the legal doors were opened to enable people with a variety of handicaps to privately challenge their denial of employment in the private sector.

RELIGION   Religion within the health care context means beliefs in a deity or supreme being that guides or influences human decisions regarding their health care. Advance directives, consent to treatment, and the use of birth control devices are often influenced by an individual's religion. Several examples exist. Many people believe that all medical technology was given to us by God and all should be used to prevent death. Alternatively, some religions forbid their members from using modern medicine because illness is a sin. God will care for the person or direct the outcome. The Roman Catholic Church decries the use of birth control other than the natural "rhythm method." These examples reflect well-known religious doctrines. Religion also has a much greater influence on one's daily health practices. Members of the Church of Jesus Christ of Latter-day Saints (also known as Mormons) have strong rules promoting healthful living and emphasizing the avoidance of alcoholic and caffeine-based beverages and of substance abuse. Studies by epidemiologists on morbidity and mortality in the predominantly Mormon state of Utah consistently indicate a healthier population and one that has a longer lifespan.

JEHOVAH'S WITNESSES

One religious group that has denied to its members most medical care is the Jehovah's Witnesses. But since these individuals are competent to make their own decisions about their lives, and since their right to do so is supported by the Patient Self Determination Act of 1990, they may allow exercise their religious beliefs by denying medical treatment even to the extent of losing their own life.

Religious beliefs are recognized ethically under the principle of autonomy. As long as they are competent, people have the right to make their own decisions. Bioethical and legal issues arise when the individual is called upon to make decisions that affect the medical treatment of his or her their children or when the individual is called upon to make decisions for another whose wishes are not known. Guardianships are frequently established by the court under these circumstances so that the decisions can be made on the basis of the best interests of the patient. Exactly where religious boundaries should be drawn and where the state should step in to assert its interests in protecting the individual are the subject of many discussions.

See also **Parental Rights.**

 RIGHT TO HEALTH CARE   Do people in the United States have a right to health care? Should health care be provided regardless of the individual's ability to pay for the services? Many people believe that health care is a right because it is a basic need. This concept is a major underlying premise of the argument for a national health care system.

A right is something that a person is entitled to regardless of whether the person possesses it or not. In our current system, people have a small right to health care; it occurs in an emergency. A person entering an emergency department will be treated regardless of ability to pay. However, people do not have a right to nonemergency services. For these services—even many that are important but not immediately required—the patient must pay, either through insurance or directly. Without some form of payment, the services probably will not be provided. In the American health care system, therefore, the only "right" is to treatment in an emergency.

Most people rely upon "third-party payers" to cover their health care costs because of the extraordinary expense of obtaining medical services. Most patients have private health insurance, Medicare, or Medicaid. Insurance is frequently paid for by the employer as a benefit. Under this arrangement, health care is not a right but a privilege guided by one's insurance contract. Many people do not realize that their contract does not cover all medical services or the entire cost of the service. It is very important for people to read their contract.

See also **Health Insurance**.

RIGHT TO REFUSE TREATMENT
See AUTONOMY, PRINCIPLE OF; QUINLAN, KAREN ANN

RISK   A risk is the possibility of a loss. Every medical procedure and virtually all medical and pharmaceutical treatments entail risk. You may lose the ability to do something you were once capable of doing, or you may experience an effect that is less than desirable.

For example, aspirin may take away your headache, but when you take it, you risk as some very serious side effects. It thins your blood, and if taken by a person between under 18 who has the influenza A or B virus or varicella virus, Reye's Syndrome may result. Beginning with a mild fever, this syndrome is potentially fatal.

In view of the risk of such complications, it is important that patients understand the nature of the medications and procedures they are about to undergo. Physicians have an obligation to explain the potential complications that could result from their service. Patients have the right to hear them and make their decision from a complete knowledge base.

Problematically, many patients do not discuss the treatment risks with their physicians because they don't want offend their doctors or waste their doctor's time. Nothing could be more potentially damaging to the patient. In order to give consent that is truly informed, the patient must understand the risks of the procedure and/or medications. If patients sign a release of liability without understanding the risks, they may have waived their right to a lawsuit without knowing it.

ROE V. WADE (AND PROGENY)
See ABORTION

STANDARD PRECAUTIONS

STANDARD PRECAUTIONS Procedures required for health care workers when working with all patients entering health care organizations (formerly called Universal Precautions). Practitioners recognize that a variety of diseases can be communicated by direct contact between persons. Some of the diseases may be minimal and some may be fatal. In either context, the opportunity for passing on these diseases should be minimized as much as possible.

Standard precautions focus upon the prevention of direct contact between an infectious source and the health worker. In dealing with *all* patients, workers are ordered to wash their hands before, after, and between patient contacts. Wearing gloves is encouraged and required if any contact with blood, body fluids, tissues or contaminated services is expected. Hand washing should occur even when the person is wearing gloves. Eye protection and masks are to be worn if any type of contact would be airborne. Surgical caps and shoe covers should also be worn. If resuscitation is required, protective ventilation devices are to be used (these devices do not permit direct contact but allow air to be moved from one person to the other).

Sharp objects are to be handled carefully. Needles cannot be re-capped or broken by hand (to avoid being stuck by the needles). If a needle stick occurs, the health organization will have a protocol for the person to follow.

The broad adoption and emphasis on Standard Precautions occurred with the threat of AIDS. Epidemiologists and other health professionals have long recognized that many diseases can be spread by not adhering to these preventive measures. Many of the precautions have been ordered used for many years. The threat of AIDS simply gave dramatic emphasis to the need to follow the standard precautions.

STANDARDS OF PROOF In deciding a case, courts demand different levels of proof depending on how serious society considers the accused's alleged misdeed. In civil hearings, generally, the court uses the "preponderance of evidence" standard. In juvenile abuse cases, the court uses "clear and convincing evidence." In criminal trials, the judge or jury must find the defendant guilty "beyond a reasonable doubt." Each of these levels is progressively stricter, demanding a higher probability that individual on trial committed the alleged misdeed. To approximate the scheme mathematically (and simplistically), one might view these levels as percentages of probability that the person is guilty. Under the preponderance of evidence standard, the judge or jury needs to be 51 percent sure the individual did the act (or failed to do what he or she was supposed to do). Under the clear and convincing evidence standard, the judge or jury needs to be 75 percent sure. Finally, to be certain "beyond a reasonable doubt," the judge or jury should be 98 or 99 percent sure that the person committed the crime.

Preponderance of Evidence: The most basic level of evidence that suggests that the party "more likely than not" did what the complaint charges or failed to do what was required. *Clear and Convincing Evidence:* Evidence indicates with high probability that one party's version of the facts is accurate. *Beyond a Reasonable Doubt:* The presented facts indicate that the accused did the act and the decision maker is entirely convinced of that fact.

STERILIZATION   The process of making one incapable of reproduction. Three types of surgery prevent pregnancy permanently. The hysterectomy is a complex surgery that removes the uterus. It is not typically a procedure intended to prevent pregnancy but is often intended to deal with other problems with the uterus. In some communities a hysterectomy is the surgery of choice to prevent pregnancy. However, the use of such a complex surgery for this purpose is declining. The remaining two procedures, the tubal ligation and the vasectomy, are based on the principle of interrupting the ducts carrying eggs (fallopian tubes) or sperm (vas deferens). These procedures are considered to be virtually 100 percent effective. They are intended to be permanent and should be carefully considered by the patient. Numerous requests to reverse these surgeries have arisen after divorce or death of a partner or child. However, the attempted reversal is frequently not successful.

Tubal Ligation: This form of sterilization is carried out on the woman. It may be performed after childbirth as an inpatient or in a laparoscopic procedure in an outpatient setting. The fallopian tubes are closed by cutting and cauterizing them or through the use of bands or clips. (Currently many physicians use bands or clips because less tissue damage results and sterilization is made more reversible.) Following reconstruction, pregnancy rates are 50 to 58 percent. *Vasectomy:* A 30-minute procedure that isolates and cuts the sperm duct (vas deferens). Each end of the vas deferens is closed by either tying the vessel (ligation) or electrical closing. The incision is closed and the patient is discharged. However, he may not gain sterility immediately. About 15 to 20 ejaculations are required before sterility is achieved. At that point, the man's semen should be analyzed. He will not be considered sterile until he has produced two sperm-free ejaculates. Most vasectomies are complication free, with some minor exceptions. This surgery is considered permanent. The patient should be aware that reconstruction is much more difficult for the vasectomy than the tubal ligation. Following reconstruction, pregnancy rates are 45 to 60 percent.

SUBSTITUTE JUDGMENT RULE

This rule is introduced when a person, now a victim, is incapable of making her wishes known. The challenge is that decisions must be made for the victim. Under this rule, a person, committee, or institution attempts to determine what the patient would do if she were competent and could make the decisions for herself.

The problem is that no one really knows what the patient would do, so the decision is speculative. Therefore many believe that the lack of advance directives or other indicators of the individual's wishes indicates that all interventions should be used. The principle of beneficence is followed, working towards the best interests of the victim. The alternative outcomes are considered and evaluated along with any information about the person that might give some indication of the her wishes should.

Advance directives are clearly the recommended alternative. The substituted judgment may or may not be what the victim would want. The absence of the victim's input makes the judgment forever suspect.

SUICIDE

The taking of one's own life. In most states, suicide is illegal.

SURROGATE MOTHERING

A relatively modern solution to the problem of infertility, surrogate mothering allows infertile couples the chance to have a biologically related child. The surrogate's eggs and the male's sperm are combined in a laboratory. The fertilized egg is then artificially implanted into a woman (surrogate) who carries it for the nine-month gestational period. After giving birth, the birth mother gives sole custody of the child to the biological father, and his wife adopts the child.

COMMERCIAL AND VOLUNTARY SURROGACY

The surrogate's actions may be voluntary or may be a commercial transaction. The voluntary surrogate is usually a friend or a relative. The commercial surrogate is brought to the infertile couple usually through arrangements with a brokering firm that specialize in providing these types of services.

Commercial surrogacy is illegal in some states. The argument is that commercial surrogacy is related to selling children. The parties are brought together by a brokering agency and enter into a contract indicating the amounts to be paid for the services to be rendered. However, these agencies are not licensed, and this is where the problem arises. The agreement is based upon contract, which sets forth the entire agreement between parties. In most surrogacy situations, however, the parties are not medical or legal professionals and are not aware of all the potential medical and legal hazards. The transaction is not normally regularly regulated and consequently may result in great harm.

In other states, unpaid surrogacy is legal, but certain legal and social protections must be incorporated into the arrangement to protect all persons involved. For example, all parties must be medically and psychologically evaluated.

GESTATIONAL SURROGACY

This recent advance in assisted reproductive technology allows infertile couples to have a child that is biologically related to both parents. What is required is that the biological parents be physiologically capable of providing the a viable egg and sperm. Viable eggs are removed for fertilization with the intended father's sperm. The egg and sperm are joined in the laboratory and implanted into a surrogate mother. The result of this form of surrogacy is a child biologically related to both parents and not related to the surrogate. The surrogate in this instance is called a carrier rather than a surrogate mother, because there is no biological relationship between her and the fetus she is carrying.

This process begins with an infertile couple being assessed to ascertain whether or not each is capable of providing a viable contribution. If both are capable, a broker is contacted to locate and match a potential carrier. A contract is written and offered, with all parties represented by attorneys (legal representation is strongly encouraged).

T

TERMINAL ILLNESS   An illness that will result in death. The physician has determined that the patient can no longer be cured and death will be the result of this spell of illness. Often the term is associated with cancer and the decision to enter hospice care (see **Palliative Care.**)

THROMBOLYTIC THERAPY   Therapy that is directed at dissolving a thrombus (blockage in a blood vessel). Because heart disease is the number one cause of death in the United States and the developed countries, much research is directed at eradicating it. In a heart attack (myocardial infarct), a piece of plaque breaks from a vessel wall and is carried through the bloodstream. When the vessel becomes too small for the plaque to pass through, it stops, and the plaque becomes a thrombus. If the thrombus is located in one of the vessels leading to the heart, then blood is blocked from the heart. The heart reacts when the oxygen carrying blood does not reach it. If the blockage lasts long enough, part of the heart muscle may die, and may cause the person to die. If the thrombus can be dissolved rapidly enough, however, minimal damage to the heart occurs. This minimal damage is the goal of thrombolytic therapy. The cells of the thrombus are dissolved with clot-dissolving medication, thus reopening the vessel and blood is allowed to flow.

TRANSGENICS   This scientific effort involves the use of animals to grow human organs. Researchers are identifying the genetic blueprint to direct the growth of certain human organs, and the medium in which the organ is grown is an animal.

Pigs are often used in these experiments. The function and size of certain organs in pigs, such as kidneys, are similar to those in humans. Therefore, researchers ask, why not create a biologically equivalent kidney to remove from the pig and transplant into humans? After all, pigs' heart valves are already used in surgery on humans. Why not consider expanding this use of animals?

The difference between this approach and xenografts (transplants or grafts from animals) is that a human genetic sequence would be introduced to the animal so that a "human" organ would be grown rather than the animal organ. Researchers believe that the organ compatibility would be genetically acceptable, making transplantation rejection less severe. A successful outcome is believed very possible because of the genetic foundation unique to this new research.

TRANSSEXUALISM

This condition involves the state of a woman being in a biologically male body or vice versa. Typically, a person's gender identity is the same as their biological gender. Some children have a fleeting experience of not being aligned with their gender identity, but it usually passes quickly. A few people, however, report belonging to a gender other than that of their biological features. Beginning in childhood, these people often have a troubled life, because they truly believe that nature was wrong. They frequently dress and act as members of the sex with which they identify. They pursue medical assistance, not to help them psychologically, but to help them physically change into the gender to which they belong.

CONVERSION SURGERY

The surgical change from one sex to another. The change can result in a positive adjustment as the individual becomes more anatomically similar to the gender with which he or she identifies. (This type of surgery is not appropriate for homosexual people because, in general, they are not transsexuals.) In conversion surgery, the individuals' biological gender does not change, because medical scientists cannot change their genetic makeup. The physicians can only modify hormonal treatments and carry out surgical modifications.

This procedure begins with psychiatric treatment to make sure that the motivation is present to undergo the lengthy procedures necessary for the change. It is followed by hormonal therapy with surgery (usually surgeries) to follow. Following the surgical changes, training must occur to help the person with movements and gestures. Surgically, the change from male to female is reported more satisfactory than the changes from female to male.

▥ TUSKEGEE SYPHILIS STUDIES   One of the earliest and longest-lasting unethical medical experiments occurred in

Tuskegee, Alabama. In the 1930s, medical scientists were attempting to learn the progression and consequences of syphilis, a disease that is called "the great impostor" because its symptoms copy or mimic many other diseases. In order to learn how this disease manifested itself and evolved when left untreated, scientists intentionally infected a variety of black men with the disease and left them untreated, even though a cure was available. In 1997, President Bill Clinton publicly apologized to the living men intentionally injected with the syphilis-causing agent. These men, now few in number, were in their eighties and nineties. They indicated that they appreciated the apology, and all, including the president, condemned this type of human experimentation.

Scientists today do not condone the this type of experiment. Institutional review boards are intended to stop any experiment of this type, should such a proposal be presented.

One question that has arisen is how to deal with the data resulting from such unethical experiments. Should the data be used? The infected individuals were indeed wronged. But why should their suffering be in vain? Why not allow the information gleaned from their suffering to be used for the good of others and ensure that their suffering is not repeated?

Many scientists believe that using the data indirectly ratifies (or condones) the experiments. They argue that other scientists may wish to repeat the study or conduct a similar experiment because they know their results will be used. They may not care about the ethical issues. Furthermore, the best means to determine the natural history of a disease (the progression of a disease left untreated) in human beings is to obtain information from untreated human beings. Therefore, if the scientist is willing to sacrifice a few for the good of many, these experiments could be attempted. The way to avoid this situation is not to allow the results to be disseminated. In this way we avoid rewarding unethical behavior.

This questions also arose concerning data from the medical experiments and studies inflicted on the Jews during their incarceration in Nazi concentration camps during World War II. Many Jews and others were forced to participate in hypothermia experiments in which they were exposed to freezing conditions so that the Nazis could learn the effects of cold upon their pilots in the war. Many were exposed without any protection so that researchers could ascertain how long it took them to die. Many types of protection were considered for the German pilots, including different types of clothing such as rubber suits. The victims' responses allowed Nazi experimenters to determine which types of protection were most effective. Clearly, these experiments were unethical and must not be repeated. But, if helpful information was gained, should the information be withheld when modern countries lose children to drowning in frozen lakes every summer? Many Jews believe that publication of the data would give their relatives' senseless deaths a positive meaning.

U

 UNIFORM ANATOMICAL GIFT ACT OF 1987 *See* ORGAN AND TISSUE DONATION

 UNIFORM RIGHTS OF TERMINALLY ILL ACT This 1989 act was intended as model legislation. It allowed individuals to provide guidance for medical professionals concerning their wishes to limit treatment that is merely life extending, should they become unable to participate in treatment decisions. Its purpose was to establish a simple procedure for the voluntary indication of a patient's wishes, should a terminal condition arise. It provided the format and forms that would satisfy even the strongest critics of advance directives. It was hoped that the model would be adopted by all states and that this uniformity would make decisions clearer and more consistent from state to state. Although it has not been adopted in any state at this time, it did motivate many states to implement living will legislation or other approaches to advance directives.

The approach was to offer the form containing a person's decisions under specified conditions. For example, "If I am prematurely brain damaged, I want to donate any and all organs, if they are appropriate for use." This condition is signed and specifically states when this condition is to be considered. Initially, the act recommended criminal consequences for not following the person's decisions. Most people following the model, however, have not elected to implement criminal sanctions. Most do not have specified sanctions. Rather, there is more of a moral requirement demanding that the reader follow the directions of the author.

 UNIVERSAL PRECAUTIONS *See* STANDARD PRECAUTIONS

UTILITARIANISM, THEORY OF   An alternative theory to deontology. At its heart is the "greatest happiness principle," which according to John Stuart Mill, indicates that an action is right to the extent that it promotes happiness and wrong to the extent it promotes dis-happiness. The utility of an act is determined by its tendency to promote or produce happiness; the right action among alternative choices is most correct if that action produces the greatest good.

There are two major forms of utilitarianism: act utilitarianism and rule utilitarianism. An act utilitarian analyzes the act and seeks to determine when an alternative in a particular case would maximize the opportunity for good or minimize suffering. A rule utilitarian, alternatively, focuses on the effects of actions. Rule utilitarians analyze policy, asking which policy, as a general rule, would maximize happiness and minimize suffering.

Act utilitarianism is the more common of the two schools of thought. Because it focuses on acts and their consequences, the individual actor is or may be separated from his or her actions. The situation itself is under the microscope. Through this analysis, even the best-intentioned person is recognized as capable of performing a wrong act. The person's intentions and feelings are deemed irrelevant; only the act and its consequences are analyzed and identified.

One of the principle criticisms of act utilitarianism is that it is very simplistic. There are many influences on any one act, and happiness or good may be relative to the person and/or context. It does not allow for a thorough explanation of an individual's or a group's actions.

Rule utilitarianism suggests that humans should integrate moral rules into our approach to governance. Rules that are themselves governed by the greatest happiness principle would have the greatest good consequences. Health care is, in fact, different from business because of rule utilitarianism. The recognition of moral rules and values hold physicians accountable to a higher moral authority. This sense of morality enhances the quality of their medical practice.

WITHDRAWAL OF LIFE SUPPORT

Advance directives authorize the removal of mechanical or technological support that makes the body's essential functions operate. Life support technology includes mechanized kidney support (renal dialysis), pacemakers to continue a consistent heart rhythm, and respirators to assist with breathing. The advance directives may also authorize the withdrawal of feeding and drinking (hydration). Under these circumstances, a person's feeling of hunger and thirst are very different than those experienced by the normal person. Medications may be administered to eliminate the desire for food and drink. The dying person has already authorized this "withdrawal" and indicates when these measures are to be taken. (See **Advance Directives; Living Will; Physician-Assisted Suicide.**) These measures are not taken unless the individual is beyond any form of therapeutic (curative) treatment or is in a persistent vegetative state.

Opponents to withdrawal of life support reflect the belief that life should be extended until medicine's tools are at an end. If we have the technology, then use it.

Proponents of life support argue for a natural death. If the patient can be beneficially treated, then the life support has a role. If the life support only sustains life when there is no possibility of a cure, it is not serving the person. Its only result to increase in the cost of dying. Therefore, when the appropriate time is identified by the physicians, and with the family's consent, life support is withdrawn and the individual is allowed to die.

The principles of autonomy and beneficence are incorporated into these decision-making processes and into the medical practices of our society. As our knowledge increases, so does our understanding of the best time to withdraw of life support.

X

XENOTRANSPLANTATION A medical procedure that transplants animal tissue (a xenograft) into humans. This idea has been explored experimentally for the past 30 years, driven by the inadequate supply of donated human organs. The concept has gained further impetus because some physicians believe that the number of voluntary and posthumous human organ donors has reached a plateau and that alternatives must be sought.

A logical avenue of exploration involves animals becoming the donors, with humans as recipients. The donated tissue may be an organ or it may be bone marrow. The type of animal selected as the organ donor depends upon the type of donation required. For example, researchers consider a close primate match as desirable for tissue transplants. The belief is that the closer the donor organ is to a human organ, the smaller the degree of tissue rejection and risk to the recipient's life. Other researchers argue that the pig is a good donor because of the remarkable similarity of organ anatomy and physiology to humans. Pigs are also less likely to have the viruses that primates closer to humans would carry.

Animal-to-animal and animal-to-human research testing xenotransplantation is currently ongoing. The organs of candidate donor animals have been transplanted into primates so that receptivity can be tested. The procedural and surgical complications are being identified to resolve those issues. Drugs negating organ rejection are also being identified and tested to make the implantation more successful. An animal-to-human experiment in San Francisco involves the implantation of baboon bone marrow into an AIDS victim, with the goal of rebuilding the immune system. The selection of a baboon was guided by the finding that baboons are essentially immune to the HIV infection. As bone marrow is responsible for white blood cell production (leukocytes), scientists are hopeful that a successful baboon xenograft would give the AIDS victim a recharged immune system and an opportunity to survive the fatal disease. (See **Acquired Immunodeficiency Syndrome; Animal Experimentation**.)

One of the first and most controversial cases of xenotransplantation was the 1984 case of Baby Fae. This baby was born with a severe congenital heart malformation (hypoplastic left heart syndrome). This malformation leaves the left ventricle too weak to pump blood through the circulatory system. The condition is fatal unless heart transplantation or another surgical procedure occurs. Medical researcher and surgeon Leonard Bailey of Loma Linda University proposed a third alternative, transplanting a baboon heart to the infant. The heart would be the necessary size. The parents agreed to the transplant. Dr. Bailey performed the xenograft. After the surgery and for the ensuing few days, Dr. Bailey was optimistic about Baby Fae's chances of long-term survival. But Baby Fae died after living only eleven days.

The publicity surrounding the surgery resulted in substantial criticism of Dr. Bailey and Loma Linda University. Reports indicated that the parents may not have been adequately informed about the experimental nature of the surgery. Further, evidence suggested that Dr. Bailey had not investigated the availability of a human donor. There was apparently a newborn heart available. Others argue that the information gained by this experiment will have major benefits for the future.

Many ethical questions were raised by this experiment and many protocols were established. These protocols focused upon the prevention of ethical violations surrounding inadequate informed consent and procedures intended to be in the best interests of the patient. The recognition of the potential for xenotransplantation was not questioned.

Appendix:
Sample Living Will

LIVING WILL DECLARATION

Declaration made this _____ day of _____ I, _____ , _____ being of sound mind, and not under or subject to duress, willfully and voluntarily make known my desires regarding the use or continuation, or the withholding or with-drawal, of life-sustaining treatment. If I am unable to give directions re-garding the use of such life-sustaining treatment when I am in a terminal condition or a permanently unconscious state, it is my intention that this declaration shall be honored by my family and physicians as the final ex-pression of my right to refuse medical or surgical treatment, including life-sustaining treatment. I am emotionally and mentally competent to make this declaration, and I understand and accept the consequences of such refusal.

If at any time I am in a "terminal condition," I direct that life-sustaining treatment that serves principally to prolong the process of dying shall be withheld or withdrawn by my attending physician, and that I be permit-ted to die naturally with only the administration of treatment deemed necessary to provide me with comfort care. THE TERM "TERMINAL CONDI-TION" MEANS AN IRREVERSIBLE, INCURABLE, AND UNTREATABLE CONDITION CAUSED BY DISEASE, ILLNESS, OR INJURY FROM WHICH, TO A REASONABLE DEGREE OF MEDICAL CERTAINTY AS DETERMINED IN ACCORDANCE WITH REASONABLE MEDICAL STANDARDS BY MY ATTENDING PHYSICIAN AND ONE OTHER PHYSICIAN WHO HAS EXAMINED ME, BOTH OF THE FOLLOWING APPLY: (I) THERE CAN BE NO RECOVERY, (II) AND DEATH IS LIKELY TO OCCUR WITHIN A RELATIVELY SHORT TIME IF LIFE-SUSTAINING TREATMENT IS NOT ADMINISTERED.

If at any time I should be in a "permanently unconscious state," I direct that life-sustaining treatment that serves principally to prolong the process of dying shall be withheld or withdrawn by my attending physician, and that I be permitted to die naturally with only the administration of treatment

211

deemed necessary to provide me with comfort care. THE TERM "PERMANENTLY UNCONSCIOUS STATE" MEANS A STATE OF PERMANENT UNCONSCIOUSNESS THAT, TO A REASONABLE DEGREE OF MEDICAL CERTAINTY AS DETERMINED IN ACCORDANCE WITH REASONABLE MEDICAL STANDARDS BY MY ATTENDING PHYSICIAN AND ONE OTHER PHYSICIAN WHO HAS EXAMINED ME, IS CHARACTERIZED BY THE FOLLOWING: (I) I AM IRREVERSIBLY UNAWARE OF MYSELF AND MY ENVIRONMENT, AND (II) I HAVE A TOTAL LOSS OF CEREBRAL CORTICAL FUNCTIONING, RESULTING IN MY HAVING NO CAPACITY TO EXPERIENCE PAIN OR SUFFERING.

IT IS MY INTENT THAT ARTIFICIALLY OR TECHNOLOGICALLY ADMINISTERED HYDRATION AND NUTRITION SHALL BE WITHHELD OR WITHDRAWN BY MY ATTENDING PHYSICIAN, IF I AM IN A PERMANENTLY UNCONSCIOUS STATE AND IF MY ATTENDING PHYSICIAN AND AT LEAST ONE OTHER PHYSICIAN WHO HAS EXAMINED ME, DETERMINE TO A REASONABLE DEGREE OF MEDICAL CERTAINTY AND IN ACCORDANCE WITH REASONABLE MEDICAL STANDARDS, THAT SUCH NUTRITION OR HYDRATION WILL NOT, OR NO LONGER WILL, SERVE TO PROVIDE COMFORT TO ME OR TO ALLEVIATE PAIN. As a further indication that the above authorization regarding nutrition and hydration is my intent, I am signing the following signature line.

_____

_____

Signature authorizing withdrawal of artificially administered nutrition and hydration

If my attending physician determines that life-sustaining treatment should be withheld or withdrawn, I ask that my physician make a reasonable effort to notify one of the following designated persons with the priority as listed below:

1. Name: _____
   Address: _____

   Phone: _____ Or: _____
   Relationship: _____

2. Name: _____
   Address: _____

   Phone: _____ Or: _____
   Relationship: _____

If I have been diagnosed as pregnant and that diagnosis is known to my physician, this document shall have no force or effect during the course of my pregnancy. However, if at any point it is determined that it is not possible that the fetus could develop to the point of live birth with continued application of life-sustaining procedures, it is my preference that this document be given effect at that point. If life-sustaining procedures will be physically harmful or unreasonably painful to me in a manner that cannot be alleviated by medication, I request that my desire for personal physical comfort be given consideration in determining whether this document shall be effective if I am pregnant.

If any provision in this document is held to be invalid, such invalidity shall not affect the other provisions which can be given effect without the invalid provision, and to this end the directions in this document are severable.

I understand the purpose and effect of this Living Will Declaration and sign my name after careful deliberation on _____, _____, at _____, Ohio.

Signature: _____

Name: _____

Address: _____
           Ohio

Note: This document may be properly signed by having _____ _____ 's signature acknowledged in the presence of either (i) two qualified witnesses, or (ii) a notary public.

The undersigned witnesses attest that _____ signed or acknowledged this declaration in our presence. We further attest that we are adults who are not related to _____ by blood, marriage, or adoption, are not the attending physician of ____ _____ , and are not the administrator of any nursing home in which _____ is receiving care. It is the belief of each of the undersigned witnesses that _____ _____ appears to be of sound mind and not under or subject to duress, fraud, or undue influence.

Witness Signature: _____

Name: _____

Address: _____

Witness Signature: _____

Name: _____

Address: _____

For Further Reading

Annas, G. 1993. *Standard of Care: The Law of American Bioethics*. New York: Oxford University Press.

> An academic text dealing with a wide variety of bioethical issues. Used in many graduate bioethics classes. Deals with ethical issues presently encountered, giving in-depth explanations of the various positions taken in arguments.

Beauchamp, T. L., and Childress, J. F. 1989. *Principles of Biomedical Ethics*. 3d ed. New York: Oxford University Press.

> An academic law and medical school text for use in courses in medical ethics or professional ethics. Text is updated as needed and covers a wide array of ethical issues.

Berkow, R., and Fletcher, A. J. (eds.)., 1992. *The Merck Manual of Diagnosis and Therapy*. 16th ed. Rahway, NJ: Merck.

> A handbook of medical diagnosis and treatment. Used by physicians, it is a standard reference tool in the clinical professions.

Bucy, Pamela H. 1996. *Health Care Fraud: Criminal, Civil, and Administrative Law*. New York: Law Journal Seminars-Press.

> A legal treatise on issues occurring within health care for the legal practitioner. Updated annually.

Cleverly, William O. 1997. *Essentials of Health Care Finance*. 4th ed. Rockville, MD: Aspen.

> Health finance for the graduate health administration student. Written by one of the premier authors and analysts of health finance in the United States.

Dill-Calloway, S. 1991. *Ohio Nursing Law*. Cleveland: Banks-Baldwin.

> A practice manual for lawyers involved in bioethical and legal issues in nursing.

Dorland's Illustrated Medical Dictionary. 1988. 27th ed. New York: Saunders.

> One of the major medical dictionaries.

Duncan, A. S., G. R. Dunstan, and R. B. Welbourn. 1981. *Dictionary of Medical Ethics*. New York: Crossroad.

> A dictionary of issues in medical ethics in the United Kingdom.

Fine, Toni M. 1997. *American Legal Systems: A Resource and Reference Guide*. Cincinnati: Anderson.

> An excellent introductory text to the foundations of the U.S. legal system.

Furrow, B. R., Johnson, S. H., Jost, T. S., and Schwartz, R. L. 1991. *Bioethics: Health Care Law and Ethics*. St. Paul: West.

> A text for use in legal classes dealing with bioethical situations. Often a companion volume to the health law text cited in the next entry.

Furrow, B. R., Greaney, T. L., Johnson, S. H., Jost, T. S., and Schwartz, R. L. 1995. *Health Law,* Vols. 1–2. St. Paul: West.

> Legal practitioner's set of information on health law. Updated as necessary.

Grodin, Michael, and Glantz, Leonard H. 1994. *Children as Research Subjects: Science, Ethics and Law*. New York: Oxford University Press.

> A book for people concerned with ensuring that children's present and future rights are protected in medical and scientific research.

Hall, Mark A., and Ellman, Ira M. 1990. *Health Care Law and Ethics*. St. Paul: West.

> An overview of the interrelations between health law and bioethics. In the Law in a Nutshell series, it is an excellent capsule of extensive information on law and ethics.

Hastings, D. A., Luce, G. M., and Wynstra, N. A. 1995. *Fundamentals of Health Law,* Washington, DC: National Health Lawyers Association.

> An introductory text on health law for legal practitioners.

Konigstvedt, P. R. 1996. *The Managed Health Care Handbook*, 3d ed. Rockville, MD: Aspen.

An advanced text for health administrators and physicians moving into the complex managed care arena.

National Health Lawyers Association. 1991. *The Patient Self-Determination Directory and Resource Guide*. Washington, DC: National Health Lawyers Association.

A compendium of information on the different laws and guideline to issues to be encountered in patient's rights. (The association is now known as the American Health Lawyers' Association.)

Nolan, J. R., and Nolan-Haley, J. M. 1991. *Black's Law Dictionary*. 6th ed. St. Paul: West.

The classic legal dictionary used as a standard reference.

Pavarini, P.A. 1997. *United States Health Care Laws and Rules*. Washington, DC: National Health Lawyers Association.

Synopsis of key legislation that health lawyers are likely to encounter and that attorneys are likely to need for legal analysis.

———. 1995. *Ohio Health Care Laws and Rules*. Washington, DC: National Health Lawyers Association.

The key legislation in Ohio likely to be encountered by health care providers.

Prentice-Hall Editorial Staff. 1995. *Lawyer's Desk Book*. 10th ed. 1997 Supp. Englewood Cliffs, NJ: Prentice-Hall.

A good basic general legal reference text.

Prosser, W. P., and Keeton, W. 1984. *Torts*. 5th ed. (supp. 1988). St. Paul: West.

Written by Keeton following the master of U.S. tort law, Professor Prosser.

Rakich, J., Longest, B. B., Jr., and Darr, K. 1992. *Managing Health Services Organizations*, 3d ed. Baltimore: Health Professions Press.

An excellent introductory text to health care services management.

Rognehaugh, R. 1996. *The Managed Health Care Dictionary*. Rockville, MD: Aspen.

The new jargon of the managed care area has created a demand for a specialized dictionary. This dictionary incorporates both the language and the acronyms the inquirer may encounter.

Shandell, Richard E. 1994.*The Preparation and Trial of Medical Malpractice Cases* (with annual supplements). New York: Law Journal Seminars-Press.

A treatise on the legal practitioner's preparation for medical malpractice cases.

Smith, James Walker. 1994. *Hospital Liability* (with annual supplements). New York: Law Journal Seminars-Press.

A corporate hospital practitioner's guide to helping hospitals avoid liability.

Scheutzow, Susan O. 1994. *Ohio Health Care Provider Law*. Cleveland: Banks Baldwin.

Part of the practice series, the law encountered in the practice of health care in Ohio.

Sultz, Harry A., and Young, Kristina M. 1997. *Health Care USA: Understanding Its Organization and Delivery*. Rockville, MD: Aspen.

An introductory text on the U.S. health care system suitable for undergraduate classes.

Tribe, Laurence H. 1988. *American Constitutional Law*. 2d ed. Mineola, NY: Foundation Press.

An excellent reference by one of the principal constitutional interpreters of the the current period.

Wolper, L. F. (ed). 1995. *Health Care Administration: Principles, Practices, Structure, and Delivery*. 2d ed. Rockville, MD: Aspen.

An intermediate text identifying the underpinnings of health administration.

Table of Cases

Index

Numbers in **boldface** indicate main entries.